Barbara Cassani is Chairman of the ⬚⬚⬚⬚⬚ which aims to win the Summer Olympic ⬚⬚⬚⬚ She is also a Non-Executive Director of Marks & Spencer.

Go was voted Best Low Cost Airline in 2001 by both readers of *Business Traveller Magazine* and the *Telegraph*. Barbara herself was named Entrepreneur of the Year in 2001 by the *Sunday Telegraph* and in 2002 received the Veuve Clicquot UK Businesswoman of the Year award.

Prior to joining British Airways, Barbara was a management consultant with Coopers and Lybrand in Washington DC and London. She received her BA from Mount Holyoke College and her Masters from Princeton University. She serves as a trustee to her undergraduate university, Mount Holyoke College.

She is married and lives in London with her two young children. Barbara's passion is sponsoring several UK three-day eventing top-level competition horses, while riding and competing at a lower level herself. She is also an avid reader of a wide range of books from biographies, nineteenth-century literature, modern fiction and mystery novels.

Kenny Kemp is Business Writer of the Year in the Scottish Press 2003 for his exclusives on the collapse of Enron and Arthur Andersen. He also won the award in 2001 for his work on President George W. Bush's family and its oil connections with Scotland. He has been the Business Editor of the *Sunday Herald* since the paper was founded in February 1999. Previously he was a staff journalist on the *Evening Standard*, *Today* and a Business Editor on *The Scotsman*, Edinburgh. He met Barbara Cassani in September 1998 when she launched Go flights to Scotland. He has written extensively about major companies in the UK and is now a freelance writer living in Edinburgh.

go

an airline
adventure

Barbara Cassani

with Kenny Kemp

timewarner
books

A *Time Warner* Book

First published in Great Britain in 2003 by Time Warner Books

Copyright © 2003 Barbara Cassani
A CIP catalogue record for this book is
available from the British Library.

ISBN 0 316 72662 1

Typeset in Baskerville MT by M Rules

Printed and bound in Great Britain
by Clays Ltd, St Ives plc

Time Warner Books
Brettenham House
Lancaster Place
London WC2E 7EN

www.TimeWarnerBooks.co.uk

This book is dedicated to my husband, Guy. Without him there would have been no airline adventure and certainly no book. He has been my partner and supporter in every way for the past twenty years. The book is also for my children, James and Lauren, who were Go fans from the early days and have always spoken generously and proudly of their mother. And finally to my parents, Jim and Noreen, for their encouragement and enthusiasm for every new adventure on which I have ever embarked.

I also want to thank Michael Coltman for helping to research the Korean crash chapter and Pamela Watson for generously sharing her book-writing skills with me. I'd also like to thank Bob Ayling, Andrew Cowen, Lynne Hodgkinson Grigg, Simon Harford, Steven Horner, Julie Naulls, Dominic Paul, David Magliano and Ed Winter. Each played a big role in this adventure story and I thank each of them for taking the time to help me tell this story and read the draft manuscripts.

For everyone who ever worked at Go, this book is for you. We built something terrific and I'll always be grateful for your help. I also want to thank you for all the contributions to this book. It is a richer story because so many of you took the time to get in touch.

And finally, I want to thank all my friends and colleagues at British Airways for some great years. I am also very grateful to all the people in British Airways who never failed to encourage and voice their pride in what we were doing at Go. As there is now no Go, I'll be flying whenever I can with my second favourite airline – British Airways.

Contents

Foreword

Subject: Your airline book
From: Jill.Milne@googista.co.uk
To: Barbara.Cassani@internetaddress.com

I'm sure you are getting loads of responses for your book, so I'll try and jog your memory as to who I am. I was originally a cabin crew and then one of John's team dealing with pilot recruitment. I don't have a particular story but Go meant a lot to me. For the first time in my working life, I was a person and not a number. My four-year journey with Go was one of the most fantastic and memorable experiences of my life. It was unique and one I shall never have the experience to repeat. I was part of a very special group of people, who all worked together as a fantastic team and created something very successful and special. – Best wishes,

Jill (Milne)

PS I would also like to let you know how I spent some of my Go money. I underwent laser surgery to correct my eyesight. What an amazing difference, it has changed my life on a daily basis.

Jill was not alone. There were dozens of other messages like this. When I considered writing the Go story, I emailed everyone I could think of to ask them for their memories to use in this book. I was still recuperating from the blow of the forced sale, and so many of the stories put a smile on my face. I enjoyed recalling inventing the Marigold award – a pair of washing-up gloves – to present to Captain Rob English for personally unblocking a loo on the plane to avoid a long delay. I'll also never forget the day 'in the business' when I helped with tidying aircraft between flights with a vacuum cleaner attached Ghost-buster-style to my back. I sucked up someone's sick and then systematically spread the smell to every other aircraft in the fleet.

Other emails brought heartening responses such as First Officer Paul Robinson's, who said: 'I had a hard time outside of work for almost three years, but the only thing that kept me going was Go and its people. It was a family, who had rows and fell out now and then, but when it mattered, we pulled together and could withstand anything. I will always thank you for that.'

Senior cabin crew member Andrew Morris got in touch to say: 'The airline was an absolute pleasure to work for and it made work every day something to look forward to. I just want to thank you for letting me be part of the success and also for making my dreams become a reality.' Then he continued: 'I have always wanted to be a pilot and thanks to the shares you gave me I can now make my dreams come true as I have just begun training to fulfil my ambition.'

And I will never forget Glo (Gloria Wright) and Phyll (Phyll Fay), two Essex ladies who were a scream in the office. On the phone with customers all day in the sales department, they worked hard for Go. They were always the first to dress up on a special occasion to add some fun to the day at work. They should have had their own television show. One was petite, the other, well, not, and they were an inseparable double act at the start of the airline. Their hard work, along with the rest of the team's, helped take Go from an idea to a successful reality. Phyll Fay even became a founding member of Go's Consultative Group, representing her telesales colleagues and negotiating pay. Her straight-talking candour and humour added to every meeting.

Our service was snappy and informal and our customers knew Go was out of the ordinary. Of course they wanted low fares, but they found that low cost didn't have to mean low quality – and they liked that. Customer John Harrison wrote me an email sitting on a Go flight in 2002. He starts with: 'Firstly, let me say that this is the first time in my life that I have passed on congratulations to a complete stranger, but I think you deserve it. I am sitting on one of your flights from Glasgow to London on a Wednesday evening and the attitude that your staff portrays is exemplary.' He goes on to talk about the genuinely friendly crew and the high-quality on-board magazine. He finishes with: 'You have created an excellent environment for your employees and it shows. If I can achieve just a few components of what you have built here within my own business – I will be very happy. Well done!'

Colleague Dominic Paul summed it up in an email to me: 'You made it clear what the company should stand for – people and customers and then costs and profit and I think we stuck to that . . . I think it's what made it such a great place to work.'

I also think it's the reason we built a successful, valuable business – one that turned a £25 million investment into a company worth £374 million in four years. This airline adventure story is for my colleagues at Go and the people who paid to fly with us.

Chapter One

The Battle Commences

From the moment our first plane took off to Rome on Friday 22 May 1998 we were in a battle to survive. We had taken on the impossible by setting up the airline in just six months, but we still came very late into the game – almost three years behind rival easyJet and two behind Debonair, while market leader Ryanair was already a highly profitable and well established airline.

No one in the airline world wanted us to succeed. easyJet had started legal action to try to shut us down and consumer protection groups opposed us. We even had detractors inside our parent company, the great British Airways. While Chief Executive Officer Bob Ayling was looking for us to grab a share of the fastest-growing, most exciting sector of the airline industry, others in British Airways felt we were another risky investment that might become perpetually loss-making.

Our stress was compounded by the unnaturally intense media interest. The press had latched on to the story of a new UK airline from British Airways being run by an American woman following the appointments of Americans Marjorie Scardino and Rose Marie Bravo to high-profile, big-salary jobs at Pearson

and Burberry. And easyJet was making the most of every opportunity to promote its own public campaign to 'Stop BA stop
Go'.

With so much pressure on us, the launch day could have
been a nightmare. In the days and weeks that led up to 22 May,
recurring fears kept me tossing and turning in my sleep. We
imagined all the customer complaints, vitriolic newspaper headlines, sneering from within British Airways and jubilation from
our arch-enemies at the other low-cost airlines if we fumbled
the ball.

But the biggest nightmare was that Go would be grounded
even before our first flight. If their legal action in the High
Court in London was successful, easyJet would stop us from
operating. We could do all the work to create a world-class
brand and service, choose routes, sell seats, find aircraft, recruit
and train flight crew and cabin crew, receive our Air Operator
Certificate from the Civil Aviation Authority (CAA) on time,
only to be forced to shut the airline down before we even began.
I could imagine the newspaper headlines quoting easyJet's
founder Stelios Haji-Ioannou saying: 'We stopped Go.'

Another bad dream was that when we opened our telephone
sales centre on 2 April 1998 no one would call up to buy a
ticket. We actually did delay opening the phones one day to
avoid any possible bad luck associated with starting sales on
April Fool's Day. But what if we were 'all dressed up with
nowhere to go'? I was terrified that the travelling public would
believe our detractors and refuse to buy seats from us because
we were 'bad guys' intent upon putting 'good guys' out of business. The thought of deathly silence in the call centre petrified
me.

The next recurring nightmare was that we might miss a per-
nickety point such as having the wrong sort of life jackets on
board. This could cause the CAA to refuse to grant us the vital
piece of paper we needed to fly – our Air Operator Certificate.

The flight to prove to the CAA that we were a quality operation had been scheduled just days before 22 May, and I fretted that we would have bright newly painted planes, trained and smartly turned out crew, a plane full of eager customers . . . but no certificate to allow us to fly.

The planes were part of another nightmare involving Ed Winter, Go's Chief Operating Officer, and Mike Williams, Chief Engineer. 'What do you mean we have no planes?' I would ask in horror. Ed would explain in mind-numbing detail that the two planes we had leased were still being repaired and weren't ready to fly. Mike would regale me with a long and tortuous story about how a small but critical replacement part on each plane was being sourced from Boeing in the US and was travelling to London via Rome. He would then tell me that the slowest part of their journey was the trip around London's M25 orbital motorway, where the parts were now stuck in a thirty-vehicle pile-up. Like the best nightmares, some were just too close to reality for comfort.

Other bad dreams featured the myriad third parties we had to rely upon for the airline to function. 'What's the matter in Rome?' I would ask anxiously. Jane Willacy, the project manager, would shake her head. 'It's the baggage handlers, Barbara. They've announced a lightning strike to coincide with the big football match this afternoon. That means we'll have luggage all over the tarmac in Rome with Go's first passengers humping their own bags. And of course, there will be huge delays.'

My own personal nightmare involved public humiliation, always guaranteed to wake you up in a cold sweat in the middle of the warmest night. In this one, Stelios and his colleagues would arrive at the terminal for the first flight, joined by a flouncing Richard Branson in wedding drag. And then Michael O'Leary, Ryanair's feisty CEO, would turn up in a kilt with a pub-load of boisterous companions. The check-in area would dissolve into chaos as they started verbally trashing Go and then me. And in the background, I could vaguely make out Sir (now Lord) Colin Marshall, British Airways' Chairman, arms crossed, head shaking in dismay, while standing beside him Lord King loudly proclaimed that women really should never be allowed to run airlines. To complete the nightmare, the calm voice of Trevor McDonald opens the ITN Evening News with full coverage of the debacle.

But it wasn't a nightmare. It went like a dream.

That morning, on the stand of Gate 14 at Stansted Airport, in Essex, our fleet of two Boeing 737-300s stood glistening in the warm sunshine ready for take-off to Rome on Go's inaugural flight. Every detail had to be perfect, so I slipped into our second-floor offices at Enterprise House to check that everything was on schedule. Jane Willacy, the project manager who had effectively dragged us into existence by her dogged determination, bloody-mindedness and endless bubble charts, smiled, hugged me and wished me luck. On my desk there was a pile of good-wishes cards, flowers from my parents in America, and a letter from Sir Colin Marshall: 'On behalf of the board of British Airways, I send all of your team best wishes for your launch and success for the future. I have no doubt that if your initial effort is anything to go by, you will achieve a fine record.'

The omens were favourable for the start of our airline battle. It was turning into a rare beautiful British day as I strolled across to the main terminal. My five-year-old daughter Lauren, looking gorgeous in her sailor-girl outfit, had arrived at the check-in desk with her godmother, Denise Pritchard, an old friend from my days at consulting firm Coopers & Lybrand in 1986, her husband Hefin, and my husband, Guy. Denise had been involved with Go's early marketing and went on to build the airline's first website. She marked our big day by giving the launch team fleeces embossed with the Go logo. We had left my son James, who was only two, at home. He was just a little too young to enjoy the occasion.

Flight GOE103 to Rome Ciampino was open for check-in, and I waved to Cheryl and Gail, who had trained all the new check-in agents. Ed Winter smiled as I approached. The flight was ready and on time, with our Chief Pilot, John Mahon, at the controls in the cockpit, and Mike Williams keeping a close eye on the aircraft's readiness. I checked in at the stylish desks with Go's branding and moved with the throng through security to the boarding gate.

David Magliano, our Marketing Director and the brains behind our branding, was waiting for me and managing the expectant press with Sue Harrison, our public relations expert. Lynne Hodgkinson, our recently arrived Finance Director, taking her last day of leisure for many months to come, would also be with us on board with her future husband, Simon. My co-author of the Go business plan, Simon Harford, and his fiancée, Ansi, were also travelling to the Italian capital, while our newly hired network planning guru, Steven Horner, held the fort back in the office.

In the hectic weeks leading up to lift-off, we discovered that our greatest rival, Stelios Haji-Ioannou, was planning to travel on the first flight, snapping up ten £100 return tickets. It was hardly a detective story, because his name gave it away. The telephone sales team intercepted his itinerary and gleefully brought it to me. I sent him a hand-written note saying: 'Looking forward to welcoming you on board.' We hoped his antics on the day would be restricted to something typically flamboyant, but nothing dangerous. He didn't disappoint. Stelios and his gang of ten dressed up in orange boiler suits that spelled GO EASYJET and made a colourful addition to the first flight.

I welcomed Stelios and his easyJet party-crashers to the boarding area with a wide smile and a jumbo-sized boarding pass emblazoned with our Go logo. The press lapped it up and it secured our event a slot on the evening news on television and radio. Next morning the *Sun* reported: 'Cheap Jet "Hijacked"' while *The Times* devoted the better part of a page, with a picture of Stelios and me together grinning. The coverage was a bonus for both of us.

We all boarded the aircraft, filling every seat with a mix of new customers and old friends and helpers who deserved their day in the sun. There were no freebies and everyone had to pay their way. Before the cabin crew began their mandatory safety demonstration, I made a little speech saying: 'This is a milestone for us and if you enjoy the trip, please tell your friends.'

I was brought up to be courteous, so I even thanked Stelios and his colleagues for 'making Go your low-cost airline of choice'. The easyJet team handed out orange promotional leaflets showing their characteristic chutzpah. They read: 'The unbelievable fare you are enjoying today is the result of a revolution led by easyJet which started in Europe some three years ago.' The Greek entrepreneur was perfectly charming, even complimenting the cabin crew on our cafetière coffee, which soon became one of our trademarks. It was all oddly civil considering that we had just been fighting Stelios in the High Court over his claim that British Airways was launching Go to undermine the competition. One of his orange-suited gang, Mike Coltman, later joined Go and became a close friend. He confessed to me that he had been a little embarrassed about being part of Stelios's stunt.

I popped into the cockpit to greet John and First Officer Rod Mayo. All was well and we were ready to go for the very first time. Moments later there was a graceful take-off, and not a flutter of turbulence would trouble us on our journey. Up at 30,000 ft, when the seat-belt lights were switched off, I began what became a regular habit, walking up and down the aircraft aisle, answering questions and thanking customers for using Go. I never failed to perform this enjoyable ritual on every single flight I ever took on Go.

The first flight was textbook stuff and touched down with the Italian capital basking in mid-morning sunshine. Dominic Paul and his new airports team welcomed us with laughter and handshakes. Still in his mid-twenties, he'd been out in Rome setting up our operations. A super-fit competitive triathlete, he was a star in the making.

It was a delightful 25 degrees and there were more press interviews – where I introduced the Go brand to the Italian press by describing us as the 'Swatch of the sky'. Then we cut an enormous Go cake and I poured a few glasses of sparkling wine for customers. Some of the adventurous headed into town for a whistle-stop tour of the sights. Simon and Lynne, their partners and the rest of the team settled into a well-known trattoria and ordered several Sambucas.

But I headed back on our return afternoon flight and went straight to the party in my 'CEO launching airline' garb for the first of Go's crazy twice-a-year parties. It was staged in a large marquee on the grass by the side of the Stansted terminal where Go colleagues had brought in food from home and some pilots were running a sizzling barbecue. I could now relax for a few minutes confident that colleagues were preparing for tomorrow's flights.

It went like a dream. We could stand up to the world's scrutiny. We even enjoyed our biggest competitor trying to hijack our launch. And we were ready to fight for our survival. Our low-cost battle had commenced. And this was just day one.

Chapter Two

An Unlikely Businesswoman

So how on earth did an American woman in her late thirties with a degree in international relations and never previously described as a low-cost person find herself leading Go into a battle for a slice of the fastest-growing part of Europe's airline industry?

I can claim to be a Child of the Sixties, born in 1960 in Arlington, a suburb of Boston in Massachusetts, but it wasn't Flower Power and Peace and Love. In fact, we were a pretty normal East Coast family where my parents worked hard and believed in the American Dream – get educated, work hard and you'll do well.

My father Jim, born just outside Boston to an Irish-Italian family, went to university after his military service late in World War Two. His degree in chemistry led him into a sales job for laboratory equipment, where he climbed the management ladder at various companies. My mother Noreen came from the harbour town of Cobh, in County Cork, Ireland, and immigrated to the US as a toddler. She was raised in Cambridge, just outside Boston. The hope and optimism of life in the New

World did not pan out for her parents and she was greatly affected by being a child in a struggling immigrant family during the Great Depression. Nevertheless, she believed, and instilled in us, that life's about 'pulling ourselves up by our boot straps'. She worked as a secretary and rose high to become the personal assistant to the chief financial officer of a leading US company.

There were three of us. My brother Tom and my sister Pat were a few years older than me, and we were at the tail-end of the Baby Boomer generation. My parents had an immovable faith in the power of learning and they were always encouraging about our academic progress and ambitions. Prone to mild exaggeration, my mother used to say to the three of us: 'Don't worry about how much university costs, I'll scrub floors to put you through Harvard.' All my life I have remained very close to my parents, and every Sunday evening I enjoy phoning them to swap tales on the week's events.

I must have been a little different even then, because I remember as a seven-year-old being asked what I wanted to do when I grew up and answering: 'Well, I want to be President of the United States.' I couldn't understand why everyone wouldn't want the same ambition and was shocked to hear about the nurses, teachers and firemen that my classmates would want to become.

I spent my teens striving to do well at school, following my nose to subjects I found interesting. We moved around a lot. I attended three schools in three different states: California, Iowa and New Hampshire between the ages of fourteen and seventeen. I never stayed long enough to really settle in, but in Iowa I was named the Most Likely to Succeed among the seventeen-years-olds!

Yet I had no early ambition to be a business person – let alone an entrepreneur. Growing up with a father who regarded his job with the kind of affection you might have for a hobby left a positive imprint on me. Unlike many of my university peers, business carried no stigma for me because I'd watched my father enjoying his work for many years. We have had many chats about managing sales forces, handling customers, and how demanding it is to work for entrepreneurs. He passed on lots of nuggets of business wisdom. One of my favourites was when he once told me how he had faced a regular problem with sales people crashing their company cars and how the problem disappeared when he asked them to submit mileage charges and use their own cars instead.

Then, without intending to, I learned a lot about day-to-day good business practice at my after-school and summer jobs. Like most American teenagers, I worked part-time, earning a few dollars to pay for extras. My money paid for my out-of-school interests. In my case it was to fund my expensive passion for riding horses and to help me build my nest-egg for college. My parents agreed to pay the tuition and housing costs for university and we were responsible for buying books and providing our own spending money. I am quoted in several newspaper interviews as 'flipping hamburgers' in my youth, but that isn't really true. An early job was at Burger King in Ames, Iowa, where we lived for a year. Mostly I worked at the front counter, taking orders, putting the burgers and fries into paper bags and smiling at the customers as I relieved them of their cash. 'Have a Nice Day' must have been tattooed on my forehead. My most mind-numbing job was matching shuffled-up cards and envelopes at a greeting-card shop. I didn't especially enjoy any of these jobs, but they served their purpose, kept my horse in oats and filled my savings for college. I was also picking up subliminal lessons about customer service; if you're polite and smile, it lightens the day.

Working as a checkout operator at a Finast supermarket in New Hampshire, when we moved back to New England, provided me with my first hard lesson in management. The manager was a bully who tried to use intimidation to get things done in the store.

'Haven't you finished packing that shelf yet?' he would shout.

'Where have you been?' if someone went off to the toilet.

One night I was petrified when the cash in my till failed to add up to the sales I had rung up – by less than a dollar. Minor errors like this caused major eruptions. It was an unhappy place. I developed a hatred of bullies and vowed in the future to stand up to anyone I thought was being unfair.

This crude attempt at management by intimidation was futile. The downtrodden employees, most of whom had been there for many years, practised passive resistance to make their lives bearable. They worked at a snail's pace, urging me to slow down too.

It was also my first experience of organised labour. Finast was a closed union shop, meaning that you were required to become a card-carrying, dues-paying member of the Amalgamated Meat Cutters and Butchers Union. It was not an option. I thought it wrong to force people to join an organisation just to get a job. I've always thought it's another form of discrimination.

The one good outcome from this job was my black and white cat, Thadeus. The store boss was going to dump a stray kitten in a bag at the side of the road and let it die because it had wandered into the storeroom looking for food. I rescued the kitten, took it home, and he lived with my animal-loving parents in New Hampshire until he died at seventeen a few years ago.

I enjoyed riding a great deal and began to take my sport very seriously, competing at ever higher levels. I narrowly missed going to the national US championships in Madison Square Gardens in New York. I needed a first place in my region and only managed to come second. It was a deep disappointment, and left me longing to get back into riding once I could afford the sport. I effectively quit at the end of high school because paying for a US private university education was incompatible with the care and feeding of a horse.

I worked hard and did well at high school and went on to Mount Holyoke College in Massachusetts, a selective liberal arts college of about 2000 women founded by Mary Lyon in 1837. It is the oldest of the Seven Sisters – a sort of female equivalent of the formerly all-male Ivy League – whose ethos is to encourage independent, critical thinkers who speak and write effectively. Having been lucky enough to be accepted at several places, I chose Mount Holyoke because it was so highly rated yet everyone I met there was very friendly. All of this was bound to suit me.

From day one, academic life at Mount Holyoke was challenging, and I recall being hauled up to see the professor after obtaining a dismal grade in my first political science course. As I sat in his book-lined study, he flicked through my papers and then looked at me through his half-moon spectacles.

'Ms Cassani, your work is falling short here. You do a good job at describing the issue but you aren't arguing a case. You should develop a hypothesis then use evidence to support your argument.'

It was very different from my high-school educational experience. Although I got my first and only C grade at university, it was a breakthrough when I finally understood. I've been arguing that way ever since!

In my second year at Mount Holyoke, I took an introductory course in International Relations from Professor Vinnie Ferraro, a young professor with a genius for putting across his passion for the subject. I loved analysing the foreign policies of the US, the Soviet Union and Europe and wrestling with all the various theories about what determined how states behaved towards each other. It was the era of Lech Walesa, the leader of Solidarity and the Gdansk shipyard protests that led to the fall of Polish communism. I even had a Solidarnosc poster on my wall. Studying these epoch-changing events became my 'major' and in my final fourth year I was elected President of the International Relations Club.

I chose to write my honours thesis on Romanian foreign policy, which seemed to have received scant academic attention by comparison with other Eastern bloc countries. Once I graduated *magna cum laude* (an American way of saying that you graduated with high honours), my paper was made available publicly. I was shocked to receive calls from Romanian dissidents in the United States urging me to help them. I hadn't appreciated that an interesting academic paper to me might mean I would want to join the fight for justice against Nicolae Ceausescu on the streets of Bucharest.

When I became a research assistant for Professor Ferraro, it struck me that you get paid a lot better to use your brains. He kindly shared the pride of authorship with another student and me when we published an academic paper on the social and medical costs of underdevelopment in Africa. I couldn't believe my luck, because up until then I'd been dishwashing in the student residence to earn spending money. I was paid $9 an hour for the research, double the rate in the kitchens. Until then, all my jobs had been pretty boring and relatively poorly paid. Now I was on to something.

Following my third year at Mount Holyoke College, earning money for my first trip to Europe and replenishing my college savings forced me out of the library research role and back to waitressing. I found a decent summer job at Saunders seaside restaurant in Rye Harbor, near my home in New Hampshire. My clumsiness was notorious, and one day I slipped on the deck and tipped a big tray of cooked New England lobsters back into the sea by mistake. To make it worse, my father was having a business lunch there that day! I wasn't the most elegant waitress but I managed to compensate for my lack of finesse with friendliness. I'd tell customers that I was earning money to help pay my way through college. And I smiled a lot. The tips were great.

When it was time to graduate with my Bachelor of Arts degree, I hadn't yet exhausted my interest in international relations. I was offered a full scholarship – including spending money – to earn a Master's degree at the Woodrow Wilson School at Princeton University. So off I trotted in 1982 with no career plan for what I would do with this fancy degree. The Woodrow Wilson School was founded by the same idealistic president of the United States who was also an alumnus and former president of the university. I admired Wilson's principled campaign for global peace and found ironic his failed attempts to get the League of Nations ratified by the US Congress. The school lives up to its namesake and is a stopping-off spot for leading intellectuals, visiting diplomats and pipe-smoking statesmen who teach seminars. I was one of the youngest graduate students in my year and was impressed by the visiting lecturers and fellow students who had come from around the world from careers in economic development and government.

The most enjoyable courses were with former US government leaders on subjects ranging from foreign relations to international monetary policy. But it was a course with international finance expert Professor Peter Kenen involving complex computer modelling that really appealed to my practical soul. The class was split into role-playing the International Monetary Fund, a Central American country and a large multinational bank, such as Chase Manhattan. It was just like a Sim City computer game, but this was in the early 1980s when you needed a mainframe computer even for simple models. We examined deep-rooted problems such as debt, poverty and the banks' risk portfolios and studied them from every conceivable angle. It was a primer in crafting macro-economic policies and a clever way of bringing to life often-intractable issues. I flourished.

By now I was flirting with a career in government or the diplomatic service. A few months working for a Republican Senator in Washington and another working for the US Embassy in Stockholm threw up doubts about taking this direction. I enjoyed living in Stockholm but I wasn't cut out for an envoy's life. My job was to report back to the US State Department on the condition of the Swedish economy. It wasn't particularly interesting work and I was positive diplomatic life wasn't for me when I was asked to give a hand with the visit of Vice President George Bush (Senior). The role was helping with the logistics for his wife Barbara, such as where to find a loo at each of her engagements. I also penned all of her thank-you notes to her hosts and helpers and even wrote one to myself. It began to dawn on me that an Ivy League degree was no protection from the mundane tasks in every job.

Nevertheless, time at an Ivy League university puts a skip of self-confidence into your stride. You suddenly have an internationally recognised stamp of approval. And by the second year of the two-year Masters programme I was itching to get a job and earn some proper money.

I met my husband, Guy Davis, at Princeton where he had won a scholarship to do research in economics after completing his BA and M.Phil. from Oxford University. He was a super-fit swimmer and I fell for his amusing, detached English style. He was also handy to have around to help with the dreaded statistics homework. Guy returned to London for his first job with Boston Consulting Group in 1983 and we began a long-distance romance. We hopped back and forth across the Atlantic until we both moved to Washington in 1984.

In the eighties, if you were in your early twenties at a top US college you had to become a professional *something*. Most of my peers aspired to be a lawyer, doctor, or professor, and even banking and consulting were becoming pseudo-professions. It was simple. In professional jobs, you hung around with people like yourself, hopefully worked on stimulating projects and you made good money. That didn't sound so bad. It never entered my head to be interested in business, let alone airlines.

When it was time to leave Princeton, I was hired by Coopers & Lybrand's (C&L) international business consulting group in Washington, DC. I liked them because the work was interesting, business was booming and Michael Huerta, a Woodrow Wilson School graduate who was working there as a consultant, made the place sound intriguing. When I arrived I was thrown in at the deep end. I thrived on defining business problems, sifting through data or information to draw conclusions and then persuading the client I was right. It was the perfect extension of what I'd been doing in university and I was being paid well!

After a couple of years on projects such as assessing debt-ridden Brazil for business opportunities and evaluating the likely prospects of a joint venture for beef farming between a Chinese group and a company in Omaha, Nebraska, I was struck by a gap in my experience as an international business consultant – I'd never lived and worked outside the United States for more than a few months. So we headed for London. It worked for Guy because he wanted to move into banking. C&L wouldn't help me move to their UK office, so I quit in the US and got myself rehired into their London office, while Guy started on his banking career with SG Warburg. Our relationship flourished and we got married in my parents' garden in New Hampshire in 1985.

In London, I was eager and willing, but perhaps I was trying too hard. When you arrive in a new country you want to get the clichés out of the way as soon as possible. London's got traffic problems, hasn't it? The English don't invite you around much, do they? And what's that strange, pale glow in the sky? I've never thought of myself as a typical American but I can imagine that to some I might have seemed one.

This being 1986, the time of the Big Bang, when the London

Stock Exchange became a truly global trading institution, wasn't being an American a good thing? Not at C&L, which was still an Oxbridge stronghold with men wearing blue pinstripe suits. Not quite bowler hats and umbrellas, but the culture suggested that they were not long gone. And I was definitely not 'Old School'. I was in my twenties, noisy and direct. At my annual appraisal I dared to ask for feedback. This was clearly too direct for their taste. My diffident boss paused, and then said: 'Barbara, you're over-enthusiastic.'

Well, that did it. If wanting to work hard and do a good job for clients was 'over-enthusiastic' then this was not the place for me. I found myself spending too many lunchtimes with friends Denise Pritchard and Pamela Watson in our regular Smithfield wine bar haunts complaining about it, so a big change was called for.

Chapter Three

The Luck of the Draw

I joined British Airways at age twenty-seven because I loved travelling. Isn't that the reason anyone would join an airline? I had a vague idea of staying for about two years, doing a bit of internal consulting and, if lucky, moving up the management ladder. The fact that British Airways was recently privatised from government ownership and facing a huge change agenda also appealed to the Woodrow Wilson School side of me. Having said all that, the biggest draw was the opportunity to travel the world for free – and in First Class! Now I would have the chance to spend time exploring the corners of the world I'd never seen before. The thought of Australia and the endless empty beaches in the Seychelles clinched it. Yes, it sounded an excellent move.

I even took a pay cut from Coopers & Lybrand, where I was still a fairly junior consultant, to join British Airways as a senior manager. But instead of working at British Airways for just a couple of years, I stayed for a decade. It was an interesting adventure as my job changed every eighteen months or so. In ten years I held seven jobs, all but one of them a newly created role when I took over. The one job that existed before me was a role we got rid of. There was just so much to change and develop at British Airways, and I was the sort of person who relished the challenge of figuring out how to do things differently.

British Airways was going through a revolution when I joined in 1987, changing from a public-sector dinosaur to a private company trying to evolve into a commercial dynamo that would report impressive results to Mrs Thatcher's new generation of private shareholders. A lot of energy was expended transforming the company into the most successful global airline in the eighties and into the mid-nineties.

From my first day in British Airways, I found myself held up as a symbol of the changing organisation emerging from government ownership; I was American and knew all the snappy eighties management jargon. It was a lot different to how I was viewed at C&L, and a lesson in how others' preconceptions can help or hinder. British Airways had been a loss-making burden on Britain's taxpayers for years but was being reshaped. Its flotation on the stock market in February 1987 was an instant success, receiving over one million applications – including mine and thousands of other small investors' buying into the emerging popular share-owning culture for the first time.

The Chief Executive at the time was Sir Colin Marshall, now the Chairman and a member of the House of Lords, who had spent ten years running Avis, the car rental giant, in the United States. He knew about marketing and everyone remembered the Avis badges and slogan: We Try Harder. British Airways was still run like a civilian arm of the Royal Air Force and Marshall wanted a seismic shift in the company's collective thinking. When he arrived, senior pilots and engineers had too much power that stifled change and snooty cabin crews patronised the paying customers. By the time I arrived, some of the changes were under way. British Airways was becoming more dynamic and even glamorous. Younger employees from outside industry were being drafted into the company, people whose backgrounds hadn't been in government. Mike Batt, the head of British Airways' Brand Marketing, arrived from Mars, the confectionery giant, which over the years has been an outstanding training ground for senior UK executives. Mike is famously quoted as saying: 'There has always been a mystique and a romance about aviation, but in terms of the principles involved in satisfying your customer, there's no difference between selling airline seats and chocolate bars.' In principle, I think he's right. Then Martin George, another chocolate industry marketer, was taken on. He had been in the confectionery industry too and became a colleague in sales and later Director of Marketing.

Marshall and his team infused the new kind of service-led thinking. And because I was American, and had had all those service industry jobs, it was second nature to me. I liked the slogans and didn't mind wearing the badges. The emphasis was on the people who served customers, but sometimes that message didn't seem to penetrate through to head office thinking. I now find it odd that I worked for British Airways for three years before meeting a customer. It was the kind of place where lower-level people dealt with customers. More recent events, such as wild-cat strikes, suggest to me that the culture hasn't changed much. In retrospect, such detachment at head office from the customer seemed unhealthy, and this perception framed my own future thinking.

Looking back, bumping into Bob Ayling, the future Chief Executive of British Airways, back in the autumn of 1988 played a key part in this story. Together with a gaggle of British Airways executives, I was in a Chilterns country house, at a management development course called Managing People First, which was related to the course that everyone in British Airways attended – Putting People First. This training was part of the Marshall Plan aimed at transforming British Airways' customer service in the eighties. Attending was mandatory and this was the last chance to make the course.

We all gathered at Chartridge, an elegant retreat in Buckinghamshire, thirty miles from London, then owned by British Airways and used for running senior management seminars. We sipped tea in china cups and nibbled the ubiquitous pink wafer biscuits. I ended up chatting to a man named Bob, then British Airways' Legal Director.

Somehow I ended up on the course with many of British Airways' senior directors. There were about 100 people including ten of the top guys. I liked Bob Ayling a great deal – and I still do. He was relaxed, intelligent and humorous. None of us at the time had any inkling that he would become our boss.

We were split into small breakout groups. Mine included Bob; Sue Moore, who moved into a senior role in Marketing in the nineties; Pat Durrant, who has since left, but he was ex-British Caledonian and Chief Engineer at Gatwick; and John Lewis, an ex-Pan Am guy, who headed the US telesales. The course helped us understand our management style. Since I wasn't managing any people, it was rather academic but still enjoyable. Bob was never a great believer in all this management development guff, which made his later appointment as human resources director ironic. I think he warmed to me because I was sparky and confident. I was the loud-mouthed ex-management consultant from the States and he thought British Airways needed a few more like me.

Bob now jokes that I was continually complaining about not being challenged enough and was always wanting a new role. I must have been a real pain in the neck. His response was to nod patronisingly and send me back to whatever I was doing at the time. In retrospect, British Airways put me through a range of roles that helped prepare me for running my own company. I didn't enjoy every one, and some of the experiences taught me what not to do, but others encouraged me to strive for higher standards. My path and Bob's would cross regularly over the next decade, but it was only in 1997 that I realised the good fortune of having been with him on that Chartridge management course.

My first few years in British Airways were spent doing the sort of work I'd done at Coopers & Lybrand, only this time it was for the same client. I helped buy a computer reservations system and assessed the potential for a clunky precursor to the web as a home airline booking system. My assessment was fairly brutal. It was a dud – and time proved me correct.

However, my interest in internal consulting began to wane as I learned that the real power is always with managers at the sharp end. It was plain to me what had to be done, but I didn't have a patch of my own. Too many British Airways managers seemed content to preserve the status quo and weren't brave enough to try something new. Who could have blamed them? The culture of British Airways rewarded politically savvy executives who didn't rock the boat.

My big break was in 1989 when an enticing job came up in UK Sales. The then Director of Marketing and Operations, Liam Strong, called me into his office.

'I know you've been keen to try something new, so we've got a suggestion for you, Barbara. You can remain here in Head Office in your safe and well-paid position as a strategist or you can take a risk.'

I was intrigued. 'Tell me more,' I thought.

'There is a position as Sales Manager for Southern England, but I have to warn you it's a tough one. I'd like you to go and meet Jim Callery.'

I nodded and agreed to explore the proposition. I went to visit Jim, who was an American and the head of Worldwide Sales. He was blunt and told me that he didn't agree with me even being considered for the job. He was convinced I'd mess it up. 'Screw them,' I thought, and took the job.

So thank goodness for Kevin Hatton, who became my new

boss. He had enormous enthusiasm and energy. He already had a half-dozen people working for him who knew how to be sales managers. He wanted someone outside the box, and he landed me. Kevin and I worked well together for my couple of years in sales. I had ideas on how the sales organisation could be improved, and he implemented some of my suggestions while keeping his eye on our revenue.

He was a great boss, and systematic about managing his senior team – we all had clear quarterly goals and talked about achieving them all the time. He was wonderful with the sales reps too. He genuinely liked them, appreciated their efforts and knew we would be nowhere without their effort. Many of these lessons helped me when I started my own business.

The best part of my job was managing a team of around 100 people and having responsibility for meeting tough revenue targets. Once a week I went out with a sales rep zooming around the highways of southern England in a Ford Escort meeting travel agents. I loved it.

I also enjoyed the thrill of the monthly sales numbers. I immediately wanted to dig into them, trying to find out what was working and what wasn't. I even liked getting them when the Gulf War started in 1991, bookings across the Atlantic dried up, and our sales dived through the floor. My biggest frustration was the six-week delay in getting data.

Two years in UK sales taught me more than I could have ever gleaned from memos to HQ. And I'd proved that inexperienced but motivated head office people can sometimes make a frontline role. It wasn't all plain sailing – I made a series of gaffes that still make me wince when I recall them today – but this too was part of my career development.

In my early days at British Airways, Sir Colin Marshall had a mysterious American named Michael Levin working with him. No one knew precisely what he did, but his name sowed fear in the hearts of the British Airways old guard. It was said that he did Sir Colin's dirty work and had an adjacent office at Speedbird House at Heathrow.

There'd been a day in the early 1980s, called 'the Night of the Long Knives', when hundreds of middle and senior managers lost their jobs as part of the company's turnaround. The folklore told that Michael Levin had drawn up the final list for those to be sacked, among them some talented airline people who prospered elsewhere.

Soon after joining British Airways, I was asked to meet Michael. I was wary of him, since he had the reputation of a bully. Putting on my breeziest manner, I wandered into his office as if daring him to fire me.

'Tell me, Miss Cassani, what are your motivations and plans for working with us at British Airways?'

Well, I couldn't really share my thoughts about the benefit of first-class travel to go to the Seychelles.

'I am hoping to move from a strategic role into line management at some stage in the future,' I replied.

He nodded approvingly and then asked about my five-year career plan at British Airways.

I laughed. 'I'm going to give it two years and see how it all goes,' I replied.

Clearly, this was not the right answer. And it got worse.

'I note your educational background here, Miss Cassani. Why did you attend the Woodrow Wilson School at Princeton instead of choosing the Kennedy School at Harvard?'

'I thought Princeton had the better programme and it was more quantitative,' I replied with characteristic bluntness.

In other words, Princeton was more difficult and Harvard was for wimps. Michael Levin then informed me that he was on the faculty of the Kennedy School. Oh dear. As I left his office, I was even more certain that I was not suited for a career in diplomacy, and even wondered if I would survive long at British Airways.

My first encounter with Sir Colin Marshall also did very little to improve my prospects. Within the first year at British Airways, I began working on the connections between IT and marketing – our electronic distribution. The senior directors decided that a partnership with British Telecom would be a shrewd move, so Sir Iain Vallance, BT's Chief Executive at the time, and Sir Colin held a summit at the top of the British Telecom Tower in west London. There we were, revolving slowly with an unfolding panorama of London below, and my job was to load the slides in the projector and hand it over to the big boys. Sadly, I had not yet developed my attention-to-detail skills. I forgot to check that *all* the slides were the right way up, and the proceedings ground to a halt to make sense of the muddle that followed.

I'll never forget Sir Colin's grave face afterwards when he had a private word with me. 'Barbara, please don't let this happen again.' I'd have jumped if a window had been open. But I learned two lessons. First, the obvious one – check everything twice, all the way through. Second, never embarrass a junior person publicly. A quiet word is more effective. His control and respect, even to a very junior colleague, was admirable.

Some of my gaffes were lighter-hearted than others. Take my first business trip upon joining British Airways in 1987. I flew on Concorde to New York – my first time on this amazing aircraft – and I'll remember the flight for ever. To start with, it all went well. I worked hard trying to keep up with the piles of paperwork that sped my way throughout the flight from my new boss, Luke Mayhew. But the fun started as we began our descent. There is far more movement inside Concorde than on a jumbo jet – especially on a windy day. As the plane hit a gust, wobbled then lurched from 60,000 ft to begin its descent, I grabbed my boss's thigh and squawked with concern. Fortunately, Luke saw the amusing side and didn't file a lawsuit for harassment!

And one embarrassing anecdote is a classic for anyone who has ever tried to blend in with the locals. I was on the verge of making that big step in my career from Head Office to Sales. The rite of passage was being introduced to the sales force of two hundred by Kevin Hatton at the annual sales conference. I realised my street credibility was nil and was apprehensive. Kevin, a Mancunian known for his sardonic sense of humour, decided to make fun of my being an American.

'This is Barbara Cassani, the newest member of our management team,' he started to the sea of faces. Then he continued, jovial but close to condescending. 'She is still trying to master the more colloquial aspects of the Queen's English.'

I interrupted spontaneously: 'Ya mean like wanker.'

The whole place broke up laughing. I thought the word meant 'wally'. Later when Guy, who had been there, explained my gaffe, I was mortified. But it broke the ice at the meeting and my warm relations with the sales force were assured from that day.

My next role at Gatwick in 1992 sounded more exciting – but it was tough. British Airways had just bought Dan-Air. I was part of the integration team, and one of my responsibilities was to find ways of selling more seats. I learned one fundamental lesson that would carry me though to the end of this story: merging airlines doesn't work.

Fundamentally, British Airways made a mistake acquiring Dan-Air in October 1992. It had been looking for a solution to its unacceptable financial performance at Gatwick. The expensive customised British Airways jets, the low productivity of aircraft and crews and the burden of the huge numbers of people in Head Office, who were not part of generating revenue or providing the service, made British Airways' costs at Gatwick very high. Only Heathrow's routes were profitable because they could carry enough business passengers who paid higher ticket prices to be profitable. Gatwick's location, further from Central

London and to the south where fewer businesses are located, was unable to attract enough business customers to make its routes profitable.

Dan-Air, set up after World War Two to fly cargo from London to Europe, evolved into a popular charter operation, but in the early 1990s it was widely believed that its deep financial troubles stemmed from developing an unprofitable short-haul scheduled network. It accumulated debts of £70 million. David James, a well-known corporate rescue specialist, came in to sort it out and sell it. With too many aircraft types, Dan-Air was an unwieldy business and its future looked equally bleak. But the employees were loyal and passionate about their airline. Even the demise of Gatwick short-haul rival Air Europe in January 1991 did not improve prospects for Dan-Air. Richard Branson offered to buy the company but seemed interested only in the airline's slots at Gatwick, not in the employees or the mixed bag of forty-four planes.

By buying Dan-Air for £1 (but picking up tens of millions of debt), the idea for British Airways was to create a hub-and-spoke operation, feeding customers from Europe to British Airways' long-haul routes and vice versa. These passengers, combined with the local customers, were expected to generate enough volume to make Gatwick profitable.

In the middle of all this I had my first encounter with the advertising world. We were trying to spark interest among flyers in the Southeast of England to use British Airways at Gatwick. The idea was to create a TV ad that communicated the wide range of routes and how easy it was to move through Gatwick's new North Terminal. I was told a production budget of a million pounds in 1992 was critical or it wasn't worth doing. It seemed a bit excessive hiring a movie set near Pinewood Studios to rebuild the Gatwick North Terminal check-in area so that a bunch of actors and one lovely dancing British Airways pilot could 'waltz their way' through the travel experience. It was a stylish advert, but I later learned from Go's Sales and Marketing Director, David Magliano, that you could create an even bigger impact from an ad that cost £80,000 – with bouncing Go circles and a catchy 1960s pop tune. Not so in those days. Spending a mint meant you really cared about your business. Right?

Away from the glamorous world of TV ads, my day job was now to integrate the Dan-Air cabin crew into British Airways. We combined the sales and marketing teams and chopped most of the Dan-Air jobs. We kept a few hundred cabin crew and expected them to be grateful they had a job. They were for a couple of weeks, but then resentment set in. As part of Bob Ayling's master plan for turning Gatwick into a profitable hub, Dan-Air was to be run as a separate lower-cost unit. Cabin crew already earned 20 per cent less than British Airways crew and we were now taking another 10 per cent off them. Then we sent them to be fitted for their designer British Airways uniforms and told them to be happy they still had a job. Oh, and we also laid off too many, so that those left had to work doubly hard to fill the gaps.

The flaw in all this was that it was disrespectful at the most basic level. We gave the Dan-Air crews a humiliating, take-it-or-leave-it ultimatum. We demanded capitulation. And they balked. Quite rightly. Some 'all-knowing' management we were. You can picture the result. Strife, strikes, bitterness and resentment replaced loyalty, customer service and contentment. I learned the hard way how difficult it is to make mergers work.

I also learned that if you want a part of the company to be really low-cost, you need to separate it completely from the rest of the business. You cannot hive off a few areas, such as flight crew and cabin crew, which make up only around 10 per cent of costs, and expect to make an overall impact on the cost position. Tackle the thing head-on if you're serious. Either separate it completely or reduce the total cost base of the company.

When Charles Gurassa, Director of the Americas region,

approached me after a year at Gatwick to transfer to New York to a newly created position – General Manager, USA – it was time to move on. I had a feeling that Gatwick was going to be a tough nut to crack and I wanted to be back in a job where I had more control over what happened. So, with some relief, I said goodbye to Gatwick and moved back to America.

In my next role, I learned even more about why airline mergers don't work. As General Manager, I helped to manage British Airways' investment in USAirways – a seriously ill airline that has been in and out of the bankruptcy court for years.

It was formed by merging several regional airlines: Piedmont (a classy Southern hospitality airline that engendered incredible customer loyalty), Allegheny (nicknamed Agony Airline by its frustrated customers) and PSA (a cutesy 1970s West Coast commuter airline that painted smiles on the nose of its planes). From the moment they chained this group of disparate airlines together, failure was inevitable. Fleets weren't the same, the cultures were at odds, and people retained their previous loyalties with ensuing company politics that boggled the mind. They didn't do much rationalising at the head offices of the individual airlines; they simply added them together.

The combined route network looked all-powerful on paper and the gains in market share were expected to be huge. Rationalisation and synergy benefits (code words for 'what money you save or earn from putting the companies together') looked amazing in the plans, but they had a flaw: they were impossible to fulfil in real life. The people running the airline were not unintelligent; it's just that it's nearly impossible to benefit from a merger without killing the company.

On paper my new US job sounded great, but in reality it was an organisational nightmare. Three bosses ran the most profitable market for British Airways and none of us was in overall charge. I was asked to be the senior British Airways representative, but wasn't meant to pull rank over the other two. It was confusing, but over time we learned to work together and the US contributed massively to British Airways' record profits.

As British Airways' senior representative in the US, I got the closest I'll ever come to that lost opportunity of diplomatic service. I lunched with Princess Anne in Washington, sat on boards of chambers of commerce and went to a host of embassy dinners. I was also responsible for meeting, greeting, briefing and often accompanying Lord King, Sir Colin and Bob Ayling on their visits to the US. I irreverently called this part of my job 'bag carrier'. It was funny to think of a woman wrestling the bags from these gentlemanly male executives!

But I learned a lot as a bag carrier, mostly from Sir Colin. His approach to US trips was very systematic and professional. He always made a point of talking to the local employees as he came off his flights. At JFK Airport he would walk down to see the baggage handlers and want to know how things were going. He also made an effort to speak to the cabin crew on board. He did it every time. And the employees in the US noticed. He wasn't chatty or even particularly friendly, but his behaviour demonstrated that those employees mattered.

Helping with British Airways' investment in USAirways was a huge learning experience. British Airways bailed USAirways out of bankruptcy by investing $400m and in exchange they agreed to fly domestic US passengers from the hinterlands to British Airways' long-haul flights for relatively low fares. That was pretty much it. Oh, it was dressed up with lots of employee exchanges and synergy meetings, but they didn't come to much.

Business was great from British Airways' perspective, with soaring profits on routes that were fed highly profitable additional business passengers. But to USAirways it felt like rape and pillage. It was inevitable that it would fall apart and it did so, dramatically, because USAirways' new Chief Executive Officer wanted to renegotiate and British Airways refused.

I learned that it is best to be clear about whether you're trying to build a partnership or have a marriage of convenience. If it is the latter, then go ahead, get the best deal you can and recognise that it won't last very long. But if you want a long-term partnership, both sides need to make money from the deal. I also learned that when bosses change, the whole game is up for grabs.

There were other tricks I picked up from my US colleagues. Barbara Cohen, the Vice President of British Airways' US Finance team, taught me a simple technique that became a cornerstone of the way we managed Go. She kept track of the ups and downs of the annual expenditure budget through an Opportunities and Risks list. This list was circulated to everyone with a budget and we all met to review it together. She encouraged everyone to raise their worries and report on their successes. Because she was managing the costs across the business as a whole, we could, for example, offset the cost of extra de-icing fluid in a cold winter with the savings from a better-than-planned return on the British Airways credit card.

It meant we avoided having departments selfishly hoard their budget surpluses only to waste them on spending that didn't much matter to the overall business. It reduced the politics between departments and gave us a real sense of joint effort and responsibility. And it worked. We consistently hit or improved our budgeted results.

During these years, our home life was going well. Lauren was born in 1992 in London and James in 1995 when we were living in Connecticut. Because Guy and I were working long hours and travelling a lot, we hired top-notch nannies to help with the children. The nannies kept us all sane and organised. Jo Dean, who was Lauren's first nanny, moved with us from London. Angela Taylor, a lovely, artistic person, made going back to work after James was born equally worry-free. Back in London, Liz Alderson maintained calm and sanity at home while Go was happening. And after James was born, I began to ride horses seriously again. I hadn't been able to afford my beloved hobby for fifteen years, but I was on the verge of buying a lovely chestnut gelding to get me back into the amateur show jumping world.

Having kept in touch with Bob Ayling through his quarterly visits to New York, and having shared my frustrations about wanting to run a separate business, I was intrigued when he asked me to stay on for a chat with him and Charles Gurassa during one of my regular visits to London. He had decided that British Airways should develop a business plan for a stand-alone low-cost airline. For years, I thought I'd been the only one interviewed and was flattered that Bob had thoughtfully come up with the airline idea to give me a new challenge. I later learned that he'd asked British Airways' Human Resources department for a list of suitable candidates, requesting that my name be included. The long list landed on his desk, amid a pile of other reports, and he recalls thinking I might be a suitable candidate. The rest is history. I can only imagine it was our decade of staying in touch and my surname coming near to the beginning of the alphabet that gave me the chance of a lifetime.

I met Bob and Charles to hear their offer: 'It's time for us to take on this growing sector of low-cost carriers in our own right,' Bob explained. 'I'd like you to prepare a business plan to set up our own separate company.' I was intrigued to hear that this airline would be the most independent subsidiary in the British Airways group.

I was thrilled, but I didn't accept right away. The first thing I did was call Guy. He loved living in Connecticut and was doing well professionally, but would he make this sacrifice? He was fantastic. He could see that this was a chance in a lifetime for me and immediately agreed to move back to London. For that, I will be eternally thankful.

Chapter Four

Projects Lupin and Hyacinth

The murmurs of the Friday evening members of the Supersonic Club were punctuated by the clink of ice cubes plopping into delicately cut crystal glasses. Sir David Frost nodded in my direction; a tanned and bleached Sting sat near the front looking suitably nonchalant; while two immaculately suited investment bankers loosened their Hermès silk ties and sat whispering conspiratorially. A friendly blonde member of the cabin crew with beautifully manicured nails and a spotless blue uniform leaned over, smiled and said: 'Good afternoon, Ms Cassani, would you like your regular?'

I looked up at her. 'Yes, a glass of still water, please.'

In fact, many frequent Concorde flyers sipped only water and declined the gourmet service because they were heading for the latest trendy Michelin-starred restaurant once they landed at New York. And I was a Concorde frequent flyer, but one who travelled for free.

I flew on this Anglo-French marvel often during the four years that I was the General Manager for British Airways in the United States, based in Queens, a few minutes' drive from Shea

Stadium, home of the New York Mets baseball team. My reason for sipping water on the flight was not so glamorous. I was heading home to Connecticut and two active toddlers. I needed to be in good shape!

This particular flight was in March 1997, and minutes later the sleek Concorde lifted its beautiful nose up into the puffy clouds over Heathrow and powered to Mach One and beyond. The magic of this 3 hours and 25 minutes flight meant we flew westwards through four time zones and I would be back in the Big Apple before we even left London on Friday evenings, in time to tuck my children into bed.

I reached forward, pulled out a nondescript A4 file from the seat pocket, and flipped open the front cover again. It was entitled 'Project Hyacinth: A business proposal for a European low-cost airline'. Here I was sitting in a £4000 seat plotting a business where people would fly for as little as £10. In fact, the irony of the situation didn't hit me until much later. I was too busy shuttling back and forth, juggling everything on my plate and trying to finish up my responsibilities in the US while working on the Hyacinth plan. Then, as we landed, an anonymous traveller from a neighbouring seat leaned over as he pulled on his overcoat.

'I'm intrigued,' he said. 'You've been working the whole journey, engrossed in your pile of figures. Would you mind telling me what you do?'

I replied vaguely: 'Oh, I work for British Airways in New York.'

'Well,' he replied, 'the last time I saw concentration like that was with Margaret Thatcher.'

'I'm not exactly working on matters of state,' I laughed. 'It's next year's budget!'

The project title for the business plan wasn't mine. It had come from Charles Gurassa, by now elevated to a more senior role as a British Airways director close to Bob Ayling. I never understood any hidden significance, since the only Hyacinth I knew was Mrs Bouquet, of *Keeping Up Appearances* fame, whose snobbish pretensions in a television comedy were a million miles from this secret project about assessing the viability of establishing a low-cost airline. The name had started as Project Lupin some time before, but for the sake of secrecy it was changed again to Hyacinth. I was never a gardener, and had never heard of these flower types.

As I opened my Hyacinth folder, I was overwhelmed by how much needed to be done. And there was only me. I bought two notebooks with Burberry-pattern covers to track my early thoughts on the project. They were snapped up in a sale – I love getting nice stuff at a bargain price – and they became my constant companions throughout the spring and summer of 1997 as I criss-crossed the Atlantic, the United States and Europe. I filled them with every question, statistic and contact detail I could muster. And I began to list all of the essentials to start a low-cost airline. On Page 1, I penned a reminder to see people who 'really know the business'. And I began to formulate thoughts on my ideal business model, jotting down: 'First Direct', the telephone banking company, and 'Home Depot', the multi-billion-dollar American DIY chain. Both are employee- and customer-focused in their approach.

Throughout March 1997 I pestered a dozen senior British Airways people to get background on what had gone on before. Most were helpful and generous with their time, but some were dubious and suspicious. I also spoke to some independent thinkers to get an outside perspective

Project Lupin had been started at least a year earlier to react to the threat of increased competition after the European Union fully deregulated the airline industry in April 1997. The process of deregulation had taken ten years and was a progressive march towards free access for EU member airlines to each other's markets and freedom to set fares without government intervention.

And the irony is that if Project Lupin had been approved and taken wing then, it might well have been able to stay ahead of the new breed of low-cost carriers. easyJet had started flying in November 1995 and Ryanair had reinvented itself into a low-cost airline by 1995. But British Airways dithered over the business case and allowed the chance for an early start-up to slip away. It would make it all the more difficult for our project, which would be a much later entrant into the market.

Talks with Dublin-based Ryanair took place in the autumn of 1995 for British Airways to buy an equity stake in the Irish business. British Airways learned that Ryanair had grown by capturing a new market among Ireland's increasingly rich and youthful population who were keen to travel to London and Glasgow in huge numbers. British Airways also helped the nascent Ryanair by pulling out of the Dublin-to-London route because of excessive losses. Ryanair boss Michael O'Leary was shrewd, able to negotiate unbelievable airport deals, and offering exceptionally low prices. The negotiations with British Airways broke down when Ryanair bumped up the price.

Then in early 1997 easyJet talks began between British Airways' senior deals director Roger Maynard and Stelios Haji-Ioannou, easyJet's founder. Born in Cyprus, Stelios, the son of a billionaire Greek shipping magnate, Lucas Haji-Ioannou, studied at the London School of Economics and took a Masters degree at the City University Business School. He was only in his twenties when he used family money to launch his airline on the Luton-to-Glasgow route in November 1995. One of their early advertising campaigns showed them at their cheeky best. The ad challenged travellers to pay the price of a pair of jeans to fly to Glasgow. There were tentative negotiations in Speedbird House in London and at easyJet's base in Luton, but again they collapsed when British Airways saw too many regulatory problems. Besides, the price tag was too steep, valuing the company in the hundreds of millions.

Bob was intrigued to see if we could set up our own for much less. I never received any information from the people who managed these discussions with both Ryanair and easyJet. We created a Chinese Wall and I started from scratch. But very quickly I realised I needed a colleague to develop this new plan and to bounce ideas around with. That was to be Simon Harford. He had joined British Airways in December 1995, having been interviewed personally by Bob Ayling. An Oxford University graduate, he had followed the traditional route into the City, joining the merchant bankers SG Warburg, then went to Insead, the European business school, based in Fontainebleau. After this, he joined the Boston Consulting Group but wanted to move into either aviation or the media.

When British Airways' strategy committee had given its blessing to the idea of setting up a low-cost airline, they expected a fully-fledged business plan. The clear mandate from the start was that the airline would become a profitable company. The British Airways board was not in the mood for yet another loss-making subsidiary, after losses of tens of million of pounds incurred following the purchases of Deutsche BA in Germany and Air Liberté in France.

From the outset, we were to draw up the plan with venture capitalists in mind, which is an entirely different and more exacting proposition than setting something up as a subsidiary to be bankrolled by the parent company. Every financial element had to be justified: proper sales and cost projections had to be made, and there had to be a definite timescale for when the business would start to wash its own face. Profitable in three years seemed reasonable to us.

The financial case presented us with a steep hurdle though. Typically, British Airways expected a return on its investment of 8 per cent on its capital projects; instead we would be required to make 18 per cent. I needed someone with strong financial

aptitude and who knew the ins and outs of British Airways'
Head Office. I had been out of the internal executive politics for
eight years. Bob Ayling recommended Simon, then in his early
thirties. Simon later said that his immediate reaction to working
on the project was: 'Fascinating, but it all depends what that
woman's like.'

So Simon flew across to America to meet me. He arrived in
New York at 9 p.m. and we went to a restaurant for a chat near
my home in Connecticut. He was completely jet-lagged yet we
talked for five hours. We hit it off and were absolutely buzzing
with excitement, although I'm sure the many injections of caffeine helped keep our brains pumping.

Within the week, Simon had accepted the job and we set
about creating the DNA for the new airline. From Easter
onwards we piled into the ideas, working sixteen hours a day, six
and a half days a week. We had so little time and so much to
prepare.

But we needed somewhere secret, away from the prying eyes
of the gossip-mongers who might spill the beans on our project.
So we paid rent for the first-floor boardroom in Whitelocke
House, British Airways' pension fund building at Hounslow, ten
minutes' drive from Heathrow. The pensions department
needed a way to recoup some of the cost of their quiet private
lair, and we were the brash loud tenants. Then we begged and
borrowed some bashed equipment and sorted a single telephone
line. It was an early badge of honour that we were able to get
the second-hand desks and chairs from another British Airways
subsidiary, Air Miles, for almost nothing. They were upgrading
their offices and let us have the old furnishings if we paid to collect them. At a time when so many dot.com companies were
splashing out on ritzy offices before they had made a single
penny, we were excited by saving money. That Hounslow boardroom would become our temporary headquarters, causing
enormous curiosity among the pension staff who wondered

what was going on in their normally sedate building. 'We'd love
to tell you, but we'd probably have to shoot you,' we joked when
one bespectacled clerk stuck his head around the door to ask
what we were up to. The receptionists, Satti, Pam and Jenny,
were just so pleasant, but they hadn't a clue about all the strange
packages of airline manuals and financial analysis that soon
arrived.

Simon felt that we needed more analytical firepower, so we
called in Peter Smith and Martin Pilkington, both partners at
LEK Consulting. They were experienced at creating the kind of
detailed financial projections that the British Airways board
members would need to approve the business blueprint. They
were among our most loyal supporters and friends, playing
important roles throughout the brief history of Go. From the
outset, Simon and I were in agreement that this was going to be
our show. Much to Bob Ayling's credit he gave us the independence that he promised me at our first meeting. We had the
freedom to get on with the job, and we did.

Before I embarked on a little hands-on market research, I
wrote up a list, drawn from my experience in the large traditional airline sector. It was entitled: 'What *not* to do.'

It began:

Firstly, hire a chief executive who is a frustrated pilot or
engineer – someone who loves the sight and sounds of the
cockpit and wants all the freebies of visiting the Boeing
and Airbus factories.
That sure wasn't going to be me.

Develop an antagonistic relationship with unions and allow
poor employee morale to eat away at your organisation.
No thanks, I'd seen enough of that in the US airline industry.

Make lots of decisions based on where you'd like to fly to

play golf or go to the theatre and don't even try to understand how each single route contributes to making a
profitable airline. Kid yourself that networks of routes can
always make money.
Not me – every route is like a product line. It needs to pull its weight.

Build an expensive central cost base, such as aircraft maintenance, that isn't able to be flexible with seasonal and
cyclical movements of the business.
Nope.

Use expensive prime-time television adverts to try and justify to customers why they should pay so much.
Been there, done that.

Run the airline in compartments so one part has no idea
what's going on anywhere else. Make sure your pilots never
meet or talk to commercial people. And vice versa.
My personal bête noire.

Use expensive travel agents who don't add extra value but
cost a packet and use an out-of-date and expensive ticketing process that means you wait six weeks for your cash
flow.
No way!

Hire people and then not pay attention to their personalities – pilots just fly planes and cabin crew should be hired
for good looks, shouldn't they?
Sorry but no; this one really winds me up.

Have a variety of aircraft sizes that fit every part of the
market; fly to any expensive airport you want and pass the
landing costs back to the customer; employ a huge IT

department and custom-build every bit of software because it's 'mission-critical'; charge customers enormous fares because they are business customers and the company pays.
No. No. No and No.

Make it really difficult for leisure travellers to get low fares, befuddle them with fares structures and confuse them with conditions in small print at the bottom of every ticket. Treat each customer with disdain and baffle them with airline jargon. Then feed them tasteless food they don't want to eat.
Just a waste of time and money.

So with the negatives out of the way, how was I going to create something different? I thought I'd go and see how the pros did it. I bought a seven-leg journey and headed out to view Southwest Airlines. I already had some ideas fermenting in my head. Now I wanted to look at them from the view of the customer in Seat 14B.

I flew from Baltimore to Chicago Midway, then from Midway to Nashville, both with all-women cabin crew who were professional and pleasant. Then we dashed off to Houston Hobby plus a quick hop to Dallas Love, the spiritual home of Herb.

I didn't go to see the granddaddy of all the low-cost airlines, Herb Kelleher. I had tried to call him and had hit a wall. They weren't eager for more visitors at this stage. Maybe being from British Airways put them off. Who knows. Besides, I wanted to *see* how they actually did it rather than hear from the top people! So it was back to Houston and over the desert to Phoenix, Arizona, in 2 hours and 20 minutes, with a 20-minute turnaround. This flight had the first male cabin crew I saw. Then from Phoenix to Las Vegas. But with no interest in slot-machines and blackjack, it was straight on to LAX, Los Angeles' major airport hub, before grabbing an American Airlines flight back to JFK.

I finally witnessed the world-famous Southwest joking cabin crew on that last leg from Las Vegas. It was an afternoon flight full of pensioners and the attendant opened her safety announcement by asking for hands up and applause for all the newly minted Vegas millionaires. It was all a bit corny but it amused everyone onboard.

The Southwest flight attendants were generally young, mostly below thirty, attractive, even quite glamorous and made-up even though they were dressed casually in khaki shorts and trousers with red or navy long-sleeve rugby-type shirts. I spoke to one senior cabin crew member who told me they could fly up to eight sectors a day in a six-day week but it was usually less. A sector is a trip from airport to airport and they were paid on a per sector basis, around $20 each. I found they had a very nice friendly and open attitude, and this was consistent among every-one I met.

I chatted to another Southwest crew member just out of col-lege who had been flying for only six months. She told me she had spent six weeks in training which had instilled the distinctive Southwest spirit, and it shone through. I was intrigued to learn that she met Herb, Colleen Barrett, the senior person responsi-ble for people and customers, and Bill Miller, the head of the cabin crew. Each gave time to the training courses for cabin crew and pilots. That was impressive. I liked what I saw, but I realised that our new airline would have to have its own identity.

Since then, Southwest has had continued success, winning Airline of the Year in 2003 in the industry's management mag-azine, *ATW* (*Air Transport World*), which again voted it best, saying: 'Thirty consecutive years of profit is a remarkable per-formance in any business, but especially in the airline industry, it borders on the miraculous. And yet, unless a volcano buries

Dallas Love Field under a mountain of lava, it seems inevitable that Southwest Airlines this year will notch its 30th year without a break.'

The award paid tribute to Southwest's continuing ability to keep its passengers satisfied and its perpetual drive to give them exactly the service they expect. 'Although it is a no-frills airline, flying on it is no hardship,' said the magazine.

Back in 1997 after my Southwest sortie, I began to sketch out my thoughts on possible low-cost routes: London to Inverness, Paris and Belfast, all four times a day; and to Milan, Lyons, Düsseldorf and St Helier, twice a day. In my jottings, I was trying to assess how many Italian expats lived in London and how many Brits had second homes in France. There was still a lot of planning and research to be done and plenty to tell Simon.

Sure, we borrowed some of Herb's ideas – so did our low-cost European rivals – but we also moulded them to suit our own contemporary European experience, basing our approach on the belief that customers wanted to have it all: low prices with great service.

At our next session together Simon and I drew up a list of priorities. Finding people to help with the skills he and I lacked was our highest priority. I needed short-term help on the business plan from an experienced operational chief. I hoped this person could help me assess external candidates who could join the new airline full-time if we gained British Airways board approval. The permanent operations chief would live and breathe planes and operations; someone who understood the complex nature and foibles of commercial pilots, and who was also robust enough not to be thwarted by the intricate politics inside British Airways. I also wanted the person to share my no-compromise view on safety and security for this new airline. Another requirement was a bright and enthusiastic all-rounder who could apply the elbow grease to any number of tasks to get our project motoring.

All this was in my mind one afternoon when I took an early recce out to Stansted Airport. The place was deserted and I sketched down its 95 check-in positions in my notebook. It was a pretty sad show, because there were 35 empty check-in desks. There were counters for Air UK, Ryanair, Jersey European, and package tour operators such as Sun World, Cosmos and Unijet, while the faded blue of ground-handling company Servisair was prominent. You would certainly need a fertile imagination to describe Stansted as a buzzing European airport at that time. I noted with amusement that Cadbury's Chocolates had its own dedicated sweet shop – a definite plus for a chocoholic like me. One of my ideas for thanking Go people and customers in later years was to buy sweets from this same shop and share them out. But there was a long way to go before this Essex airport would emerge as our favoured choice.

On Monday 24 March 1997, before heading off on my Southwest trip, I was in British Airways' remarkably tatty former headquarters at Speedbird House, next to Hatton Cross Tube station, hustling for more information with several meetings. One was with Lloyd Griffiths, a senior BA Flight Operations manager, where it was even suggested I check with the company's government affairs department to ensure that it was OK for an American to be running a subsidiary of a British company. (The British government – like all major EU countries – insists that control of its major airline remains in British or EU hands.) Bob Ayling tackled that thorny issue by becoming our chairman. Our path to launch would be littered with issues like this. At first glance, it looked insurmountable, but with a little creative thinking it was quickly dealt with. Lloyd and I talked about how to attract pilots to the new venture and manage flight crew and he suggested I speak to British Airways' Chief Pilot at Gatwick, Ed Winter.

Earlier that day Dominic Paul's name cropped up when I went to see Dr DeAnne Julius, a fellow American who was then

BA's chief economist. A few years later she was spirited off to set the UK's interest rates by becoming an original member of Eddie George's Monetary Policy Committee of the Bank of England. DeAnne was helpful and told me that Dominic, who had worked in her strategy department, had just turned twenty-six and was making a name for himself after opening the Kiev operation for BA. Despite speaking almost no Russian and little financial support, he had made it profitable within eighteen months. Just what I was looking for.

Neither Ed nor Dominic had any idea of the roller-coaster ride that lay ahead but, to their credit, they both agreed to at least listen to my sales pitch. I had already failed with a number of other colleagues because the project was seen as far too risky.

Simon and I had more meetings with the LEK brains that week, and it wasn't until Thursday that I phoned Ed to introduce myself.

'Hi, Ed, it's Barbara Cassani here. I wondered if I could come and talk to you about a special project I am directing. I think you'll find it interesting.'

He was extremely friendly, and even remembered me from my days as the sales and marketing cheerleader for loss-making Gatwick, although we had never been introduced. He said he would be delighted to meet but he was leaving the next day with his son Eddie on a skiing holiday to Whistler in British Columbia.

'What time's your flight to Vancouver?'

'Oh, it's not until the afternoon,' replied Ed.

'Then I'll come across in the morning and we'll talk at the airport.'

My own temporary weekday lodging was at the Hilton Hotel at Heathrow, so next morning I nipped through the Easter weekend rush and linked up with Ed before he flew out.

Poor nine-year-old Eddie sat forlornly playing with his GameBoy beside their Salomon ski bags plonked on a trolley, while Ed and I talked shop. From the moment I met him, I liked his can-do attitude. He also had gravitas. I reckoned we could use a bit of that on the team.

Ed Winter's pedigree as a pilot and then a senior BA manager was exemplary, and it would become an essential element of our success, although initially Ed said he had no intention of joining us. He was in his early fifties and qualified to retire on a generous pilot's pension in five years. But Ed was willing to give us the benefit of his knowledge, and, as he became more involved, he was seduced by the lure of creating his 'dream airline'.

To this day, he remains a pilot's pilot, a safety-conscious aviator whom I picture walking around his car to check all the tyres before beginning every journey. He began flying planes with BOAC, the British Overseas Aircraft Corporation, in 1967, flying the work-horse Boeing 707, and he became a captain ten years later. He loved flying the early Boeings, but the politics of global airlines forced British Airways to change tack and he undertook an aircraft conversion course to fly the Lockheed L-1011 Tristar, the long-haul jets of the 1970s with the distinctive Rolls-Royce engine in the tail.

Ed became the assistant flight manager for the British Airways' Tristar programme, which was the first rung on the management ladder. And then as the Tristar began to age, he changed fleets and became involved in the technical assessment to choose between the Airbus and the next generation of Boeing. He even lived in Seattle, where he worked alongside Boeing's flight specialists to ensure that each new 737 plane met all the specifications that British Airways required. Effectively, Ed's job was to add more costs to the planes British Airways was buying from Boeing by selecting extras, whereas life in the low-cost sector was about stripping out all those bells and whistles and taking vanilla planes (with no added extras) off the shelf.

After a spell as Chief Pilot of British Airways Regional, when he enjoyed the freedom of running a separate operation in the UK, he moved back to Gatwick, where he was Chief Pilot responsible for the full range of aircraft including the Boeing 747s. But it was his understanding of where costs could be cut, his uncompromising attitude to safety and his affection for the smaller Boeing 737 that would be prized assets for our operation.

As we chatted in Terminal Four, I asked Ed what he thought about low-cost airlines, and he said he could clearly understand the emerging rationale and why British Airways had to do something concrete in the face of increasing competition. He had been involved in tough industrial relations issues with pilots and witnessed first-hand the inertia against radical changes inside British Airways.

'I can see what needs to be done to make things more efficient,' he told me, 'but I've become more and more frustrated by British Airways' restrictive agreements with the flight crews. As the Chief Pilot, I can see what might be achieved, but it is very difficult to revolutionise an essentially conservative group of people such as airline pilots. But if you start with a clean slate, then you can do it differently.'

It was a fundamental truth, and a hurdle that we would have to overcome if we were to become a truly low-cost operation. But listening to Ed's observations and then receiving his good-natured encouragement was reassuring for me at this point. As he headed off to the departure lounge with a now grinning Eddie, he agreed to continue our discussions as soon as he returned.

Meanwhile I had to keep everything moving. When I emailed Dominic asking him to contact me that weekend at home in Connecticut, he thought I was pulling his leg – he was used to British Airways' senior managers putting business on hold after lunch on a Friday until Monday morning. But he called me up and we agreed to meet in London the following week. A

London University economics graduate, Dominic was part of the British Airways management intake of 1993, and one of his first tasks in the office of DeAnne Julius had been helping assess the implications of macroeconomic trends on international air travel over the next ten years. She was impressed by this efficient and perceptive young man who at one time had aspirations to become an academic.

Dominic had been posted to Vienna to gain some hands-on experience working in aircraft dispatch, ticketing, baggage handling and helping to run the BA operation. He then received a call asking him if he could step in temporarily to head the tiny Baku operation in Azerbaijan, on the Caspian Sea, which was taking advantage of the disintegration of the Soviet Union and the booming oil sector. For a 23-year-old it was an unbelievable opportunity to run a station, serving a frontier town, then emerging from years of ethnic strife.

The international airlines were just beginning to taste the potential market in the former Soviet Union. British Airways already flew into Moscow, St Petersburg and Baku, but not into Ukraine. Then, at Christmas 1995, Dominic was asked to go to Kiev to open a new BA route. He was given two and a half months to get it going, and he did it.

With so much latent demand, it ended the year as one of British Airways' most profitable routes. Increasingly rich Ukrainians, now free to travel, were able to fly to London on five flights a week, then take Concorde to New York to see their expatriate relations. Dominic recalls passengers arriving with bags full of $20,000 in cash to pay for those flights. Even in Ukraine, anyone with money – no questions asked – wanted to fly with the World's Favourite Airline. Later we would be lucky to earn that kind of money from 250 customers travelling on our low-cost airline.

The Friday after Easter, I was squatting in a colleague's office in Speedbird House with Dominic smiling at me across a desk.

'It wasn't so much an interview as a sales pitch from you,' Dominic later recalled. 'It was a very exciting proposition joining a project examining a new airline and it looked as if you'd already made your mind up about me. I didn't really have to say a great deal, I just nodded my head vigorously. You seemed to know what you wanted.'

Little did he know how desperate I was for an intelligent and capable helper. Dominic was enthused and I suggested he have a chat with Simon, who was in another office downstairs.

'That was the real grilling,' he said about the session with Simon. 'He was much more difficult and intense and wanted to know exactly what I had been doing. It was a touch of good cop and bad cop, but later I hit it off superbly with Simon.'

Dominic still had to hand over Kiev to another manager, and for the next few months he too was leading a double life, running his Ukrainian operation while becoming more immersed in our project. He even spent a few nights on a mattress sleeping in the back of his father's Volvo estate in the pension building car park. The nine-to-five pension people were becoming increasingly alarmed about our after-midnight work sessions and other bizarre behaviour.

Dominic became our intellectual handyman, darting around and taking on a variety of tasks. 'There wasn't really a clearly defined role for me at that time. I was a jack of all trades, but my speciality of running the operational side of airports was soon useful,' he later recalled.

With Dominic on board and Ed agreeing to help with the business plan, I turned my attention onto my frantic personal life. Guy was busy at work with Wall Street corporate dealmakers Wasserstein Perella in New York, so I was on my own to house-hunt in London. I allocated just one day and kept my fingers crossed. Guy had seen a new housing development on the Thames in West London advertised in the US edition of the *Financial Times*, and I checked it out. We snapped up one of the last plots and moved in August 1997. There was no time for decorating, but we managed to get curtains for the windows thanks to our first-ever nanny and now friend, Jo Dean, whose parents owned a soft-furnishings shop in Colchester.

Ed, Dominic and I realised that the first big decision and negotiation would be finding the right airport in which to base the airline. After some basic research by LEK, Simon and I had decided on London, so we began to look at the options. Would it be Luton, Stansted, or even Biggin Hill, an old Royal Air Force base south of London? We struggled to get the airports to understand that while we were owned by British Airways, we weren't British Airways. The name got us in the door, but it was a struggle to make them understand that our cost structure needed to be Ryanair, not Concorde.

Chapter Five

Operation Blue Sky Is a Go

We didn't have too many friends inside British Airways. After you counted Bob and Charles, you were hard pushed to rub together two more senior British Airways executives who thought it was a good idea to launch a low-cost airline. Well, they all had their fiefdoms, domains and profit-centres to protect.

But Bob's support reassured us that we would be independent and left alone to get on with it. And that turned out to be a true blessing for us. We needed to have low costs to be competitive, so we simply couldn't be tied to the apron strings of British Airways, with its traditional structure of pay and conditions, expensive overheads and operating procedures appropriate for a global, complex airline. The new outfit needed to be built for a much narrower purpose: safety and low costs. But this caused growing friction within British Airways.

Many former colleagues at British Airways didn't think it was a clever idea to create a new company that might cannibalise the existing business, but I think they missed the point. The world had changed forever in a deregulated market. Europe would never be the same for traditional airlines. A new, more profitable sector was emerging. Why shouldn't British Airways participate in it and reap the benefits for its shareholders? Certainly, British Airways needed to continue to reduce its own cost base, but if we could pull off having the best low-cost airline as well as the best full-service airline, that would be a coup indeed for shareholders.

And Bob Ayling knew the low-cost market was happening around him, whether you joined the game or not. He liked to cite the example of Ford, the global motor giant. 'They produced one of the most successful cars ever with the Ford Cortina,' he once told me, 'but they knew it couldn't go on for ever. So they scrapped it. They had to evolve and to find fresh products for the changing market. That's the same with British Airways.'

And our job was to develop a new low-cost brand that British Airways would be proud to claim as its own, but not one that would cause confusion with consumers. For me, developing the brand of a new low-cost airline was a lot more than just coming up with a name and some fancy design. It needed to guide everything in the business. I began scouring London for an advertising agency that could give Project Hyacinth marketing wings – and pronto. The prospect had dismayed me: I didn't want our plans to be hijacked by a bunch of pretentious creatives out to impress each other.

This was new ground for me, so we asked several firms to make a pitch. Remember, at British Airways it was Saatchi & Saatchi or nothing for over a decade. The launch of a new airline had agencies positively salivating – but there were to be no illusions about bloated fees. One handy piece of advice from British Airways Head of Advertising Derek Dear and other experts was to 'look at the credentials of the principals' and make sure you know who's going to be doing your work. That was to be a critical factor.

Throughout the summer of 1997, London was packed with dozens of trendy agencies vying for work as the dot.com gold rush approached. So I went to see Kevin Gavaghan, who had been a founder of First Direct when it was launched in October 1989 by Midland Bank. I admired this bank's 24-hour, 365-days-a-year offering, which made using your account so much easier if you were a busy professional who couldn't get to a branch. Indeed, from our kitchen table in Connecticut, Guy and I arranged our mortgage in London with First Direct.

Over beers around the conference table after a visit to his new IT-based training company, Kevin told me about HHCL, or Howell, Henry, Chaldecott, Lury and Partners, who were among the most innovative agencies in the 1990s and had been behind the First Direct branding and advertising launch.

It was a sunny June afternoon when I arranged to visit them in their offices just off Oxford Street. Kent House, in Great Titchfield Street, is a sturdy 1930s Art Deco-style building. I strode past the ground-floor commissioner and up to the fifth floor to be greeted by HHCL's beaming receptionist. The office was bright, with windows facing out onto central London below, a herring-bone wood-block floor, crimson walls and aluminium skirting board. It felt friendly and contemporary, with the scent of fresh lilies in the air.

The place was alive; casually dressed designers sat attentively at their Power Mac computers, account executives wandered around talking to clients on their mobiles, and bike messengers regularly delivered packages.

Two of the principals, Adam Lury and Rupert Howell, greeted me and took me into one of their 'Huddle' rooms – a glass office slightly bigger than a phone box – that would become so familiar. I had met Adam Lury briefly at my home away from home, the Heathrow Hilton, and he had impressed me.

'Who would you have working on this project?' I asked.

'Well,' said Rupert, 'we just recruited this guy who is about to start with us. He's David Magliano, who will be the business director on this project. He has worked on retail sales accounts for Ford and Pepsi. The senior planner would be Mark Piper, who has great experience in the travel industry; and he would be supported by our partner, Axel Chaldecott (the C in HHCL), who has been the creative director on a number of high-profile launches, and myself.'

I was listening, and then they offered something that clicked with me.

'We're prepared to share some risk with you on this. If your business plan doesn't get approval by British Airways, then we will charge you at cost price. But if it gets approval, then we'd like to take our normal profit margin,' he said.

'It sounds interesting,' I responded as I quickly jotted everyone's name and cv into my notebook.

I still had some others to visit, but I felt instinctively that I could do business with this bunch. From the outset, I could see that they were on the same wavelength as me. They shared my view that no-frills needn't be cheapskate. I liked their principals and I liked their principles.

I quickly made up my mind, dismissing the other contenders, and a few weeks later HHCL were conducting focus-group consumer research in North London. First there would be a 'brand-storming' session with eight to ten potential customers, then a series of focus-group workshops in the UK to try out some of our ideas and identify who might travel with us. We wanted to know if free food on board was important. Did they mind paying up front for seats with a credit card? Was a linkage with a big airline important? As the project developed David Magliano increasingly took the lead.

Then we moved the focus groups to Europe and had the same conversations. I knew the timing was tight, and it would have been laughable at British Airways to conduct only two focus groups per country, but HHCL took it all in their stride. At a couple of hundred thousand for the pre-launch work, it was going to be one of Project Hyacinth's biggest expenses to date, but we were fleshing out the service and personality of the company. And they would help us understand more about the kind of person who would enjoy flying with us.

The feedback from our groups was fascinating. The airline had to be relevant to Italians, Swedes, Germans and Spaniards and not just to the British. The European focus groups were very positive.

Some said: 'I love the idea of lower fares but I don't want to be uncomfortable.' What did they mean by 'uncomfortable'? I wanted to know. For the Germans it meant safety. They didn't want to fall out of the sky, and here being associated with British Airways and its safety record was a plus factor. In Italy, it was: 'I want to know my credit card details will be secure.' For British people: 'I don't want to be embarrassed to tell my friends.' Particularly among the educated middle- to upper-income British, who were brand-conscious, there was the worry: 'Oooh, what does this say about me?'

So I wanted to pull those simple elements together. I wanted it to be friendly, safe, and nothing to be embarrassed about.

HHCL pushed ahead with this basic brand-building work and introduced us to the design company Wolff Olins in September to take our raw ideas the next step towards reality. They had developed First Direct and Orange, so I was sure they would understand our ideas. They set out to deliver the external design elements by mid-January 1998, including items such as airport signage, uniforms and boarding passes. We made life easier for them by scrapping the idea of luggage labels, which no self-respecting low-cost airline wastes money on, and exempting sick bags, where I thought: why brand a bag when plain white does the job?

There were also the aircraft's livery, seat fabrics, head-rests, curtains, carpets, seat-belts and on-board wallpaper to sort out in only sixteen weeks. It was going to be extremely tight. Again we dumped some standard airline items, like curtains by the galleys. We wanted our cabin crew to be in constant view of customers and vice versa. No hiding behind the curtain at our airline!

Wolff Olins's quirky creative director, Doug Hamilton, would be overseeing the project along with project manager Jane Speller and other designers such as Robbie Laughton. The fees worked out at £270,000, which was a huge amount for Go, but if these guys could deliver on time they were worth every penny.

I began to hear troubling rumblings from Bob Ayling's top Executive Team meetings about 'valid business concerns' within British Airways. Martin George, the Marketing Director, was deeply anxious about Project Hyacinth using, in any way, the British Airways name and logo. His colleague Dale Moss, the Sales Director, was increasingly worried about undermining support from travel agencies who would lose their commissions from Hyacinth. Mike Street, the Operations Director, was fearful that cabin and flight crew would see Hyacinth as a threat and cause a strike. David Spurlock, the Director of Strategy, wasn't convinced about developing a low-cost operation and felt that, if it had to go ahead, it should be aimed at destinations chosen by British Airways. He did not agree that the subsidiary should develop its business independently, and certainly not on routes like Milan, where British Airways made a lot of profit.

Beyond this senior group, there were many, many more who pronounced it as sheer folly. Even Charles Gurassa's team of regional managers out in Spain and Italy faced a blinding headache when they understood we were going to be independent. It meant that the regional general managers in Italy, Spain and Portugal had to compete with us directly on the Rome, Milan, Bologna and Faro routes. Having worked in sales,

I admit that must have been extremely uncomfortable, causing strains with local customers and suppliers. Interestingly, British Airways pilots and cabin crew were unfailingly positive towards us. Every time I flew British Airways for five years they were encouraging and liked our style!

I could never understand why British Airways did not do their own analysis of the new low-cost airline subsidiary's potential impact on the mainstream business. Simon and I tried to think it through, but we neither had the base information on British Airways' mainstream business, nor was it our brief. It meant that the British Airways board would get only half the story. There were a number of Strategy Group meetings, which included all the senior British Airways directors, but no one would really stand up to Bob's decision – yet they did not conduct their own evaluations of the impact on British Airways' own European business.

I was frustrated at how much time was being squandered. I suspected the delays were a form of passive resistance to the project and was concerned that without a lot of pushing, we wouldn't be on the next British Airways board agenda. In one memo to Charles Gurassa on 19 September 1997, I said we were 'ready and eager' to present the case for a low-cost airline to the board. But I raised my concerns, saying: 'I have been surprised that there is little commitment from the Strategy Group to fulfil the Chief Executive Officer's request to review the implications of Hyacinth on the British Airways Group.' Surely this was a 'go slow' form of passive resistance?

Who would calculate the revenue losses to British Airways from Hyacinth or work out how two very different brands would operate together in Europe? Had the risk of doing nothing been assessed? One director told me it wasn't a priority. So I fired off both barrels. 'No one has taken ownership of evaluating the impact on British Airways of not doing Hyacinth and allowing the low-cost sector to grow without British Airways' participation.' In a way, it was none of my business if they chose to go ahead without understanding the impact, but it offended my analytical instincts. Hyacinth was a hot potato and the politicians in Head Office steered clear of it. Ironically, just days before the business case was to be presented to the British Airways board, Simon and I were asked to think through the implications for the main airline. I don't even remember the contents of the work. We weren't the right people to be doing it.

This foot-dragging made our need for independence all the more important. If British Airways had any practical role, we would slow down, and the business plan and our low prices would be diluted. We were to walk a fine line for months. Yes, we were owned by British Airways, but customers needed to know that they were not going to get British Airways. It was a separate brand, service, rules, sales – the whole shooting match.

The business plan covered three years; beyond that, we would probably need more capital to grow. Being a completely separate entity would help make a private sale, flotation or even debt financing much more straightforward.

For me, it was also a personal decision about what I wanted to do professionally. I did not want to run the company if it would be hamstrung by British Airways' numerous departments who didn't believe in the project and who would grind us down at every turn. We were already late entering the market and we'd need to be nimble to survive.

Simon and I continued our flurry of meetings to try to sell the idea to the doubters before the British Airways board meeting in Prague. British Airways' quaint, but expensive and time-consuming, tradition was to move the board meetings around the world like an Elizabethan royal 'progress'. In the autumn of 1997, it was Prague's turn. Some executive directors, who might have been expected to have an opinion about low-cost flying, remained neutral, either for political reasons or because they genuinely weren't sure. Derek Stevens, the Chief

Financial Officer, never revealed his personal thoughts, and Roger Maynard, who became the second chairman of the new airline in 2000, was also reticent about airing his views. To this day, I'm not sure what Lord Marshall really thought of the strategic decision to set up a low-cost carrier.

The business plan Simon and I had prepared was to be presented to the British Airways board at their meeting at the Inter-Continental Hotel, Prague, on Friday 10 October 1997. We had all the key facts to hand and thought up tricky questions we would have asked ourselves. We were eager to be unleashed on the British Airways board. We knew that in the first year each flight cost us around £5,000 for the plane, pilots, crew, fuel, check-in, baggage handling and maintenance. The sales and marketing costs in the first year were huge at £22 per passenger, but were a necessary investment to build the name and reputation of the company. The dollar exchange rate was critical because fuel and aircraft leases had to be paid in dollars. We budgeted $1.56 per £1 and could benefit or lose millions depending upon the fluctuating exchange rate. A captain would cost £57,000 per annum in base pay, and he or she would fly 810 hours per year (that's 25 per cent more than a British Airways captain would fly, but still well within the Civil Aviation Authority's limits). We knew it all by heart.

And in that early plan, we asked for £20 million in capital and hoped to squeak into financial break-even in the second year. We eventually slipped break even to year three, and for a bit of elbow room Derek Stevens wisely suggested capitalising the company with £25 million. He was right of course.

Many of the directors, including Bob Ayling, Sir Colin Marshall, Captain Colin Barnes, a former Chief Pilot, businessman Michael Davies, Dr Ashok Ganguly, a former Unilever director, Baroness O'Cathain, who previously ran the Barbican arts centre, Sir Robin Renwick, the former British diplomat turned banker at Robert Fleming, and Ray Seitz, the former

American ambassador to Britain, were travelling out to Prague on the British Airways flight.

I stood in the galley bending the ear of one of the directors for most of the flight, while Simon sat lobbying another. We continued over drinks at the hotel that evening. Next morning Simon and I rehearsed our presentations for the last time, pacing up and down the top-floor ante-room. I was confident about our ability but a little nervous as I pondered how the board might react.

Our proposal was the last item on the agenda that day; special projects always came at the end of the board meeting and the directors were obviously getting peckish. It was shoehorned into twenty minutes or so, as the board wanted to finish on time to greet their local dignitary lunch guests. Some directors were not overly keen on the project, which they said could become just another subsidiary folly.

One would have thought that the future of British Airways' European strategy would be a huge topic; instead they simply reviewed the paper that Bob had introduced onto the agenda. Simon and I gave a slide show and we told the gathering that a substantial new segment was emerging in the European short-haul airline market for low-priced, no-frills, point-to-point services. We emphasised that easyJet, Ryanair and Virgin Express, the Brussels-based airline that Richard Branson had purchased the previous year, were already established and growing rapidly. We also understood that both Air France and Lufthansa were considering joining the game.

The board listened attentively as Bob stressed that British Airways should not miss this new opportunity. He pointed out that even if British Airways didn't enter the low-cost sector, its revenue would be eroded as the emerging low-cost rivals wooed passengers from British Airways standard services. He told the board he wished to defend the revenues and capture that value by launching British Airways' own low-price airline. He outlined how he had rejected buying an existing company and asked us to detail our plan for starting a new low-cost airline. A new company with a more suitable code name of Operation Blue Sky, was to be launched in the spring of 1998 and initially would be wholly owned by British Airways.

By now, Bob was becoming a very high-profile public figure. The new Labour Prime Minister Tony Blair had confirmed the decision to proceed with the Millennium Dome, and Bob was chairman of the New Millennium Experience Company, responsible for ensuring that the Dome at Greenwich opened in January 2000. It was meant to be a celebration, but it became a huge white elephant, pilloried by the press as the costs overran. It eventually cost over £800 million to build and open. It is said that Sir Richard Branson had already turned down the chairmanship saying that it was going to be a complete waste of money. But Bob had taken on the task because Michael Heseltine, the Deputy Prime Minister in the previous Conservative administration, asked him as the head of one of the major sponsors, and he felt a civic responsibility to do what he could. Perhaps Bob should not have stayed on after Barry Hartop, the first chief executive, resigned in 1996 when their original budget was rejected by the Commission. But he did, and in the end more than six million people visited the attraction. While his critics said his involvement in the ill-fated Dome and the London Eye took him away from his core responsibilities at British Airways, he was always clear about his strategy to enter the low-cost sector.

The board asked questions that suggested they felt that close proximity to British Airways would destroy the business model. All in all it seemed that they were resigned to possible failure but were willing to risk £25 million to back the CEO's whim – a small amount for a board used to buying 747s at $100 million each.

The board were close to backing our plan but wanted a bit of extra work done. They wanted us to go back and reconsider buying an established low-cost player. We went away, reviewed the options, and by the end of October reiterated our views that the players were either dramatically loss-making (Debonair, Air One in Italy) or too expensive for less than 50 per cent ownership (easyJet and Ryanair).

By November it was official. The board approved the Operation Blue Sky plan and were adamant that we receive no more than £25 million for the first three years. Further, in the event of failure the costs of winding the business up would be limited to £29 million, to include any redundancy costs. Some on the board, however, reiterated the Strategy Group's concerns about the possible cannibalisation of British Airways revenue. There was also genuine alarm that it might cause further unrest with the already jumpy unions and employees. An official strike in the summer of 1996 had caused huge disruption and cost the airline £125 million, and Bob's lack of finesse with employees had harmed his reputation in the City.

It had been close, but we had done it. Given the cloudy looks on faces as we left, we couldn't go back to that bunch for more money, so we had to make it work. It was galling to me to sense the air of resignation that assumed we would fail. It reminded me of the half-hearted job offer I had received to join UK Sales a few years back.

Again I thought, 'Screw 'em, we'll create the best low-cost airline in the world and it'll make money.' And after that session we began the countdown. With a target launch date in April 1998 we had just twenty-five weeks from the nod to build this new airline. Now it was really going to happen. Operation Blue Sky was a go.

Chapter Six

Mother of Two Launches Airline

We had no planes, no employees and only an interim name, Operation Blue Sky. We did have an airport to reveal when I stood up in front of the press for the first time to announce our new airline to the world on Monday 17 November 1997.

Choosing the base airport while trying to get final sign-off from the British Airways board had been a nightmare. Just days before at our regular weekly Whitelocke House meeting, we'd been preparing for our public announcement, but negotiations to find our base were dragging on. We couldn't announce the launch of an airline without saying where it would be based. It was bad enough that we didn't have a name or any aircraft yet.

'Our talks with Stansted are coming to an end and they're finally putting a deal on the table that looks good. The final meeting is next Tuesday and we should know then if we're in the right ballpark,' I told our working group.

The zeal we brought to airport negotiations was decidedly un-British Airways. It was folklore that Ryanair was paying nothing, or at least very little, in airport costs across Europe.

This was radical for me to get my head around. I had come from British Airways in the USA, where we had spent more than £15 per passenger at some airports. We eventually found out that Ryanair were probably paying around £1 per passenger at Stansted. This was versus a rack rate of £6 – the standard price before any talks. It would be tough to match, since they had negotiated this rate when the airport had been virtually empty. In our business plan we had prudently assumed around £4 per passenger. Our aim was to get nearer to the £1 per passenger deal rather than the £6 rack rate.

We had no preference between Stansted or Luton, so Dominic and I went to meet Mike Hodgkinson, a senior director then the Chief Executive of the British Airport Authority plc, which owns Heathrow, Gatwick and Stansted, and the then Managing Director of Stansted Airport, John Stent. BAA assumed we were just a Trojan Horse for BA – and sort of winked every time I said that we were a separate airline. It was infuriatingly funny.

We examined the offering of each airport over a three-year period and tried to make the deals comparable by translating all the charges into a cost per passenger, assuming that we would carry about 399,000 departing passengers, on 6,257 flights, using four aircraft. Luton's charges declined over time as we grew, but the first-year charges were still close to £1 million more than Stansted's. We haggled over the price for several weeks, and at one stage seriously thought of going to Luton, since they were easier to deal with, but Stansted emerged as the better choice for us because they could more easily handle our anticipated growth and were cheaper.

And we finally negotiated our own Ryanair-type deal on routes no one was flying. BAA insisted on a mind-bogglingly complex agreement that required a specially trained accountant to work out, but we got there.

With the name of our base airport the only hard piece of

news, I stood in the offices of Brunswick, the City public relations agency in Lincoln's Inn Fields, on 17 November to tell news reporters, business and transport correspondents and television cameras about our new low-cost airline. Wearing my favourite black Jil Sander dress (half-price at Harvey Nichols' winter sale!) and a silk scarf made me feel bigger and tougher in front of this daunting crowd. When meeting people later they would say: 'Aren't you that scarf lady?', but I'm afraid my poise that morning was no more than skin-deep.

Moments after 7 a.m., a prepared statement was fired down the wire to the London Stock Exchange's Regulatory News Service to provide news to the City's major financial investment companies and the Reuters and Bloomberg news agencies. 'British Airways sets up own low-cost, no-frills airline' was a snippet being digested by the fund managers, investors and analysts as we arrived at Brunswick.

It wasn't unexpected. There had been a leak to the *Independent* newspaper a few months before and the 'secret' seemed common knowledge to most people in the aviation business. But there was a surprisingly strong interest in British Airways' decision to appoint an American woman in her late thirties as the chief executive. I now faced a barrage of one-to-one interviews, first with the Press Association to get the news out as early as possible to the regional evening papers, then with London's *Evening Standard* to make sure the story hit its influential second edition. Then it was broadcast lights shining in my eyes as the BBC, then Sky, cable and local television and radio stations asked me about what was going to happen.

'My new airline will fly to the best cities in Europe, at the best prices and offer the best no-frills service – that's my pledge to customers,' I told the gathering as digital flashbulbs popped.

There was a great deal at stake for Bob Ayling and the British Airways board and the announcement could have triggered a big share-price fluctuation, so I was clear that my key points had to be driven home at every turn from day one. Yes, this was going to be a start-up business, a separate entity that would offer the customer genuine low-cost travel, but it was backed by British Airways. And it would create more than 150 jobs in the first year of operations. Fortunately on that announcement day the share price barely wobbled, remaining unchanged at 663.5p a share.

We never had enough money for glossy advertising campaigns, so we had to use public relations as a weapon to get the equivalent of millions of pounds' worth of advertising in the news pages. The low-cost airline businesses already had strong well-known characters. Like them or loathe them, O'Leary, Stelios and Branson were larger than life and were faces the public could easily recognise.

Brunswick are one of the best PR outfits in London, and they were appointed as fire fighters by British Airways after the cabin crew dispute, which had had a shattering effect on the airline's morale. Our launch now needed kid gloves if it was not to spark another walk-out. Bob Ayling was pruning the traditional airline, taking out costs of £250 million, and it had caused considerable grief. A strong pound was also damaging BA's profitability, as had been the public furore over the introduction of BA's ethnic tailfins, the multi-coloured motifs which downplayed the 'British' aspect of the organisation – and prompted the famous incident when Margaret Thatcher dropped her hankie over a model plane to express her distaste that the Union Jack had been removed from the airline's livery – which was only just dying down.

James Hogan, a partner in Brunswick, had been a broadcast journalist in the BBC News and Current Affairs department, running *Question Time* and Election Night special coverage. He now ran what he called 'High Impact Day' like a military operation.

'I'm a control freak,' he would say. 'I've run the BBC's elections night coverage and major documentary series. Everything has to be scripted and everyone must know what to do. If a client is standing in front of the media and turns to me and says: "What do I do now?" then I have failed in my job. So sack me.'

And as we were new to the media world, I was to be meticulously groomed.

'The key messages need to be carefully controlled, and we'll have to think long and hard about how we do this,' Hogan told me.

The *Sun*'s headline made me chuckle – 'Mother of Two Launches Airline' – but I wasn't going to make a song-and-dance about being a superwoman running a business; that was never my intention. I was simply a chief executive who happened to be female.

The press's access to me was to be strictly rationed. I wasn't going to speak to everyone and anyone; there was a logic and purpose so we could send out the clear messages we wanted.

It wasn't my idea to face the press that morning. Charles Gurassa and Bob Ayling pushed me into the front line for the first time. Charles must have known that I would attract attention, because he kindly warned me to brush up on my interviewing skills. But I needed 'babysitting'. I had some experience facing the press in the United States, but the London pack, I was told, would eat me alive if I didn't put on a good show. BA's executives wanted to keep control of the situation; after all, I was just a 'rookie'.

For Brunswick, the British Airways public relations contract was a substantial honeypot, and they weren't going to allow a Yank to mess up this lucrative relationship. James Hogan hauled me through several mock sessions of interviews and questioning. I was prepped to perfection, anticipating every kind of question. His younger associate, Nick Claydon, who went on to become head of communications at British Airways, became a valuable sounding board, advising me on the journalists I could trust.

It was all worth it, because the news conference went smoothly and I even managed a few off-script one-liners. My lippy asides had often landed me in trouble as a child, and as a young executive. At last they could be turned to my advantage. When one reporter asked me if I would be doing Branson-esque stunts, I said: 'You won't get me jumping out of a cake at the launch party.'

As the announcement spread, easyJet went ballistic. Stelios lashed out immediately, saying that British Airways was indulging in anti-competitive practices. In characteristically colourful language, Michael O'Leary said: 'BA has no idea how to run a low-fare airline. I know more about flying Concorde than Bob Ayling does about running a low-cost airline, and I've never flown on Concorde.' As far as they were concerned, war was declared.

One of the most bizarre memories of this early period was the 'Beauty and the Beast' advertising campaign that ran in mid to late November 1997, when easyJet ran full-page ads costing upwards of £15,000 per paper per day in the quality national newspapers to demonise Bob Ayling and portray me as an attractive Mata Hari trying to infiltrate the low-cost sector to put all the 'good guys' out of business. The ad exhorted the European Commission to act to deter British Airways from dastardly deeds. It ranks among my personal favourites as an advert for its sheer ridiculousness. Of course, Guy saw the amusing side and fell about laughing to see me promoted to 'beauty'. It explained a lot about the fury we were causing at easyLand, easyJet's Portakabin headquarters in Luton.

They wouldn't leave it alone. In a follow-up ad on 23 November in the *Independent on Sunday*, easyJet reported on names suggested by the public for the new British Airways subsidiary. Suggestions ranged from Bully Airways from Paul Cave from Carshalton Beeches to British Aircrimes from Peter Orne in Milton Keynes, and even Air Rhubarb, attributed to the British Airways 747 Fleet at Heathrow. It was getting very personal.

With the help of the Brunswick team, we carefully built up my press profile, and there were acres of cuttings to show for it. The London broadsheets seemed to lap up my appointment, and the mid-market tabloids loved the idea that a woman had broken through the 'glass ceiling' and was in charge.

There were, however, undertones of admonishment about my decision to be a working mother. In one feature article in *Marketing* magazine, I talked about my ambivalence about being seen as a champion for working women.

> There is a moral judgement underlining some of the press commentary which I find distasteful, because I have spent my whole life accepting people as they come and not being prescriptive about the way other people lead their lives.
>
> I'm not going to throw myself in front of the press and say 'Aren't I wonderful, I'm a mother and have a really high-profile job'. I've got the wherewithal to make money smooth my path; I think the women who are really amazing are those who make £20,000 a year, have two kids in school and a husband who works shifts.

I was regularly asked about my work–life balance. The question perplexed me. If you aim to be at the top of whatever you do – be it sports, academia, theatre, politics or business – you give up a big part of your personal life. That's the trade-off. Finding enough time for my family was a real struggle, but it was for all my male colleagues too. I worked after both children were born because I enjoy the stimulation of life outside the home. That's it in a nutshell, and I've explained it in these terms to my children. And Guy knew exactly what he was getting into from our very early days as students together, when I was already in a hurry to get on.

My message to other women has always been very simple: if you have the choice financially, do what makes you happy – and this is likely to be different things throughout your life. And keep talking to your partner about what each of you expects, particularly if child-rearing is involved. Many men who appear very egalitarian still have traditional views about raising children. The last piece of advice I give is to stop listening to other people. Make the right choices for you, your partner, and most importantly your kids.

And then there was the approach by *Hello!* magazine to come into my home and photograph me in full glossy colour with my adoring husband and attractive children. I just couldn't believe it. For goodness sake, I was just running a company! And we weren't even in business yet. I was very wary of the attention because we had not yet proved ourselves. In three years' time, I would be the first one to brag if we achieved our objective to break even and were on our way to becoming Europe's best low-cost airline, but we hadn't done a thing yet. It offended my down-to-earth New England sensibilities.

The cattier comments made by seasoned hacks stung and caused me to become more cautious. Boris Johnson, the bluff blond journalist who was later to become a Tory MP and editor of the *Spectator*, was one of the first. I don't know what his problem was. In his *Telegraph* back-page feature, he portrayed me as a ditzy British Airways stooge who couldn't even figure out what to name the airline. James Hogan advised that I would have to become thicker-skinned and learn to shrug off derogatory comments. This was my introduction to the press. My reaction was to withdraw and refuse most of the profile interviews on offer.

But there was a host of other people to meet. James commandeered a lunch each week in my diary and I was whisked off

to a variety of appointments with editors and television journalists. I was even in demand with cabinet ministers. Then there
were more invitations to speak at conferences and business
breakfasts. And I was even invited to No. 10 Downing Street to
have bacon and eggs (which I refused in favour of a lighter
croissant!) with Tony Blair and a bunch of hip-and-happening
technology entrepreneurs who were changing the face of Cool
Britannia. When I look back, virtually all of us have either lost
our jobs at the hands of the technology bust or our companies
were merged into oblivion.

In these interviews I was regularly asked where I came up
with my approach to running the airline. I just did what felt natural. The idea for a quality low-cost airline was simple; it was
just devilishly difficult to do. Some of it was copied from what I
saw and read, but we made a lot of it up as we went along.

One place where I learned a lot about simplicity and following your gut was in the paperback *Made in America*, by Sam
Walton, the founder of the Wal-Mart group – the largest discounter and retailer in the world. It's a bible for many
entrepreneurs I have met because its message is so plain and
simple. Sam Walton claims he didn't have any big idea. He
once told the *New York Times* that when he started in Newport,
Arkansas, in 1945: 'I had no vision of the scope of what I would
start.' But he knew about value and his customers. His story is
humbling and simply remarkable. He led the development of
Wal-Mart from a single store to become the world's largest
retailer – all achieved by lowering prices and giving customers
more of what they wanted.

You see, I'm a magpie, drawing from my experiences as a customer, airline executive, waitress, grocery store and checkout
operator, as well as being a student of leaders. My heroes
weren't the business leaders in massive corporations who are
fêted in glossy business magazines like *Fortune* and *Forbes*. I
admired people such as Teddy Roosevelt, the bold American

president who had the vision to set aside millions of acres to create one of the best US legacies: many of the great national parks. I admired Sir Ernest Shackleton, the Antarctic explorer who touched the extremes of human endurance and whose leadership skills brought home alive his entire team after being lost on the Antarctic ice for eighteen months. Then there was Harry Truman, the president who got the job because of Franklin Roosevelt's untimely death and together with Stalin and Churchill became the unlikely third party in the trio that structured postwar Europe at Potsdam. All were people who rose to the challenge to do great things, even though they were personally flawed. Greatness on the world stage comes from playing the hand you're dealt to perfection. Business wasn't much different, and each of these people helped me think through the challenges at Go.

To help new recruits understand what I meant I handed out copies of the book *Nuts!* by Kevin and Jackie Freiberg. It's the amazing story of Southwest Airline's growth and success. Admittedly, it was a suspiciously uncritical account, but it did help me explain what we were aiming for at Go. Quality, because we have pride in what we do; low costs so we can push prices down as low as possible for customers. Simple really. Just relentless. While all the interviews and media noise in the autumn of 1997 were helpful in presenting the project in a more positive light, that profile was a waste of time if we didn't get cracking to have an airline ready to fly in the spring of 1998.

Chapter Seven

Go Direct from A to B with Osca on the Bus

Operation Blue Sky was now approved, announced, and the money was in the bank. It hit me that there was a lot to do and no one around to do it. We were naïve and confident because we hadn't yet fathomed the enormity of the task ahead. But I did realise that we needed to get organised.

Enter Jane Willacy with her world-class project management skills. She could organise the Olympics! She became the fixer and organiser who picked up all the guano at Go in the early days before we took off. Petite, in her early forties and a real dynamo, she was a freelance consultant who was acclaimed at British Airways as the project manager who introduced electronic ticketing to the airline. The system had an impact on virtually every corner of British Airways' mammoth operations, and Jane's skill pulled them through the ticketing labyrinth, earning her the praise and respect of the airline's top executives.

I had known Jane vaguely before, but I was impressed when Charles Gurassa and Martin George, British Airways' Marketing Director, independently recommended her for Operation Blue Sky. I made contact at once and urged her to be

part of the start-up team. She recalls her decision: 'I was heading to Bath for a long-planned weekend and wrestled with the
idea, thinking: "It's not often you get the chance in life to start
an airline. I'll do it." So I phoned and apologised to the other
people I was supposed to start work with. They were charming
and understanding, so I began immediately at Operation Blue
Sky.'

She started work in October 1997 shortly after the board
gave us the preliminary green light. Now there were five of us at
Whitelocke House: me, Simon, Ed Winter, Dominic Paul and
now there was Jane. And soon we were joined by Glynis
Alghanim, who had worked as a temporary secretary with Ed
Winter and who later became my personal assistant. But we had
to multiply very quickly, finding people to fill the jobs.

'Uh, one problem though,' said Jane, once she'd assessed the
road ahead. 'If you're going to launch in the spring, you should
have started on the first tasks six months ago.'

'No problem, we'll just have to do more tasks in parallel,' was
my can-do logical reply.

She was scary because she was so focused. Much later, she
admitted that the feeling was mutual. She was an expert at getting all the boxes ticked and the jobs done. If the most
immediate task was to get a newly acquired aircraft ready for a
flight, she would dash off to the airport at 5 a.m., to pick it up,
getting down on her hands and knees to scrub the floors and
seats. And she would stay there until the job was done. She
would take cake and buy sweets to encourage laggard contractors to 'get a bleedin' move on'.

'She is a brilliant organiser. We thought we'd done so much,
but when Jane arrived she raised the bar,' Dominic said later.

One of the first things Jane did was help us understand that
we had two launch dates: 1 April 1998 for selling seats and 22
May 1998 for our first flight. To be selling seats in just twenty-
five weeks from the British Airways board meeting in Prague

then flying six weeks after that, we needed a detailed plan for every single area. I jotted them down in one of my notebooks. First, we had to continue our search for aircraft that we could lease and operate. This was an early priority, since the longest lead-times were on negotiating lease contracts, conducting maintenance checks and registering the planes with the Civil Aviation Authority (CAA).

Another equal first priority was to get our own Air Operator Certificate from the CAA. Some new airlines simply pay an established airline to provide the planes and pilots, as easyJet did to achieve a five-month start-up, then later obtained their own operating certificate. Since we were already late to the game, we wanted to be fully up and running as a separate fully-functioning airline on day one.

Next, my own highest priority was stepping up the recruitment of the top team. Ideally, they would be in place by December so that they could recruit their own teams. Third, in the commercial area we needed to choose a booking system and set up the telephone sales centre. Jane took the lead here. And of course there were the name and brand. David Magliano was managing this at HHCL, with a lot of input from me and the others.

Ed was still doing his full-time job at British Airways as Chief Pilot 747 and 777, as well as working pretty well full-time on Blue Sky. He was also given the job of Concorde's Chief Pilot and was preparing for a pilot's course. But on Christmas Eve he decided he could no longer resist the excitement of starting up an airline. He joined me full-time, giving up the cosy life in British Airways and his chance to fly Concorde.

Other critical operational matters were on the top priorities list: negotiating the destination airport contracts and selecting and training ground handling agents (in every airport) was a top priority. We needed a full service engineering organisation lined up, and computer systems to run the daily operation. We also needed to start recruiting pilots. Captains would be on three months' notice, so if we didn't have offer letters out to the first group of pilots early in the New Year, we'd be in trouble.

Jane's job was to take my rough-and-ready list and systematically detail everything we needed to do to make these things happen. She drew dozens of huge charts with lots of bubbles to describe the sequential steps by area, which caused nervous laughter among the project team at Whitelocke House in Hounslow. It was an impressive sight to see the hundreds of steps required to hit the first flight date in May 1998. If we'd taken the time to think about the daunting nature of the exercise ahead of us, we probably would have failed. We confidently went forward, knocking each bubble of activity on the head week after week. Every bubble was partially coloured when a task began, and then fully coloured in when completed.

'It was difficult to comprehend the enormity of the project,' Jane said later. 'I'd sit at home staring into space trying to think what I might be missing.'

Jane even recalls trekking down to see Ed Winter in Heathrow and asking him about what processes were needed. In her typically abrasive style, which revealed more about Jane than anything else, she said: 'Ed's a lovely man, but like a lot of pilots he needed to have everything on a plate. It's the way pilots are . . . they are mollycoddled all their lives. I'm amazed some of them can actually fly planes. Anyway, I went to see Ed and talked through all the processes to get a handle on what needed to be done, and poor Ed ended up adding more and more to his own To-Do lists. But we all got there in the end.'

Her assessment of Ed's planning skills was typically blunt and, I think, rather unfair on this point, but she did reveal to every one of us that our previous project work had not prepared us for the enormous challenge of creating something from scratch.

Our Hounslow office was getting busier by the day, with

Simon squeezing in more and more partitions and desks for the new people who were arriving almost daily. It was like the cabin scene from the Marx Brothers' film, *A Night at the Opera*; we didn't think we could get anyone else in, then we cleared another tiny space. Some of our helpers were borrowed from British Airways and we paid for their services. There weren't many, but we were grateful for their early help. For example, Jim Cameron put together the bare bones of a schedule. Then he returned to the relative tranquillity of his British Airways role.

Every bubble on Jane's chart was a lot of work. Consider one – getting aircraft. First they had to be identified, and an engineer needed to look at the plane and the technical paperwork (in South America or Asia or wherever the plane happened to be). Assuming we were still interested in the plane and the price, we negotiated the lease, which was the easy part (although it took weeks of discussion and thousands of pounds of time from a solicitor). Repairing and getting it ready for service was a mind-numbingly complex and expensive task. Repainting it in our airline colours cost £39,500 (plus an extra £700 if it was for the orange colour), replacing seat covers cost around £10,000 per aircraft. We decided that we wanted 148 seats in order to have three loos (easyJet chose 149 seats and just two loos). This one decision had enormous ramifications on the cost and timing of preparing a plane to be used. If we only flew short hops of less than an hour to Scotland, two loos would have been acceptable, but on a two-and-a-half hour flight to Rome, I wasn't prepared to inflict that much discomfort on our passengers.

On one of our leased Boeings, an overhead luggage bin, the type that clicks shut during the flight, was cracked and we needed to replace it.

'Let's have a poll,' I suggested playfully. 'How much should it cost?'

I guessed $5,000 because I reckoned the plastic container

was worth $2,500, then I doubled my estimate since every part of a plane was sold at rip-off prices.

'You're nuts, that's far too high,' said one of the team, and guessed $500. We all got a shock. The cost of a new bin and door (which meant the panel beneath had to be replaced too) was more than $50,000.

Jane left the airline once we were up and flying, but returned for another few months in 1999 when we were tripling the size of the airline and needed someone to help us digest the growth. She remains the best project manager I have ever met, and I know that our first plane took off in large part due to Jane's determination and meticulous planning.

In those early days, I trusted Jane completely to come up with the list of actions needed to launch. This put her under severe pressure, but I knew she could take it. She's just that kind of person.

With Jane on top of the project planning, I spent my time trying to sift through the decisions that would be critical to the success of the business. Our primary objective was to be low-cost. But I was also aware that we were the fourth entrant into a busy low-cost market in London. While we were unique, because we had the high-quality backing of British Airways, we were latecomers.

My personal problem – which had nothing to do with the business model – was that I didn't want to work for a cheesy operation trying to beat Ryanair at its own game. They are the 'market stall' operators, David Magliano would often say, run by a self-styled Irish common man. easyJet was owned by a rich Greek family and took up the position of 'brash underdog bad boys'; while Debonair, owned by an Italian-American, was struggling 'trying to be a bit traditional, with a couple of frills'.

I knew there was something else. I wanted to be proud of our service and brand, especially because it was low-cost. It just struck me as nonsense that low-cost meant low fares but

crummy service. When I flew with Ryanair it was perfectly
acceptable, but a bit like a cheap flying pub. I didn't want to be
part of that. The trick was figuring out how to have good service without undermining the low-cost structure. At British
Airways, we always persuaded ourselves that customers would
pay for the nice additions we offered. In the low-cost game, I
knew customers wouldn't pay anything more for nice service.
We were mostly doing it for ourselves; for our own pride.

Our early attempts at being low-cost were a bit theatrical
because we were not naturals. Ten years of expensive bad habits
at British Airways justifying high prices to customers by adding
bells and whistles to the product don't die overnight. I was
excited to think I could be part of a business where you simplify
your offering for a broad universal market. British Airways had
the frustrating problem of trying to serve too many customers in
different market segments. The net result was over-promising an
undeliverable service to customers, watching your costs skyrocket and then needing to charge high fares. I wanted to turn
the tables on all of that. We put the business plan together
taking the lowest costs we could find in each cost category from
anywhere we could find a comparison. Anywhere in the world.
The plan was now to put those radical targets into action.

Certainly Southwest Airlines gave me confidence to believe
you could run an airline that was enjoyable to work for, popular
with customers, safe and profitable. For me, Southwest was the
pathfinder, but we were not based in Texas and I was certainly
not Herb Kelleher (a whisky-swigging, larger-than-life character). And, in Europe, Ryanair and easyJet were innovating.
Ryanair's operating efficiency was awesome, while easyJet led
the way with internet bookings.

But while Ryanair and easyJet had copied large chunks of
Southwest's thinking, neither came anywhere near matching
Southwest's achievements. What makes Southwest a truly great
company is that it is simultaneously profitable, has an efficient

and punctual operation, treats employees like they matter, and inspires enormous customer loyalty through low fares and good service. No other airline in the world had done that. Well, until we came along.

As the countdown continued at an alarming rate, I turned into a control freak. It wasn't for any other reason but my insecurity over which decisions would be important either to the cost structure or to customers. Jane did what she was paid to do. She banged on about hitting our timing targets and I scoured our activities for decisions that would affect us in the long run.

The race to the first flight was unnerving and hard work, but it was the decisions that would last for ever that really worried me. We had huge decisions to make about what kind of airline we would be after the launch. We continually agonised over whether or not to have our own employees at check-in. We opted for lower costs and less complexity by using subcontractors. The first handling agent at Stansted, Servisair, hired a stand-alone special 'Go Team' and we couldn't have done better ourselves. Unfortunately, the cost of the contract skyrocketed after two years and we saw a dramatic change for the worse when we changed contractors. I'm still not sure we made the right decision when we were setting up the company. And I was acutely aware that some of our choices would be wrong. We just tried to minimise the number of mistakes.

Ed had very clear ideas on how to make the operation low-cost in a way that was consistent with the high safety standards of British Airways. David and I knew our sales and marketing costs would be high at the start, but the percentage cost versus sales needed to drop quickly in those first few years. We didn't have the luxury of time, so we all worked rapidly making decisions that would have warranted, in an ideal world, many more months of consideration.

Ed chose a state-of-the-art computer system for managing operations that would allow us to grow. We probably looked daft in the early days centrally controlling our tiny fleet of four planes on a sophisticated computer system that could manage the ins and outs of hundreds of aircraft when you could have done it on a couple of pieces of paper, but that was OK. We wanted the airline to have a solid platform for growth. This was a wise decision.

We found it challenging matching our benchmarked competitors on aircraft costs. It is difficult to lower costs when you are forced to lease planes. BA didn't want any more aircraft on their balance sheet, which meant we couldn't buy planes using borrowings. Similarly, BA did not want us to sign leases for longer than around five years in case Go went bust, so we didn't get the best deals. In the summer and autumn of 1997, Boeing 737–300 aircraft were in high demand.

Ed scoured around the aviation world for nearly-new planes that could be leased at the budgeted amount of $235,000 per month or less (like oil prices, plane leasing is in dollars and is priced like a commodity, changing almost constantly). He found some at the independent German airline Germania. The airline had a solid reputation for quality engineering, so we expected the planes to be in good shape. Ed and I flew to Berlin several times to discuss terms and availability. Managing Director Dr Heinrich Bischoff was holding out for $252,000 per month per plane, $17,000 a month more than our budget allowed. I thought he was bluffing. He wasn't. The planes went to Delta Airlines in the US (to set up their so-called low-cost subsidiary Delta Express). Other aircraft were either too old, in poor shape, too expensive, or not available when we needed them.

I phoned Bob Ayling despondently: 'It's so frustrating. There's no use setting this airline up if we have to pay that much for used planes. It would be better to pass up the chance to get into the low-cost sector than to strangle it at birth with high aircraft costs.'

'Be patient, something will come up soon,' he replied.

I've never been long on patience but he was right. The Asian crisis in the autumn of 1997 saved the day. Aircraft lease prices plummeted because airlines all over Asia cancelled new orders or shed entire fleets of aircraft. In just a few months we had secured the first three planes within the budget. It was my first lesson in the volatility of the aircraft lease market. The worst decision any airline can make is to buy or lease planes at the top of a market. An overpriced aircraft becomes a millstone that will hang round the airline's neck for years.

So we were able to secure the first handful of planes at the amount we budgeted: $235,000 per month. Leasing aircraft less than ten years old at that price was a coup. An important factor in securing the planes from GE Capital Aviation Services (GECAS), the aircraft-leasing division of the huge US conglomerate General Electric (GE), was that British Airways would guarantee the leases. If we had not been a subsidiary of a large, financially sound company, we would have paid hefty up-front deposits and the maintenance reserves would have been payable in cash. Instead, we correctly accounted for the hefty reserves in our financial accounts but did not need to stump up the cash. In the early days, being owned by a large company was a big financial benefit to a start-up business.

And I'll admit it, suppliers took us more seriously in those early days because we were owned by British Airways. But the links were more limited than was thought. In the very early days, we were assisted by around a dozen people from British Airways in different areas. We paid consulting fees for all these people and replaced them as soon as possible with our own employees. We wanted some of them to join us, such as Simon Harford and Paul Heighway, who put in place Go's low-cost, outsourced IT approach, but we couldn't persuade them away from the mother ship, although Simon remained actively involved in Go as a non-executive director on our board. There were some who came to us, such as Adrian Covill in engineering and Franz Plachy in purchasing, but in general, if you were happy at British Airways you wouldn't have the fire in your belly to join a struggling, low-cost airline start-up. Only those who were dissatisfied or itching for a business adventure would want to leave.

And the discussions continued with Stansted Airport. The announcement of our choice had been made before the final contract was completely nailed down. Dominic was deep into the details, wading in with a number of requests. Could we have ten check-in desks in our preferred location? And would it be possible to have all the systems and baggage belts installed in time for a spring launch? He also raised the issue of security and immigration, especially at summer peaks, wanting to know how the airport would ensure a maximum queuing time of five minutes at the security points. Their efficiencies would help us minimise our turnaround times. Saving minutes and even seconds would become crucial for us.

On Tuesday 25 November 1997, John Stent, Stansted's Managing Director, replied with his final proposals. It was clear they now knew we were a separate outfit. 'We understand that Operation Blue Sky operates independently from British Airways and that this relationship, and any contract, will be directly between Stansted and Operation Blue Sky, and not involve British Airways.'

The last part of the airport contract was office space in Enterprise House, a functional office block just three minutes from the main terminal. We would have preferred cheaper premises, but the proximity to the terminal meant the entire company could be located together and the crews could walk from the office out to the aircraft. Because of the steep rent, we all huddled together and used open-plan desks to justify the convenience of our location. We would move in on a cold morning in early January 1998.

With the base airport contract circle coloured in on Jane's

project bubble-chart, we needed to select a name before Christmas. Items like signage, with months of lead time, were waiting for the critical decision. Both HHCL and Wolff Olins were frantically preparing a shortlist of potential names for the big unveiling meeting.

We were all in Wolff Olins's trendy refurbished offices near King's Cross, sitting around the big table in the workroom. There were mugs of coffee, bottles of water, a bowl of fresh fruit and chocolate brownies placed in the centre of the table. This was going to be a marathon session.

David Magliano opened by reminding us of the aims of Operation Blue Sky. 'The airline is for people who pay for their own travel. Not the sort who get their company to pick up the tab. Remember, Blue Sky will be the friendliest, most affordable and most punctual European airline by making personal connections with the customers and by delivering the slickest, most professional operation in the low-cost arena. It is to be confident, modern, stylish and active.'

All the ideas had been whittled down to five names and concepts for this crucial presentation. Nick Howarth, another of the fresh-faced HHCL team, held up the A2 boards produced by Wolff Olins, with each of the names displayed on the fuselage of a Boeing 737. Lose four. Choose one. Now.

The five contenders were 'A to B', which used a tiny plane symbol between the A and the B. It was neat and clean. Then there was 'Blue Sky', which had been used a few days earlier as the pre-launch name. The third was 'The Bus', the fourth was 'Go Direct', and the wild card was 'Osca Airlines'.

David Magliano loved simplicity, and at first, A to B was his favourite. 'It says exactly what is in the can,' he argued. 'It is simple and no frills. People talk about going from A to B and it is a good expression.' But what also appealed to David's wry sense of humour was that it said BA backwards.

The one problem was that there was already a company

called AB Airlines, and our offering was too similar and would be confusing to the public. It wouldn't work.

Blue Sky also had its advocates among the designers, yet it didn't have the same positive connotations in Europe as it did in the UK. Blue-sky thinking and the sky's the limit are rich images if you speak English, but our European focus groups showed that for a young Italian or a Spaniard it had no real resonance. Blue sky meant a blue-coloured sky; something commonplace and rather mundane if you live in the Med.

Osca, taken from the Alpha, Bravo call-sign alphabet and shortened from Oscar, was proposed because it had a pro-Euro operatic feeling, rhyming with the opera *Tosca*.

'It stands for a Europe that is young and not xenophobic, because we've all been travelling on EuroRail and we know more about Europe's rich culture and diversity,' Nick explained. But there was no outright support. It was put on the list purely to create a character called Osca who would become the face of the airline, a concept that was used in 2002 when bmibaby was invented by British Midland with a small cartoon baby as its spokesperson. After seeing their efforts, I was glad we hadn't gone for Osca. So the name was dumped.

That left The Bus and Go Direct. I wasn't sure. Throughout the 1990s there was a spate of companies using the Direct moniker to signify to the public that you had to phone: First Direct, Direct Line, Direct Holidays. They had no high-street offices and shops, which kept costs lower because all the transactions and bookings were done on the telephone. The more Go Direct was bandied about around the group, the more it began to resonate.

'What if we just drop the Direct part and call it Go?' I suggested.

'It's unusual for a verb to be used as a company name,' noted David. 'But I think that makes it far more immediate. There is a shampoo called Wash and Go, but no one will confuse us.' And with that, Go Direct was shortened to Go.

So now we had The Bus and Go.

A few days later, as nearby Oxford Street was filling up with Christmas shoppers, we met up back on the fifth floor at HHCL to finally decide what our airline would be called. We had only eighteen weeks left until a pencilled-in selling launch date of 1 April 1998, so we were cutting it fine.

The Bus was the most highly regarded concept among the Wolff Olins designers. Their experience of buses must have been so much better than mine; I pictured ancient double-deckers billowing exhaust fumes. It was intended to show that low-cost air travel would be as easy as taking a bus. Getting on and off would be simple. Again, it was straightforward, and it was gathering support around the room. Heads were nodding. Nick then asked me to picture what the name might look like on a business card or a piece of headed notepaper. So I put my foot down.

'Hold it,' I said. 'I'm sorry, guys, there is no way I am going to be the CEO of a company called The Bus. I prefer Go,' I added hesitantly, waiting to be shot down by the experts.

There was some laughter, and everyone acquiesced. There was a palpable sense of relief in the room. At last, a decision. Go was fresh and different.

Later that evening I hunched over the kitchen table at home while Guy and I sipped some wine. He listened intently, then quipped: 'Well, it sounds like "Go Direct from A to B with Osca on the Bus" is the slogan you're looking for.'

I burst into exhausted laughter. Guy could have made it as an advertising copywriter.

Go would be the airline's name, but there was now only a short window of time to give it a real identity stamp. Doug Hamilton, at Wolff Olins, and his team set about creating designs that encapsulated all of our thinking. Everything, from seat fabrics to check-in counters, which had already been ordered, now had to incorporate the design in double-quick time. And Christmas was looming, when everything would grind to a halt. So, back in Hounslow, Jane Willacy prepared another one of her famed bubble charts to ensure that we beat the clock.

Doug, a Glaswegian who had spent thirty years in the design industry, working on projects for Cellnet, Orange, Virgin Atlantic and Channel 5, understood instinctively what the livery would look like.

'It is a designer's dream to get the opportunity to work on creating the image for a new airline. What we wanted to create was cheap and chic,' he said. He and his team adapted a sans serif type-font called Akzidenz Grotesque, which is used on the New York City subway signage – you can see it if you take the green Line 6 of the subway from the Bronx to Brooklyn Bridge. You might notice a striking resemblance to Go's design.

'What I like about the typeface was that the lower-case letter G was so strong,' Doug recalls. 'It looks very clear and crisp wrapped around the tail on an airline. If you were looking up, you would be able to make it out from the ground after take-off.'

The word Go would have a special typographical cut, and contrary to what became a popular myth, it didn't start in a circle. It was simply black and green. When Doug showed Bob Ayling the designs the British Airways chief executive was highly impressed too.

'That's wonderful. What colour is it?' It turned out that Bob was colour-blind and couldn't make out some of the tones.

David Magliano had impressed me with his keen intelligence and down-to-earth nature. And I liked him. I was now conducting interviews, and needed someone of his calibre as Go's Marketing Director. I'd hired a headhunter to find continental Europeans with strong sales and marketing backgrounds; and I'd met one or two likely candidates, but I hadn't been convinced. So just before Christmas I was sitting with David having a coffee in a Pret, just off Oxford Street.

'Would you be interested in the role?' I asked him. 'You don't have any sales experience and it would be a huge challenge. But I just can't find anyone else!' I added jokingly.

He was due to head off to Poland on holidays with his pregnant wife, but we agreed to discuss it over dinner at Nico Central near HHCL. Then he said he would love to join Go.

'I'd really like to do this, Barbara,' he said earnestly.

And he claims I absent-mindedly replied: 'Fine, I've just a couple of more people to interview.'

He nearly gulped, but I then assured him: 'No, no, the job's yours. I want you to do it.'

David, who had come from a down-to-earth Italian family, had gained retail advertising experience at Ogilvy & Mather making value-for-money ads, and was really instinctive about what we were trying to achieve. I'm sure the engineering degree from Oxford University and his brief time at Shell in Scotland made him more practical and harder-edged than your average London-based ad man.

He recalled in an interview later: 'I really enjoyed working with Barbara. She was inspirational and I was fully committed to the project. I never even resigned. I didn't get a chance to do that. Barbara informed Rupert Howell of HHCL while I was away in Poland, so it was all fixed when I came back.'

Even before the name was sorted, we still needed to get moving with our launch advertising campaign. It was late December and we were back at HHCL for a top-rank gathering of advertising executives. It was a mammoth two-hour presentation in which we would try to epitomise our culture as an airline. I had great expectations.

There were homely pictures of 'Ed Winter' walking around the planes kicking the tyres, then dozens of photos of people in arty poses that said zilch to me. One by one, the images kept coming past me, and the life was draining from my face.

Rupert Howell nudged me and said: 'Barbara, you'll love this.'

Then another grim image would be flashed up.

Then someone else piped up: 'This one will make you famous. Believe me.'

I gasped. There was a picture of a sheep in Trafalgar Square with a phone number on it. This was the last straw.

'Well, thanks, everyone,' I said curtly.

I turned to David.

'Can I have a word?'

We went outside the room and David later recalled in an interview: 'I thought I was going to be blasted with both barrels; she was so livid. But I later realised this was only a single-barrel blast; both barrels was when she got really mad.' Among the HHCL team, that day was known as 'Black Friday'.

The next presentation was even worse: another strange collection of photographs of nondescript people that said nothing but: 'Mmmmm, isn't this so arty?' There was even a picture of a scruffy street person carrying some tatty old bags full of clothes. Was this our target market? Surely not? And the photography cost an outrageous £55,000.

'It's all North London bullshit,' was my hot-tempered response to David.

'Please, Barbara, Soho-centric bullshit,' he replied, living in North London himself.

We really should have waited to develop the launch advertising after agreeing the name and design. It seems obvious now. Armed with the distinctive Go logo, the HHCL team bounced back beautifully, and I can still remember seeing for the first time the clean graphical ads that became so well known. And I knew we were being cheeky devils to use the tag line 'the low-cost airline from British Airways'. But it was so right. Simple. Clean. Made an unspoken promise about quality and a spoken promise about low prices and simplicity. Perfect.

Chapter Eight

Cheap Frills

I struggled to find a way of explaining to new recruits how we were different. That is until we used a bit of mathematics. Everyone was eager to 'do the right thing' for our newly minted airline, but the explaining took for ever. So we developed shorthand. The clean graphics of the brand helped, as did the broad definition of the people who would travel on Go. We were for everyone – not just the young and trendy.

My favourite shorthand was a concept that spilled out from a fertile session between David Magliano, HHCL and Wolff Olins. It's an equation that captured the idea that most of the time Go's service and brand would be the lowest-cost possible, incredibly simple and appropriate for a commodity industry. But every once in a while we would surprise customers and please ourselves with something you wouldn't expect from a commodity service. The formula is 3X + Y, where 3X means all the basics done cheaply and simply and Y is for the little surprises (which wouldn't cost much) that would make Go Europe's best low-cost airline.

The Y most associated with me was Go's coffee. There was no

way that Go could afford to provide free coffee. It would cost hundreds of thousands of pounds, even in those early years. And some of our competitors like Ryanair and easyJet didn't even serve hot drinks. But it just seemed inhuman to ask a customer to get on an early flight without giving them an opportunity to buy a decent cup of coffee. My kids think I'm addicted to Starbucks, but it must be an inalienable right of the hard-working business traveller to get a tasty fix of caffeine. Our team sipped and tasted different types of coffee. They came back proposing something similar to British Rail tar. Yes, it's black. Yes, it's hot. But it was disgusting and downright insulting to pay for.

Cath Lynn was charged with recruiting, training and managing everything to do with cabin crew. She was also CCO, or Chief Coffee Officer, which should have been a board position! I am sure she wanted to kill me. But we persisted, and when Cath and Franz Plachy, a Mr Fix-it who had a wonderful knack with our suppliers, came up with cafetière or plunger coffee from Costa Coffee, I sat up and listened.

'The crew will brew the coffee fresh on every flight and we can charge £1 per cup,' suggested Cath.

It made a double-digit profit margin and would convey quality in the way all our best 'Y' initiatives would. Sure the ground coffee was messy, it was hard work in the galleys brewing up the stuff, and the loos suffered from grounds being chucked down them, but it was still a perfect 'Y' that made us different, and customers noticed.

Another important 'Y' was part of every flight with Go. Every low-cost airline worth its salt asked customers to queue up to board with no assigned seat. With 150 customers and just two check-in positions, it guaranteed long queues because only specific check-in desks were able to give out sequentially numbered boarding passes. The number would indicate how early you could board your flight. Early numbers would board first and get a better choice of seats.

For the airline it meant that ticket printers weren't needed under each check-in desk. The idea was to reward passengers who came early and to intimidate passengers arriving later to hustle them down to the gate. With the lure of those talented retailers cum airport operators such as BAA, more and more passengers were delayed on their way to the gate, keen to find that latest bargain in the airport shops. Consequently, airlines were being hit by delays as they waited for these laggard shoppers. Many people have asked me why airlines don't just leave without these shoppers. The short answer is – their baggage has been checked in. No airline can accept the security risk of flying an aircraft with the bags of a 'no show' customer. It's illegal. And finding one person's bags in the hold of a 737 can take thirty minutes or more. So we wait, miss punctuality targets, burn up valuable crew and aircraft productivity and annoy the rest of the passengers.

Why wouldn't Go do what all the other low-cost players were doing? It seemed simple to me. It was just too dehumanising to make everyone queue up like cattle. It was stressful enough catching flights. Why make finding seats together with your family, friends or colleagues an unruly scramble? I was a parent with young kids and found the cattle queuing method causes anxiety and uncertainty. Why wouldn't all my customers think this? And even if you don't care about parents and their children, what about business people? By definition, they arrive later, usually pay more because they don't pre-book when fares are lowest, and are the most stressed-out flyers of all. I was very suspicious of claims of fewer delays and cheaper check-in.

Dominic and Ultan Kenney's time-and-motion tests showed there were no quantifiable differences in boarding times using the different methods. Ultan worked at British Airways and was the king of the check-in queue. He was a huge help setting up our ground handling in those early days.

They tried every combination and could not come up with conclusive evidence that seat assignments slowed down check-in or boarding.

Sure we had to buy ticket printers, but they were already there at many of our airports and the costs were minimal. In fact, it meant that every check-in desk could serve any customer, making check-in more efficient and providing shorter queues. We also found that customers went straight to their seats instead of milling about in the confined quarters of a 737 aircraft looking for the perfect spot at the window. But what I specially liked was that by making flying less stressful and more enjoyable it helped passengers feel they mattered. That was what a proper airline did, wasn't it?

Another 'Y' was the city guides brochures that we sent out to every Go customer. It was a trendy low-down on the city they were travelling to, and helped with useful phone numbers and a few options on hotels and restaurants. It covered hostels for backpackers all the way through to five-star choices. Our customers wanted to go to more places and we would help them by keeping them better informed and up to date. We, too, were excited about travel.

The guides were put together by Denise Pritchard and signalled to our early customers that Go was different, classy, fun and useful. Early on, an itinerary was posted to every customer, so we popped a city guide into the envelope. Later, with the internet, you simply printed out your own itinerary, which saved us big money in processing and postage but the guides didn't work any more. The solution was clever. Our on-board magazine (produced by another company and costing us almost nothing), tucked into the back of each seat, became the city guides. As a customer took a business trip to Edinburgh, we could whet her appetite for a weekend away at the Guggenheim in Bilbao. We wanted people to do more of what we named our airline: Go. Even when we carried 4 million people a year, the cost of producing the magazine (because of the advertising space sold) was tiny at £50,000.

Uniforms were another important 'Y'. We needed an outfit that wouldn't cost the earth, was comfortable, flattering to all sizes of women and men, and could be made very quickly. The early focus groups we undertook around Europe told us that a uniform was important for building confidence in customers that the airline was serious and safe. If the crew look sloppy or the aircraft interior is tatty, it raises questions about the airline's maintenance standards. In reality, there is no necessary link, but I draw the same conclusion myself as a customer.

We needed to kit out the team with a budget of just £200 per uniform. Our budget was daft. Someone told me that because British Airways used the Irish designer Paul Costelloe and gives crew so many pieces of clothing the cost is nearer to £2000 per crew member. I don't know if this is the right number, but you get the picture on the challenge of our budget.

So with this incredibly difficult brief and the countdown ticking away, we looked at our first uniform designs. Jane Willacy assumed that with three aircraft operational by May 1998 we would have 44 cabin crew and 19 ground handlers, rising by the end of our first year of operation to 108 cabin crew and 44 ground staff. Each Go person ended up with a coat, two jackets, two jumpers, three T-shirts, two skirts or trousers and a scarf.

Quite a lot of kit. It was this challenging brief that we took to our uniform designer. In the early days, I told the world that Joseph had designed our uniforms. Well, he had. Not *the* Joseph of Kensington and the Paris catwalks, but our Joseph Mitchell at Wolff Olins. He's a talented all-round designer who sketched out a basic grey trouser suit with a colourful T-shirt and for women a scarf tied in an elegantly simple looped style – not like the Queen with an Hermès headscarf.

The uniform makers produced the suit, the team made

changes to make it more wearable, and that was that. It was distinctive, comfortable and professional without being stuffy. The British Airways uniform always made the wearer look a bit like an old-fashioned headmistress, and the Virgin red suit and red stilettos were clearly designed by an oversexed man. Can you seriously imagine that those shoes are comfortable after a twelve-hour flight? Get real. Equally, the easyJet shirt with 'I'm easy' printed on the back was not the message we wanted to give out. I wanted Go cabin crew to feel comfortable, look good and spend their time worrying about our customers. I didn't want our women crew worrying about their underwear showing when they went along the aircraft shutting the overhead bins, or afraid they would have to fend off lecherous approaches because of the cute phrase printed on their T-shirts. No way. Not in an airline run by a woman!

We didn't want the kind of people working at Go who would want to wear those sorts of uniforms. We wanted friendly, humorous, professional people who would make customers feel comfortable. We found the right people based on their personalities, not their size, shape, sex, sexual preference or age. I was warned about the accent of the Essex natives, but it was part of who they were and it worked. Our cabin crew came to us just right, and we liked their little foibles and differences.

I persuaded Kay Foster to join us for a few months. She had been a British Airways cabin crew manager whom I'd met in New York, where she'd moved on to run telephone sales, and she was leaving the company to do something new. When she started with us in early January, she went straight in to meet Jane.

'We'd like you to prepare a detailed plan of what needs to be done to organise the in-flight service in time for the first flight,' Jane requested.

A couple of hours later Kay returned to see Jane after assessing the state of affairs.

'I can't possibly recruit and train cabin crew in time,' she said. 'Not from a standing start.'

'Oh, don't worry,' Jane replied. 'The engineering department won't have the aircraft ready in time either, but I don't want to change the target start date yet in case people relax.'

She's got to be kidding, thought Kay. *Relax?!* It was eight months before she had a moment of relaxation.

Kay now rang an ex-British Airways colleague, Stuart Iveson, an experienced cabin crew manager with the training and technical experience needed for obtaining the Air Operator Certificate, and pleaded for help and advice. A few days later, Stuart set up a meeting with eight former British Airways people, including John Steans, in a pub. John later became a good friend, a co-investor in a gastropub and introduced me to his partner, Nick Turner, who is a top-level three-day eventing rider and instructor. We jointly owned a horse called 'In for a Penny', also known as Bertie, and 'Some Day Soon', also known as Edward, ridden by Lucy Kemplay, an up-and-coming rider. All these former BA people gave their experience and expertise freely. It was this kind of remarkable spirit and cooperation that helped us get going. And I was grateful.

We didn't pay more than market rates for our cabin crew or anyone else, we were just really picky about who we would let join us. You can train for most skills, but not for personality. Training isn't what makes someone use humour to diffuse a difficult situation, or be considerate about their colleagues. It is something you're born with.

Go cabin crew were a mix of people – some quiet, some loud, many different nationalities, a range of sizes and shapes and all ages. We hired them if they had the right personality and wanted to offer good service. We didn't want just young and pretty blondes; we didn't want clones. One of Go's values was 'Be Yourself'.

At the start, Go was only taking on fifteen new cabin crew

every four to six weeks, and we didn't need thousands of new applications, but we were being deluged with interested candidates. When David Magliano casually mentioned that we were looking for cabin crew during an interview with the top Italian newspaper *Corriere della Sera*, over 3000 unsolicited and enthusiastic applications poured in during a six-week period. Replying to everyone became a problem, yet it was out of the question not to respond – it became enshrined as part of our developing culture. So Kay Foster and a few of her fellow consultants just found the extra time to respond.

Cabin crew candidates were assessed, participating in a contrived group exercise with other candidates. Sometimes the exercise was to work together and use magazines, scissors, a glue stick and a piece of poster board to create an ad to help the Go marketing department. We didn't care about their artistic skills, but it was helpful to see how people behaved towards colleagues in a stressful situation. The one-on-one interview wasn't a good way to find people who work well as a group – and this is fundamental to finding good cabin crew.

Indeed sometimes you pick up on someone's character from an unexpected angle. One day on my way into the office, I walked in behind two very smartly dressed women. They definitely had the look of cabin crew jobseekers. I was just a few paces behind them and carrying my requisite two heavy bags of overnight paperwork. As we approached the door, one of them pushed through the swing doors, caught my eye and allowed it to swing shut in my face. Oh dear! Not what we're looking for in our cabin crew.

I popped in to see John Steans, who was running the recruitment session, and described them. Later in the day he told me that one had been rejected. She was a marginal candidate and my information on her, well, manners, tipped the balance against her. I just didn't want people like her serving our customers. It was that simple.

Because of the long notice periods for captains, we began recruiting our pilots while we were still in the pensions building in Hounslow and HHCL's offices just off Oxford Street in London. Ed Winter and I saw pilots after they'd been through their flying check on a simulator. In our interviews we wanted to find out what kind of people they were. Many pilots are staid and cautious and are not accustomed to being interviewed at trendy ad agencies. These interviews were a signal that we wanted flexible people, as much as skilled pilots. Ed and I agreed we wanted pilots to become involved and learn about the whole business, and not to work in cliques. Even during the times when qualified 737-trained pilots were at their most scarce, we turned away people who wouldn't fit in. In some airlines, pilots become too domineering, creating tension with other colleagues and management.

Ed and I rejected the first captain we interviewed because she was too concerned about the perks and benefits she was hoping to get. It was a shame because it would have been a nice touch to hire a woman, but she could have poisoned the place with comments about how much better everything was in traditional airlines.

Our pilots were a crucial part of our success. We worked through issues, talked and listened openly. It wasn't an age thing. We had some wonderful British Airways retirees who worked hard for us when most of their mates were knocking a ball around the golf course. Similarly, some of our youngest pilots had paid to train for their first commercial pilot's licence from savings and borrowing, and their enthusiasm and energy added to Go's vitality. Others who had worked in a number of airlines knew how bad it could be to work at an airline that endlessly mucked around with your roster, treated you like a number and kept you segregated from the rest of the airline.

And remember, a traditional short-haul airline pilot might fly 650 hours per year, whereas a low-cost airline pilot will fly between 800 and 850 hours, which is still well within the 900 hours safety limits imposed by the Civil Aviation Authority. Cabin crew flying hours were similarly greater at low-cost airlines. Other low-cost airlines had similar levels of productivity, but at Go we tried harder to respect pilot and cabin crew rosters. We might ask for operational flexibility, but we would never take it for granted.

This may sound like a minor issue, but respecting crew personal time and only infrequently changing their flying schedule goes a long way to achieving good morale. A simple solution, but not that common in airlines. We didn't always get it right. In the early days, when we changed things around because we were making mistakes and late route decisions, we used up a whole heap of favours. I owed them all a lot.

So getting the right people and treating them fairly was at the top of the list of what would make us successful. It was our most important Y.

Someone once said that Go was for 'the middle class'. And even that we were 'the Waitrose of the Sky'. I only shop at Waitrose for a treat. I thought Asda or Tesco was far more appropriate to describe Go. In America almost everyone described themselves as middle class, even multimillionaires or struggling single working mothers. I brought this definition with me. I know the term has different connotations in the UK, but I ignored the British class thing. Who wouldn't want to be middle class? To me, it meant nice and decent quality, not snobby and exclusive. And that was what we were aiming to do at Go with $3X + Y$.

Chapter Nine

easyJet Doesn't Stop Go

We were entering the final countdown. Jane was just like the NASA controller who directs the rows of technicians at Mission Control in Houston. Right up until lift-off NASA doesn't know if it has a space mission. The tension was also running high at Stansted as we counted down the eight weeks until we started selling and fifteen weeks until the first flight.

The name Go was unveiled to the public on Friday 30 January 1998, and I faced the press again with more self-confidence and determination. The destinations and fares were still to be confirmed, but we had now thrown our hat into the cut-price ring. At that same moment, easyJet was hiring solicitors and barristers to make their first legal bid to thwart Go. They were preparing a legal action to stop British Airways from setting up a low-cost airline. We became very concerned that until the lawsuit was cleared up, potential customers would shy away from Go.

David Magliano was on the treadmill at the gym in Swiss Cottage when he saw the news flash up on the big screen with the freshly minted Go logo. 'Blimey, it's made the news. It's a reality at last,' he thought as he burned off the calories. David had now joined the management team and was already making an impact. The brand was his brainchild, and he was busy working on setting up the telephone sales centre and the marketing campaign that would generate phone calls from the travelling public.

Wolff Olins created the coloured circles. They were clear and simple. The coloured signs resembled the sixties game Twister, and it had a wonderful Carnaby Street feel about it, *circa* 1966. When the celebrated modern artist Damien Hirst saw our adverts he was furious and had his solicitors write to British Airways' Marketing Department to complain that his ideas had been ripped off. Apparently, Damien had done some pictures of coloured circles and felt he owned the shape. British Airways sent back a letter saying it was nothing to do with them. It was pointed out that coloured circles weren't really all that new. But they were direct and effective.

Our name Go fitted with us but wasn't perfect. When we tried to register www.go.com, we found it was owned by the gigantic Disney Corporation. We also couldn't register Go as the name for a UK limited company. It was my idea to use Go Fly Ltd, which then became the logical choice for the website. We also later discovered that a French travel company with go in its name wasn't too pleased with our moniker when they threatened to have our aircraft impounded in Lyons. But in those early days it was perfect.

By now there was a fresh surge of media interest as I stood in Brunswick's office to announce our spring start-up. As I held up the computer-generated photo of a plane with a Go tailfin, I was thinking: I hope nobody asks me about the planes. Because there aren't any yet. And to my relief, nobody did.

Back at Enterprise House, the two launch days were now firmly set on our calendars. Everyone I spoke to was excited yet worried. The public's expectation was growing, with more and more calls asking us when we'd be open for business. We all knew how much there was still to do, and a little gem in Jane's yellow notebook bible summed it up: 'You can't enjoy something you haven't done.' That's the way we all felt. So back to work.

Jane Willacy put on her time-and-motion hat to check how long each and every task would take at check-in. As we moved towards our launch the bubbles on her charts were being coloured in at a satisfying pace. But cutting the time it took to turn around an aircraft and get it back in the air was essential. Our task was to cut it to 20 minutes, down from the current 30 (which was still better than the 50 minutes at traditional airlines).

So Jane set out with a stopwatch to see how long an oil tanker would take to pump aviation fuel into a Boeing 737, how long it would take to clean a cabin. Then she set up a demonstration to work out how long it would take to issue boarding cards, check identity passes and arrange seating.

The demo started with the passenger shuffling forward at check-in (5 seconds). Then came her amazing eleven-step guide for Go's check-in people.

1. Smile. Ask passenger for their passport and destination (visually check if baggage looks like it needs to be checked in). 'Hello, can I have your passport please. Where are you travelling to today? Can you put any bags to be checked in on the belt please?' (7 seconds, no document fumble time included).

2. Assign passenger to flight by checking computer; type in the flight date and flight number (3 seconds).

3. Check the name in passport, valid date and photo, and any obvious signs of forgery (5 seconds).

4. Retrieve the booking from the computer, find the passenger's name, check passport and confirmation slip, and display seat map (3 seconds).

5. Ask for any seat preference – window or aisle – assuming choice is available (5 seconds).
6. Check in the passenger (3 seconds).
7. Then place the bags on the conveyor belts after weighing them (5 seconds).
8. The bag tags and boarding cards printed automatically (15 seconds).
9. Attach tags to bags, attach baggage reclaim sticker to boarding card. Remove any old bag tags (10 seconds).
10. Then ask the security questions. 'Could anyone have interfered with your baggage?' If they fail the question, escort passenger to Out of Gauge (near Domestic Arrivals and can handle non-standard-sized luggage or extra security checks). 'Have you been given anything to take on board?' If they fail, ask: 'What is it?' If unsure, escort passenger to Out of Gauge (5 seconds).
11. Hand passport and boarding card to passenger, point out departure gate and time. 'Thank you, please go straight through security, Mr Smith, and take the train to the satellite where your flight departs from Gate 14.' (Show the map.) 'To take your seat you must be at the gate 20 minutes before departure.' Goodbye (10 seconds).

Total time 71 seconds.

We compared this with other airlines and we were able to trim a few minutes off check-in; unless of course there was the dreaded paperwork fumble. That could use up minutes. We eventually found a way to hit the 20-minute turn time needed, and one Edinburgh departure even did it closer to 10 minutes!

And the trials went on. One Saturday we advertised in the local newspaper for people to come along and help us go through the motions. We had 150 'passengers' all milling around the desk, which was chaotic but enormous fun. Jane,

Dominic and Ultan Kenney were standing there with their stop-watches barking commands like Hollywood directors. 'Stop, stop. Let's do that again. And can we be a bit sharper,' they would shout.

We had a wheelchair passenger to get on board via a ramp, and one or two people role-playing as pregnant women with cushions stuffed up their shirts. Then when everyone was on board, we went through the safety procedure and the sale of coffee and sandwiches.

'Come on, come on, this has to be done much quicker,' urged Dominic.

We even caused operational mayhem when the pilot for our trundle across the tarmac made a jokey announcement about the 'departure' of the Go flight. Somehow the radio frequency was picked up by Stansted Air Traffic Control, and it took a few minutes of embarrassment to explain what we were up to.

Meanwhile Ed Winter and Jane Willacy were wrestling with the one piece of paper that was of paramount importance, the Air Operator Certificate (AOC). One of Jane's earliest jobs on joining the start-up team had been to contact the Civil Aviation Authority, which regulates all aviation functions in the UK, and she asked how quickly it could be approved. She was shocked by the response.

'Nobody's ever done it in less than eighteen months,' said a curt voice replying from the CAA's Gatwick office.

Gulp, sharp intake of breath.

'Well, just send me the details of all the steps,' she replied. It was going to take many more weeks to write down all our procedures, covering a host of directives from pilots' flying procedure, aircraft documentation and flight safety to baggage handling, before the inspectors would give us a rubber stamp. We needed to write meticulous manuals about every fine detail of our company. We became so concerned about failing to get this vital certification that we considered using another company's airline operation to start, but that was not an acceptable option. Everything had to be done to get our own AOC. Our ability to start the airline on time depended on it. And as we moved into 1998, it became a laborious exercise that pushed the whole team close to exhaustion. Ed Winter, as Chief Operating Officer and the 'accountable' executive in the eyes of the CAA, led the effort. He was supported by Mike Williams for Engineering, John Mahon for Flight Crew and Stuart Iveson for Cabin Crew. We also had to pass a test over financial robustness, and Simon Harford led those efforts. It was a huge team challenge helped along by Jane's prodding.

Once we had submitted our AOC application and the hefty technical manuals, we had to bite our nails and wait for the Civil Aviation Authority to respond – we were told this could take anything up to six weeks. During this time, the CAA's Flight Operations Inspector, Gwyn Williams, read through everything and produced a list of comments and instructions to ensure that our airline would competently run a safe operation. Ed hounded and hounded and was in daily contact with the CAA. He kept us primed about what we needed to do next. With this kind of pressure, it was difficult to be certain about when we would be ready for launch. One early goal had been April, but it didn't take Jane long to realise this was not possible. So instead we aimed for 22 May.

Beyond our internal world, our competitors were actively expanding their own claims to the low-cost sector. Ryanair, easyJet and, to a lesser degree, the Brussels-based Virgin Express stepped up their own growth campaigns. One-way fares meant some ferocious pricing, and Michael O'Leary was about to increase his European flying by adding new routes from Stansted to Venice, Pisa and Rimini and blowing his own trumpet about his company's increasing profits. Stelios, who dubbed us 'BA-go', kept telling customers not to be fooled by 'short-term special offers'. He maintained that our real strategy was to force him out of business and initiated a High Court civil action in London. The aim of the legal action was to ground Go.

It was a media circus, but it raised Go's profile in the UK, and generated the equivalent of hundreds of thousands of pounds worth of advertising for us. Stelios said that Go had a 'photocopy of the easyJet business plan'. I had to laugh at that one. Then he continued: 'Go has been given permission by BA to lose £29 million and then close in three years having put its rivals out of business.'

Where he got that nugget of information I'll never know. That was the figure prepared by Simon and me to answer the question from our grilling at the British Airways board: 'How much would it cost to shut down Go in three years?' It was for their eyes only, yet I read it in the press. From my perspective, none of easyJet's claims resembled my view of reality. Surely it was all just a huge public relations stunt for them.

It fell to Simon Harford to deal with the legal aspects on top of his financial responsibilities. Simon and I were sure in our own minds that there was clear blue water between British Airways and Go. Yes, we were a subsidiary, but we paid for everything from our own budgets and there was an obvious paper trail between ourselves and British Airways.

In fact, Stelios was suing British Airways and not Go, so British Airways hired top counsel David Anderson QC, one of London's leading competition lawyers, and Jonathan Sumption, QC. easyJet used the services of Robert Webb QC, who some months after the court hearing became, ironically, British Airways' General Counsel. He told the *Financial Times* that he bumped into Bob Ayling at Waterloo Station which led to Bob offering him a job.

Simon spent countless hours shifting through documentation and preparing briefs for the lawyers, and I sat at home late into the night correcting submissions and checking the facts. Then we were dragged in to give evidence to the solicitors at

Linklaters, who were building British Airways' defence. We spent hours on our affidavits, checking them once more and correcting them again. This was too important to be left to chance. I believed the case might fizzle out before going to court, because I couldn't see how easyJet could possibly argue that we were being illegally cross-subsidised.

When easyJet filed their papers, Simon and I pored over them and felt they were riddled with inaccuracies and unsubstantiated statements. Then we filed our detailed response. All told, British Airways must have spent hundreds of thousands of pounds defending the case. At this stage they asked the judge, Mr Justice Tuckey, to 'strike out' the easyJet claims as 'unsustainable'.

Stelios, egged on by a coterie of new-found pals such as Sir Freddie Laker and Sir Richard Branson, believed he could genuinely stop us. Sir Freddie's advice to Stelios was reported as: 'Sue the bastards.'

What irked me most about easyJet's fatuous claims was that we didn't use British Airways' systems for operations, telephone sales, reservations, the internet, scheduling. None of them was right for us. We needed simple and low-cost, not sophisticated and global. You pay a premium for sophisticated and global. Our reservations system provider was based in Utah and now boasts a huge array of low-cost airline customers. We were one of their earlier customers, along with easyJet, to be followed by Ryanair a few years later. The system was low-cost, reliable, and easy to use with a minimum of training.

While we worked on our legal defence, the race to recruit and train the call centre sales team – and train the trainers – was under way. We had to start selling our airline seats. Before that we had to order the chairs, the desks, the computer system, the telephone exchange and the headsets that would have to be in place at Enterprise House. Then the flights and fares would need to be loaded into the reservations system. We made it a lot easier by selling every seat at £100 return in those early weeks. The complexity of a multiple fare structure would come later. The new sales people even came in one weekend to paint the pillars in the sales centre to match Go's coloured spots. Lauren, James and other employee children joined in with their brushes.

And the phone system would have to be tested and retested to ensure it was capable of handling thousands of calls. Once flights began we took 7200 calls a day, rising rapidly to over 10,000 a day. At Go a new employee could be on the phones taking bookings in a week, and later that came down to days.

With the clock ticking ever louder, life became very fraught. Phyll Fay, one of the Essex ladies, recalls 2 April when we opened for business. The large office clock hit 9 a.m. exactly, and everyone in the office watched silently as the first seconds ticked away. Twenty seconds, no call; thirty seconds, no call; forty seconds, no call; forty-eight seconds, briiiinnng, briiiinnng. It was Go's first customer and there were muted cheers in the office.

'My first call was so scary it must have taken fifteen minutes to complete,' Phyll recalls. 'We had so much support from our team leader Roy. He just kept walking around and saying: "Come on ladies, we can do it, don't forget everything is £100 return."'

It was a crazy start that first day, but soon the calls dwindled. During this slow period when we had a call centre big enough for six aircraft's sales but only had two planes, the team practised by ringing each other.

Our first adverts appeared in *Time Out*, the London entertainment weekly, on 1 April 1998 in the classified travel section on page 165. In fact the ads nearly caused heart failure, because the magazines hit the news-stands twenty-four hours before we'd opened the call centre. We were concerned we'd be ridiculed in the press, but fortunately we got away with the glitch. Our first ad was a half-pager with the heading: 'the new low-cost airline from British Airways'. Then it gave the essentials: the phone number, Rome, Milan, Copenhagen and the price, £100 return. As David would often say, it does exactly what it says on the can.

As our self-confidence grew, we shunned the expensive, glossy media, but in those early days we stumped up for a full-page colour advert in *Vogue* with primary coloured circles, making the brand look like a new fragrance just on the market. It read 'London, Milan, Rome' along the bottom and had the name Go in one of the circles. It looked chic. The most exciting moment, though, for me was when I trudged onto a Tube platform in London to catch a train and was awestruck by an enormous Go poster. The airline became something real for me that day in April 1998.

And as the arrival of our first planes approached there was still a long list of items to finalise. Way back in August 1997, I had approached Julian Metcalfe, the co-founder of Pret a Manger, and we had begun discussions about selling fresh sandwiches on our planes or at the gate. It was something I desperately wanted to do to make us different. He said he wasn't sure the logistics would work, but could see that it was a chance to give his delicious chicken and avocado sandwiches an entrée into Europe. Pret a Manger was one of the companies that inspired the Go brand, and I was eager to bring the same zeal to flying in Europe as Julian had brought to the simple sandwich. But it was their commitment to high quality that made them shy away from sandwiches being stored on the aircraft. I was sorry we couldn't work together, but the discussions gave us the confidence to put together the deal with Costa Coffee. The cafetière coffee, fresh sandwiches and pastries were good quality and would earn profits.

While coffee was one of our smaller details to iron out, one of our biggest and most important contracts was choosing an engineering provider. Mike Williams, Go's Chief Engineer, negotiated very low-cost engineering services from a world-class maintenance provider, FLS Aerospace, which took away the risk of spiralling engineering costs. In my research, uncontrollable engineering costs had put more than one US airline out of business. That's how important this contract was. We paid for all our maintenance requirements at an hourly rate except the heavy D checks, which literally take large parts of the plane to pieces, test every aspect and rebuild it again over a few weeks. It meant that the more we flew the more we paid, but in winter when we would reduce seasonal flying, our costs would drop too. Making big cost items such as engineering scalable could be critical to our survival. Mike put the deal together, then he and Simon Harford spent weeks getting it captured in a commercial agreement.

FLS had built a huge facility at Stansted and was running at half capacity. Mike Williams had developed his thinking while working at British Airways in Gatwick, when it struck him that he could outsource the entire engineering activity safely and cost-effectively. It was his intellectual curiosity to do things differently, coupled with his decades of engineering skill, that convinced Ed and me to hire him. In those early years he added to our productivity in our highly profitable summers by pushing all the month-long aircraft checks into the unprofitable winters. Countless decisions like this made us low-cost and nimble.

It was unheard-of for a new airline to accept new aircraft and prepare for CAA certification with three engineers. That's what we had: Mike Williams as Chief Engineer, Adrian Covill as Engineering Manager, and Martin Wingar, who specialised in shepherding our new additions into the fleet. And on the day the two planes arrived for the first time in April, Go was full of excitement. A Boeing 737-300s – G-IGOC, the purple plane known to us as Ken, and G-IGOE, the pink plane known as Barbie – flew into Stansted and we stood on the desks in

Enterprise House to see them landing on the Stansted runway. There were cheers of delight, and even some tears.

I received an enthusiastic call inviting me to come and see our first plane. We drew names out of a hat to take people over to the hangar to see Ken. A small group of us then went to the Northside of the Stansted terminal to see this beautiful, brilliant white plane with two white engines and glorious purple painted on its underside. It looked very classy.

'But I thought the engines were going to be purple too,' I said in a very offhand manner, not thinking of the consequences. 'I thought they were on the computer-generated mock-up of the plane.'

There were some gulps from Mike and Adrian – two of the engineering trio.

The next day I was invited back and the engines were now daubed deep purple too. The painters had worked through the night, sourcing specialist paint from Belgium, and it broke the budget. It was then that the true power of the CEO dawned on me, and how I had to watch what I said in future. It was also a classic example of Go's can-do attitude that would continue to startle and impress me. And it must be said, the engines really did look good!

From the planes' arrival we had less than three weeks until the first flight, and every day they were not flying they cost a small fortune. Lynne Hodgkinson and Jane had to check the insurance was in order and spent time understanding the charges we would pay to the governments of the UK, Italy, France, Germany, Denmark and Switzerland for flying over their countries.

Then G-IGOC (or Ken) had to have its maintenance, air-worthiness and noise certificates checked and approved. It needed an aircraft radio licence along with its certificate of radio installation. Then it required a full run for its two CFM56-3B1 jet engines and air tests to see if there were any defects.

Much of this work was contracted to FLS Aerospace at Stansted, and they burned the midnight oil in their hangars on our behalf. Ken sported the phrases: 'Just Go' and 'Go Today'. Then it was the turn of G-IGOE (or Barbie), with a wonderful pink painted underneath and on the engines with its slogans: 'Go Together' and 'Ready to Go'. In their distinctive liveries, our Go fleet would become favourites for the plane-spotters. The colour scheme was less popular with the Civil Aviation Authority. An inspector spotted the pink underside and was heard to mutter: 'Now they're really letting the women get too close to the aircraft.'

When we considered our aircraft identification symbols, we just planned to move through the alphabet following G-IGO . . . A, B, C, D. But Franz Plachy pointed out that calling our early planes GOB and GOD was not a smart idea. So G-IGOC was our first plane.

Our fourth plane, a Boeing 737-3Q8 G-IGOF (a.k.a. the Hulk, because it was an odd shade of green), was leased from Indigo Aviation and it wouldn't arrive until early May, which gave us little time to have it gutted, cleaned, repainted and ready for its flights. It was to be painted brilliant white too with a green underside and engines, and the slogans, 'Go Now' and 'All Go'.

One of the last laps for gaining the Civil Aviation Authority's approval for an AOC was the 'Proving Flight' to Copenhagen. The flight, piloted by Chief Pilot John Mahon, went out to Denmark to show we were capable of running a commercial airline, and an anxious Jane ensured that the turnaround was as sharp as possible. It was surreal. Ed and I were among the tiny group of passengers on board. Nobody even got off in Copenhagen. We held our collective breaths for the flight out and back.

The CAA proving flight was stressful for everyone. We threw people such as Jules Gleeson and Jo Cassidy in at the deep end.

Jules had a huge amount of experience, starting with Dan-Air in 1985 and then spending six years with Virgin Atlantic and Airtours International, but hadn't been flying for five years when she went on Go's very first training course for cabin crew. Anyone with more than one and a half years' experience was made a No. 1 (the most senior cabin crew member), and they were expected to groom the new recruits who had no flying experience.

'Ohmigod, they can't mean me. I haven't flown in years. I can't do it,' said Jules. 'Of course, Go showed me that I could,' she said later.

The proving flight needed two crews of three members, and Jules was designated No. 1 on the outbound sector, with Jo on the return.

'At the time,' Jules recalls, 'I was terrified of the responsibility thrust upon me. Confidence wasn't my biggest attribute. It was sink or swim. However, I usually stay afloat and I began the detailed preparations and a time plan which would be monitored by the CAA's representative, Nick Butcher. My fellow crew, Jamie Burns, Emma Mitcham and little Sarah Ross, were all very nervous but the strong team spirit, prevalent even at this early stage, pulled us through a day which became one of my proudest achievements. I received a magnificent bouquet of flowers from Ed Winter and the team.' Jules now lives in Tasmania and is shaking up the Qantas call centre there.

The CAA inspectors thanked us earnestly and had a non-committal private chat with Ed Winter. We started a waiting game now. Would we get approval in time?

Even if we did get the certificate, there was another outstanding possible blockage. easyJet's lawsuit claiming that British Airways was unfairly helping Go to set up an airline had come in front of the High Court in London with Mr Justice Tuckey. The decision was set for Wednesday 13 May 1998, just nine days before Go's first flight. We had sold hundreds of thousands of pounds worth of flights. I didn't attend the hearing. I had too much to do at Go and, besides, easyJet was suing British Airways and not Go. Simon Harford drew the short straw and sat in court watching the Greek Cypriot entrepreneur, who sat in the public benches fiddling incessantly with his phone cum personal organiser.

In our view, Mr Justice Tuckey fudged the issue. He refused to strike out the claim but granted us the right to fly. It was a draw. In a press statement I said it was 'a vindication of Go's right to fly'.

We were cleared to fly. That was all that mattered that day. My relief was evident in the statement: 'While there will be a further hearing at some time in the future, the judge refused easyJet's request for an injunction, which means that Go has got the go-ahead.'

Stelios, leaving the High Court, said: 'We feel a lot better protected now that the courts are on our side. It's a sign that judges will now be taking a closer look at the actions of big bad British Airways.'

After we launched it was obvious that Go was a completely separate business. The lawsuit did have the desired effect of keeping Go completely separate from British Airways. My worry had been that we might be allowed to do our own thing at the start, but then the tentacles would start to envelop us. Thanks to easyJet, we were left to develop our business in peace.

It was now touch-and-go for the AOC, and Jane was politely harrying the CAA on the phone every few hours to see when we would have full approval. Then the following Tuesday 19 May 1998, only days before our inaugural flight, a 12-page fax spilled through from the CAA Inspectorate. 'Go Fly Limited of Stansted, having satisfied the Operator Certification prescribed in JAR-OPS 1, has been found competent to conduct commercial operations.' It arrived with just three days and counting until the first flight.

Between cramped offices, second-hand furniture, no company cars, no free parking, outsourcing and general penny-pinching, we developed an enduring low-cost culture in Go. Given our heritage as part of the high-cost British Airways, this was an extraordinary achievement. We were now operational and ready to take off on Friday 22 May 1998, a miracle of superb planning, teamwork, good luck and sheer bloody-mindedness. That about summed us up.

Chapter Ten

Wanted: Airline Adventurers

Dominic Paul had the stamina to dance on until the early hours in the marquee and still made it to work in excellent spirits. He had flown back on the late Go flight from Rome on launch day, partied like a demon, grabbed a few hours of sleep on the floor of a house shared by cabin crew, and next morning, Saturday 23 May 1998, he was bright and cheerful as he headed into Enterprise House.

I phoned in from home to check my weekend messages and then spoke to Dominic, who was heading up Go's efforts to set up airports across Europe. He recounted a few tales of the previous evening and told me everyone had had a superb time. Then he moaned: 'Oh my God, there's so much to do, we've got to launch our Copenhagen service in less than three weeks.' I heard his theatrical gulp, then a laugh down the phone. His enthusiasm was infectious.

Go's arrival on the scene was already shaking up our rivals. All of a sudden both Ryanair and easyJet were serving hot drinks (albeit crummy instant coffee) and sandwiches. easyJet was still after us in the courts and even painted an aircraft and plastered London buses with the protest 'Stop BA Stop Go'. The Consumers' Association initiated an investigation into predatory behaviour in the airline industry, focusing heavily on British Airways' decision to establish Go. Independent research was also initiated into public attitudes towards British Airways and Go. The results surprised the Consumers' Association's *Which?* magazine because it showed that British Airways' entry into the low-cost market validated the safety and acceptability of the sector in the eyes of many people. Go's existence made easyJet and Ryanair more desirable to fly with. Of all the criticism chucked at British Airways over the years, no one can say it is unreliable, unprofessional or that it ever compromised on safety. Ironically, British Airways' ownership of Go gave people more confidence to use low-cost travel and it fed the phenomenal expansion of Ryanair and easyJet.

And in the spring of 1998, strong consumer confidence and an economy surging ahead led to unprecedented optimism nationwide. The dot.com mirage was still shimmering brilliantly, excitement was in the air because Northern Ireland was voting for peace in the Province, and the FTSE 100 share index was still on the way up, pushing towards 6000 points. There was still much anticipation for Tony Blair's first Labour government, and London was at the heart of Cool Britannia. Britain, and indeed much of Europe, was soaring and people wanted to travel. It was boom time in the UK, and pundits were talking with exuberance about the days of slump and recession being gone forever because of our technological progress.

Go was now a tiny but real European low-cost airline. The flights to Rome for the next few days were almost fully booked and everything appeared in excellent order. We were the adventurers who had created a new airline in a breathtaking six months. Now we needed a customer service and operational machine that would work well each day, every day. And we needed to keep growing fast. Achieving all this meant that we needed to get organised. Good management and great people would be the key to making the company a success for years to come.

We aimed to make Go a better, more fun place to work than anywhere any of us had worked, but we didn't have many concrete ideas. We relied on a few basic beliefs, just as we had relied upon $3X + Y$ for the product and brand. But we had no handy shorthand for explaining what we were looking for, so I ended up getting involved in a huge range of workplace and people issues. Often I could instinctively sense how to resolve a problem and it must have been confusing working with me in the early days because it was more a case of feeling our way through, rather than using tried-and-tested ways of managing.

The plan anticipated us growing to seven aircraft before Christmas. One aircraft arrived in each of June, July and September and two in November, on top of the two we had at the start. To keep up with this rate of aircraft growth, we were hiring people at a tremendous pace. On launch day, we had 90 Go employees and needed to hire 30 people every month up to Christmas 1998, when we would hit 300 employees. It was a logistical nightmare trying to hire and train hundreds, but finding the *right* people was what we worried most about.

Many of us had started in traditional, large, cradle-to-grave companies like British Airways or Sainsbury and we knew we did not want that sort of culture. People happy at a big company wanted rules and joined because they needed to be part of an established successful business. Among the top team in the early days, many were from large companies: Ed, Dom and Mike Williams were from British Airways, Cath Lynn from Sainsbury. We had been oddballs in our organisations: people who wanted to try to start again keeping the best parts of these leading companies, but dumping the bureaucracy. Fortunately, some came from entrepreneurial backgrounds: Andy Holmes from easyJet, Lynne Hodgkinson, John Mahon and Steven Horner.

We had some heated debates about flexibility versus chaos and structure versus bureaucracy. To some, any constraint was bureaucracy, but to others, a big fat rule book would have been more comfortable. We tried to develop the instincts of an entrepreneur but use the method of a corporate manager. If we could take the best of both, we'd be nimble and systematic, which would help us grow fast, become true discounters and meet all our objectives: financial, punctuality, safety, customer satisfaction and happy employees. That was the plan.

So for recruiting people, it seemed sensible to aim for oddballs like us from large companies or budding entrepreneurs. We wanted people who didn't need thick rule books and who were more flexible and happy to let their own personalities shine through. The right people would feel becoming a quality discounter was the clever way to manage an airline. Cost cutting wasn't about miserably squeezing budgets, it was an exciting challenge to think up clever ways of doing things differently to get our costs down.

Ed Winter and John Mahon, our Chief Pilot, had the task of finding pilots who would buy into this philosophy. Finding suitable candidates was not easy. John was an ideal Chief Pilot for us; he loved the swashbuckling approach to starting up an airline. In those early days, he and Ed set the tone with their passion and by sheer force of their personalities were able to attract some brilliant characters who enjoyed flying the Go way.

Pilots are a peculiar breed. For most of them, flying an aircraft is a lifelong love affair. At what they affectionately call 'The Office', they twiddle the controls of 54 tonnes of complex technology. There can be few more exhilarating experiences than piloting a plane on a clear evening heading home to London. I've certainly had the privilege to sit in the cockpit at

33,000 ft and view the Alps or the patchwork of the British countryside. You can see how it draws people into flying for a living.

And we attracted the passionate flyers. Pilots such as Welshman John Reed, who amused us with his sketches and ended up as Go's unofficial cartoonist, Figment. He started flying Dakotas with Cambrian Airways in Wales back in the 1960s, and had been a British Airways captain for twenty-three years. He retired at fifty-five in November 1997, and when he was doing his round of goodbyes he popped in to say cheerio to Ed. Ed asked him if he would like to fly with us, but he declined the offer, saying he was heading off to deepest Wiltshire, where he planned a new career as an artist.

A few months later, bored rigid, he was watching the Nine o'Clock News when an item about Go Captain Bryan Bliss being arrested in Italy flashed up on the screen. He emailed one of his irreverent caricatures to Ed, with a scrawl along the bottom saying: 'If you can't get Bryan out of jail, I'll have his job.'

There's more about Bryan later, but within a couple of weeks John was back flying as a captain at Go and, as he said, 'enjoying an unexpected two-and-a-half years of an Indian summer to my flying career'.

'It was great fun,' he recalled, 'but I found myself doing as much work in ten days as I had previously done in twenty-eight days at British Airways.' He was flying more because British Airways' captains belong to a select club where the number of hours they actually fly has been reduced through decades of industrial agreements. John's flying almost doubled at Go compared with what he would have done at British Airways, and this was at the heart of why we were lower-cost. There was nothing illegal about this, but it did mean that as a pilot you flew a lot more.

There were dozens of other characters like John; some from

careers at other airlines, some retirees who had a compelling desire to fly planes. The retired British Airways pilots came with some built-in advantages. First, they were trained to fly the British Airways way, which was the standard we maintained at Go. Also, since many worked part-time, when the inevitable glitch occurred with the rosters or we had an operational problem, we were able to wheedle a few more hours' flying. They gave us great flexibility in those early days. We did make one or two mistakes, and brought in British Airways guys who couldn't cope with the informal, can-do Go culture where everyone pitched in without being asked and no one bowed and scraped to captains, or in fact to anyone (that included me too!). They didn't last long.

We also hired young pilots who had recently qualified. They were both enthusiastic and skilful. Many had arrived from other careers and adored flying Boeing 737s. We had former policemen, doctors and aeronautical engineers in our flight cockpits. They all appreciated the opportunity to do what they loved.

The wide variety of people in flight crew was mirrored in other parts of the airline. Cabin crew was full of former teachers, students, mothers, train assistants, BBC reporters, dancers, entrepreneurs and shop assistants, as well as some who had flown before as cabin crew. You name it, someone at Go had done it before. Since virtually everyone had experience of other workplaces, most expected faceless management, incomprehensible rules and anonymity. Instead they were greeted by friendly recruiters and welcoming training days and handed the Go Directory. This was a straightforward handbook to help colleagues at Go to make their way through the day-to-day issues of working. We wrote in plain English and used a question-and-answer format. We all brainstormed the logical questions we'd want to know in a new job and came up with the answers. We encouraged their help in making life better – both for employees and customers – and provided clear guidance on how to deal with everything from payroll problems to employees' personal travel. It was all part of making Go the kind of place we would want to work if we were in their shoes.

The top team were not a conventional bunch, nor could anyone ever describe us as clones. I'm someone who is never happy with the status quo. An entire team like me would have driven everyone nuts. At this early stage, there were just three directors and me – the founder directors. Ed took care of all things operational, Lynne ran all financial matters and anything administrative, while David was responsible for revenue and routes, with Steven Horner initially working for him. I chose people to offset each other's weaknesses, yet let strengths shine through. A perfect example is me and Ed Winter. My operational experience was very limited, and without Ed we wouldn't have had an airline. His thirty years' experience, calm personality and open-mindedness made us a complementary pairing.

At one point, the team felt we wanted to work better together but it wasn't happening. We found an expert who gave the directors plus a few others questionnaires to fill in about ourselves. The results helped. I was an 'adventurer, warrior' who loved to make a quick assessment then jump in and do things, rather than reflect and observe. Ed had very similar traits to me. No real surprise; we were the warriors blazing the path for the new airline. David Magliano's strong 'observer' tendency led to more reflection before action. Lynne Hodgkinson's strong analytical traits made her more cautious and more likely to be independent from the team. Together we rubbed off the sharp edges on each other's personalities, skills and experience. We made bold but considered decisions. I use the word team cautiously in business because it is often misused. At Go we really were a team. Each of us grew to perform at a higher level than we could have as individuals.

Our directors' weekly meetings evolved from decisions about

minutiae to far more strategic sessions. On big decisions that affected more than one department, we had open sessions to thrash out the pros and cons. My aim was to find a consensus. If we couldn't achieve a unanimous decision, I would navigate us through getting to a decision. The airline needed clear decisions to keep moving. This applied to everything from big sales offers through to new aircraft contracts to the schedule for the next season.

In the latter half of 1998, it was important to keep a very tight control on all decisions that would affect the basic fabric of the company. There were so many areas where initially we'd only considered the broad policy, but reality forced us to spell things out in more detail. I felt the need to be highly involved to make sure the direction was being set correctly. There was a real tension between being low-cost and taking care of customers. If you'd never had a nine-hour delay at an airport before, you didn't have a tried and tested way of handling it. We agonised over the early decisions to try to develop a pattern for dealing with the same situation again. We began to function better, though, once we'd hired people who were sticklers for high achievement and really worked together. After a few months I didn't need to make every decision. Nevertheless, until the day I left I always got involved in changing any of the special 'Y's.

Low cost didn't mean we were unfriendly and dictatorial. It just meant we couldn't afford a plush working environment. Instead, we tried to make it interesting. Early on, for instance, when the initial telephone calls slowed down, colleagues put down their headsets and headed down to Liverpool Street Station in London for a day out, handing out promotional plastic cards with Go's phone number. Their enthusiasm for Go was infectious and won over huge numbers of customers. Some members of the public thought the Go people looked dodgy, and one man tried to run away from Gloria Wright, a.k.a. Glo, when she chased him up the escalator to give him the card with Go's phone number.

Later on we introduced 'shadowing', which allowed you to spend up to a day with a colleague understanding his or her role in the company. Telesales people shadowed cabin crew. Flight crew shadowed the ground handling team or operations control. I even had a few shadows who came along to see what the CEO did. One went to Denmark and watched me do a dozen interviews with the press about our Copenhagen route and another shadowed me around Stansted. We wanted everyone to see the business from as many perspectives as possible. It made work more fun and it made the airline better.

I took a special personal interest in meeting and greeting new employees while they were in training. Often, I would wedge these 'hellos' into an already packed diary. Alan Caistor, Senior Cabin Crew Member, recently got in touch to tell me how he remembered 'having to introduce myself (along with thirteen other newies) to our CEO, and then a few days later while getting myself a coffee, that same CEO saying hello to me by name as if we were old friends. It might seem like a small thing, but when you are new and the CEO not only acknowledges you, but actually remembers your name, you know right from the start that this is someone you will enjoy working for.'

The first few weeks were also the perfect time for giving out the Go wristwatch. It was Go branded, and we ordered a thousand (at about a pound each!) to dole out to all recruits. It was a chance for me to meet new colleagues and be sure they felt welcomed. I was trying to instil a sense of the buccaneering adventure we were all sharing and, frankly, use it as an excuse to say hello. At the conclusion of the month-long cabin crew training, a tradition emerged of a proper graduation ceremony with a cabaret (produced by the crew!), families in attendance, champagne and the watch presentation and a photo with me.

Having a quick word with colleagues was one of my favourite pastimes. Helen Flack, Go's first woman captain, emailed me recently to say she missed being able to chat to the CEO in the ladies room. 'I enjoyed that,' she confided. And so did I. Some of my best conversations were in the ladies room.

There was always a lot of laughter in the office and Sarah Hargreaves, who started in the call centre before moving into Go recruitment, reminded me of one episode. 'I was working in the call centre and you plugged yourself into my phone to listen, which made me more nervous than I was already,' said Sarah. 'The customer was being difficult and arguing over an issue that is long forgotten. Then he yelled: "You tell that Barbara Santini" . . . then you flicked on the headset microphone and said "Yes, what would you like to tell me?" He went silent, it was fantastic.'

That's not to say we didn't have issues and problems. Running a low-cost airline means saying no to a lot of genuine concerns and requests because of the need to control costs. Take, for example, on-board food for crew. One captain formerly with a traditional airline felt it was a safety issue because hungry crew would potentially suffer from lapses of concentration. We had long debates. My argument was that we were a low-cost airline that did not provide meals to other employees. Southwest Airlines did not provide on-board free food for crew, so why should we add this cost? Ed Winter had spent too many weeks as a management pilot at British Airways haggling over menu complaints and seeing crew food that was thrown away. He felt it was unnecessary from a safety perspective and a waste of money. We encouraged the captain with the complaint to come up with a creative solution. He found microwave meals that would be delivered to Go's offices and stored in a vending machine. The hungry crew member could buy it then warm it up in the office or on board in the aircraft's oven (we reinstalled one oven per plane to accommodate the crew food). We stuck to our guns on the cost issue, but encouraged a creative way of addressing a genuine concern.

We also made hiring mistakes. The most shocking were where basic honesty had broken down. I was devastated when a cabin crew member was caught stealing the charity collections we'd made on board. She showed no remorse and sneered at us for making it so easy to take the money. We had our share of disciplinary problems, but, in my experience, fewer than most companies.

Most of the hiring mistakes were people who thought they'd like the buccaneering environment but needed much more direction to do a good job. Others thought that low cost meant low effort. Unfortunately, that poor performer is a drag on the rest of a team. Everyone deserves colleagues who can pull their weight. A cabin crew member who cannot complete the service quickly and efficiently affects customers, but also undermines the other cabin crew on the flight. The same goes for telephone sales team members – where teams compete for sales incentives.

Overall, we were happy with the atmosphere in the company, but it could always be better. I fretted for years on how to manage telephone sales. In the first couple of years, we could not push employee turnover in telephone sales much below 100 per cent per year. Much later we got it down to 35 per cent, but it was a struggle. This frustrated me enormously. It is a tough and repetitive job, where the prospects for increasing your salary are limited, but it is a crucial sales and customer service role. The impression made on the phones could define the entire airline in the eyes of a customer.

When telesales colleagues came looking for more money, I'd say: 'We pay the market rate. Not the top end and not at the bottom. It's in the middle. We're a low-cost airline and that's the best we can do.'

'But it's not enough, we need a pay rise,' some would say.

'Well, I'm sorry, but that's what the market rate is. If you don't like it, you should look at doing a different type of job.'

We encouraged them to apply for other positions. We had dozens of ex-telephone sales people successfully move into other parts of Go. For others, they needed to consider going back for new training for a better-paying job. It may sound a bit callous, but that is the real world and we tried to be honest with people.

Not having shares of stock in Go to give to early employees was frustrating. It would have helped in the first few years. So in our early days at Whitelocke House, Ed and I came up with the idea of giving everyone the chance to earn a 15 per cent performance bonus. Our thinking went as follows: It works to motivate management and salespeople, why not everyone else, like pilots, cabin crew and the finance team?

We linked a chunk of the performance pay to the company's targets, part to the individual or their team, and finally a bit was linked to their behaviour. The corporate measures determined my own bonus: profits, punctuality, customer satisfaction, and later we added colleague satisfaction to the measures. (I was also judged on safety.)

It was a genuine attempt to get everyone behind the idea that together we could make Go successful. We thought extra money would be a carrot. Yet there were endless discussions on how to make the bonus system work fairly, how often it would be paid, what to do if someone disagreed with their boss.

I became very worried when some of our very best cabin crew popped into my office to voice their concerns. 'You seem to think the reason we're friendly with customers and pitch in to help is because you're dangling the carrot of performance pay,' they challenged. 'Well, it is insulting to us; we just don't work that way.' That sure made me sit back and rethink.

It went on and on. It became a recurring debate, because it was difficult to make it fair yet the bonus amounts were critical to making household accounts balance. Paul Sterbenz helped bring the issue to a head. Paul was retired from Southwest Airlines, where he'd worked for many years, and was now a consultant to Ed and me. Eventually he joined Go as a non-executive board director commuting to London from Dallas. He encouraged us to put performance pay to a vote within the airline. Who better to ask? The money was supposed to make people feel motivated about doing a good job for Go, and it wasn't. And when the vote was a resounding 82 per cent of colleagues wanting a 10 per cent increase in base pay instead of the potential to earn 15 per cent in performance pay, we undid the system, added 10 per cent to everyone's base pay and moved on. Despite me believing in it passionately, across-the-board performance pay just didn't work at Go, and I accepted that.

Then there was the thorny issue of trade unions. I had seen how stultifying it became when restricted practices crippled innovation and progress at USAirways. We set up a Consultative Group which would be the forum for discussion and pay negotiations. Membership would include union representatives, elected employee reps from each part of the airline and Go's management. We wanted a different approach for unions and employee representation. We invited any union to apply to us to become one of the two recognised unions. Initially we recognised unions at Bob Ayling's request to avert industrial strife at British Airways. Later we embraced the approach because we thought it right to give people the choice of being represented by a union.

Common sense suggests that if you prevent a free-thinking person from exercising their right to choose a union, they will want it even more. This was precisely where Ryanair and easyJet found themselves. Both airlines fought union recognition and ended up in contentious votes to bring the unions into the airlines.

The 'beauty contest' we ran was a break from tradition in much of British industry. We copied the innovative approach taken at a GE/BA engines factory joint venture in Wales and set up a Consultative Group that would combine managers, employee representatives and unions. We asked the unions to accept the principle that until the company broke even financially there would be a wage freeze. I knew this would be a tough decision to accept, but we were creating a substantial number of new jobs and were expecting several years of heavy losses. In every early employee discussion, I made it clear that we needed to hit the break-even point in three years to survive. New employees had this carefully explained and then were advised that, sorry, there would be no pay rises in this period.

We met with the AEEU, the Transport & General Workers Union and several others. We worked with BALPA, the only pilots' union in the UK, to get them to accept the basic tenets of working together. We offered them a seat on our Consultative Group and explained that the committee only had power to negotiate pay, and that its primary role was for consultation between management and employees.

We chose the AEEU, then run by the progressive Ken Jackson, and BALPA, then headed by Chris Darke. In the beginning, they shook their heads in disbelief at the way we intended to run things. They were suspicious, and thought we were plainly naïve, but we won them over. Then we assisted them in their recruitment efforts at Go. The AEEU set up a desk in our tiny canteen to explain the union and how being a member could help protect employees from management and injustice. All this seemed a bit comical in those early days when I would say Hi as I made my way past the union salespeople to buy my tuna sandwich from the vending machine.

Union membership was very low to start, and by mid-2002 we estimated that about a quarter of our colleagues chose to be represented by unions. We worked well with the union full-time officials and the Go reps to find the real issues and work them through together.

Through the Consultative Group we included employees in

important decisions and we shared how the business was doing – warts and all. We never developed an 'us-and-them' attitude in the committee and I put that down to Ed's (then later Dominic's) professional chairmanship, the work of the other managers and efforts from union and employee representatives. We worked well together on the committee not because we had to but because we wanted Go to be successful and a good place to work. It just seemed the right way to run a company.

We held an election not long after launch to select the employee representatives. Mo Oliver, Ed's colourful, well plugged-in assistant, was elected to represent the office-based colleagues; Phyll Fay, known for telling it like she saw it, represented telesales; First Officer, then Captain, Peter Hogston, sensibly and humorously represented pilots, and Antoinette Ferry, a single mum from Scotland with a heart of gold and an inquisitive manner, represented cabin crew.

The Go union reps, Rick Fitch for BALPA and Kevin Lovelock for the AEEU, also sat on the Consultative Committee. Rick, a well-regarded captain, and Kevin, an energetic cabin crew member, good-naturedly moved between the company, the union and the members to find resolutions to issues. Both Kevin and Rick were particularly helpful when supporting colleagues who were in a disciplinary meeting for some problem at work. They helped their colleagues prepare and defend themselves. Discussions could be heated, but we resolved problems at our quarterly sessions.

The basics of the way the company would work evolved over the years, but in those first months after launch we stamped a personality on the place and it worked well. It wasn't perfect, but I felt comfortable that it was already better than anywhere I'd ever worked, and that was good enough as a starting point.

The place was very exacting and demanding. A bit like me. We were doing so many things for the first time – which made it interesting but exhausting. Lynne Hodgkinson recalls sitting up until 3 a.m. with a young accountancy intern preparing one of the first-ever cost-analysis papers for our weekly management meeting. Exhausted and bleary-eyed, she presented the analysis the next morning and she reminded me of my comments: 'Well, that's great, Lynne. Now what we really need is to look at it in a slightly different way to get to the root of the issue. When can you have it done?'

To survive we needed to keep improving the way we ran the business. Success would not come to us because we were nice people who tried hard. Every few months, another push was needed to keep the emphasis on low costs and hitting our targets. There was a constant need for reappraisal of the routes we flew, our cost structure, the marketing spend and our yields, and this became instinctive to us all.

'Oh, no, here she goes again,' was a regular cry from those who were affected most by the changes.

'Stop pushing so hard, can't you back off for five minutes?' my fellow directors would say. 'The pace is relentless.'

Yet I always felt that if everyone in the company could see things from where I was sitting, they'd understand this need for change. The key was communicating, and however hard we tried, we never did enough. I constantly felt we needed more. We tried anything and everything to stay in touch with our colleagues. I recorded a weekly telephone message on the state of the business that could be accessed from home – particularly useful for cabin crew and flight crew who were not office-based.

We made quarterly business presentations where I revealed some sensitive information which people respected and was never leaked outside. We invented Go TV, a Powerpoint presentation updated weekly and set up on a continuous loop visible to anyone walking through the office. Our company newsletter was funny as well as interesting – including film reviews from

Steven Horner. Doughnuts and coffee for a 5.30 a.m. start with cabin crew and flight crew was one of the best ways to chat about the business and answer questions. We ran two day-long courses for new people (called Let's Go) and another as a refresher (called Let's Go Again). The courses ended with a dinner hosted by me or one of the directors. I also hosted low-cost dinners for informal chats at a nearby Pizza Express to get to know colleagues. The dinners mixed crew with accountants and colleagues who dealt with customer complaints. I enjoyed every dinner. By the end, I'd taken over 500 colleagues out to dinner. That's a lot of pizza.

There is a story I like about a traveller passing by two brick-layers and asking what they are doing. One says he is laying a brick wall, while the other says he is building a cathedral. I wanted us to be building a cathedral. Some roles may have been more glamorous or highly paid than others, but everyone made a huge contribution. And in that first year, we introduced one of the best things we ever did – the Go MAD recognition programme. MAD stood for Make A Difference. Kay Foster, my former colleague from British Airways in New York who set up Go's cabin crew, thought it up and I immediately loved its fun and irreverent feel.

We asked colleagues and customers (through our onboard magazine, *The One Line Guide*) to nominate Go colleagues who had made a difference. Among the first winners was Frank Bishop, a Go captain, who had single-handedly unloaded all the bags from an aircraft in Milan because the local baggage han-dlers had disappeared. He came off the flight, and was heading to the crew hotel for the evening, when he noticed that the Go passengers were milling around waiting for their bags. They had been there for some time.

He nipped behind the conveyor belt and found the trolleys of bags with no one around. Without telling his colleagues, he unloaded the bags and returned to the group heading for the hotel. When one of them finally found out what he'd done, he became a natural candidate for one of our first awards.

Another early winner was Peter Griffiths, a pilot who came to us after a career in the Special Branch. He popped in one day to tell me about a marketing idea he had thought up while driving round the M25 that might help with the revenue problem I'd been talking about in a recent briefing. Could we sell Go gift vouchers to get the cash in and encourage travel as a gift? I pushed him David Magliano's way, and by Christmas 1998 we were selling the vouchers. Normally pilots don't come up with workable marketing ideas, but his brought in revenue and encouraged the idea of our brand: travelling is great but more travel is better. The idea won him a Go MAD for flight crew contribution to selling seats.

Some Go MAD awards were for all-around good guys. In some areas of the company, it was much harder to find dramatic opportunities to help out. Karin Green in Finance won an award for being so nice; she contributed something special every day to the company and even organised bowling outings for the department and making birthday cakes for Finance colleagues.

Twice we put all the previous winners into an election and asked everyone in the company to vote for a super winner. Sheila Mahon and Nicola Judge won this honour from the votes of their colleagues. Sheila, a bubbly member of cabin crew, helped out a customer going home from Rome whose purse had been stolen on the way to the airport. She lent the woman money and took a genuine interest in her wellbeing. The woman repaid the money to her and wrote to me about Sheila's kindness, generosity and trust.

Nicola Judge also showed an exceptional generosity of spirit. Nicola, a telephone sales agent, took a call from an elderly man in Northern Ireland trying to get one of our cheap fares to Scotland. She patiently reviewed the timetable and prices, finally securing the booking. When she asked for his debit or credit card the line went silent. It turned out that he didn't have one, nor did he have any friends or relations who could buy the seat for him. Nicola reached into her own bag and put his flights on her personal card. He said that he'd repay her by posting a cheque, but it never came. Her colleagues commiserated but called her gullible. Then one day some weeks later, she got a call from the Belfast check-in. A very agitated man was insisting on speaking to Nicola. When they spoke, it was her Irish friend who had the cheque for her.

As the top prize, I donated two weeks at our family beach house in Florida and we flew them out and gave them a hire car. Not high-cost but heart-felt.

Awards were presented every couple of months in a public ceremony outside my goldfish-bowl office and in the middle of the daily hubbub. Everyone stopped working – we even brought people in off the phone or guests out of meetings for a few minutes to be part of the fun – and we clapped and congratulated our colleagues. Glynis handed out the fruit juice and crisps as we chatted for a few minutes more. The prizes were definitely not the reason for getting a Go MAD award. Dinner for two was just a token and so were a couple of bottles of wine.

One prize really encapsulated Go: parking spaces made available for rent to senior Go executives were given away to Go Mad winners to use for a month. Our landlords at the BAA were shocked. But in fact we scrapped them entirely when prize winners didn't choose to use the parking places and some of the senior team and others in the know snuck in instead. Cabin crew remarked on it and so I returned the parking places to the BAA. The culture of Go was more important than parking places. Besides, it was the inexpensive little green Go pins that we all coveted – afterwards worn on the lapel or pinned to the security pass lanyard with pride. I hope they will be a collector's item one day.

Go didn't just have a handful of stars standing under a spotlight waiting for the next chance to shine. The airline was full of everyday heroes who just did their jobs well and pitched in when it was needed. The number of people nominated was staggering. From start to finish there were almost one thousand Go employees and partners from FLS and ground handling companies nominated for Go MAD awards. It was a company full of people who really Made A Difference.

Ideas for recognising people abounded. One of my favourites is when David Magliano, Oliver Wigdahl (who headed up sales), Fred Kochak (who headed up pricing), Steven Horner and Dominic Paul (who was now doing business development) all dressed in black tie and escorted all the telephone sales people who had sold a million pounds of Go flights in white stretch limos to London to take a private ride on the London Eye followed by dinner at the smart Oxo Tower. Naturally, Glo and Phyll were there, and a highlight of the evening was the limo passing through home villages to drop off the telesales celebrities. The neighbours never stopped talking about it! When I commended David for the creativity of the idea I also wondered at the cost. His response was classic: 'The limos were cheaper than you'd think, the London Eye gave us a group discount, and because we ate before 8 p.m. we got a deal at the restaurant.'

To keep the communications flowing, I didn't mind jumping up on a desk in the sales centre to update everyone or hand out a Go award. I remember doing it once when a journalist from the *Sunday Times* had just finished an interview and was shadowing me for the afternoon. She wrote a catty article about how Go's people were duped by what was dubbed a 'Go moment'. The most telling reaction was from the people who had heard me that day and then read the offending article. They were spitting mad and wanted to send a letter to the editor. I loved that kind of passion and loyalty, but advised them that letter-writing was probably a waste of a good stamp.

I also got into the habit of doing a few things. John Reed (or Figment) designed a Go birthday card and I sent one to every employee at Go until the day I left in 2002. I borrowed the idea from Herb and Colleen, the founders of Southwest Airlines, adding my own chocoholic twist. In each card Glynis, then Julie Naulls, my assistant from 2000, would put a chocolate bar or pack of M&M's. I know there was some ribbing at my expense in the cockpit, but the sweets got shared around and someone's day was celebrated. I'd be sent home each weekend with a stack of cards to complete and I sometimes grumbled, but got help from my daughter Lauren addressing the envelopes, which left me time to think up something personal to say to each colleague

Books from Lauren and James's shelf at home were an inspiration, and after a quick order from Amazon every new Go baby received a copy of *Hairy Maclary from Donaldson's Dairy*, the story of a mischievous dog in New Zealand. Later siblings received a lovely illustrated book of nursery rhymes.

Saying thank you is a big part of running a business, and I still don't think I did it enough. On our first Christmas, the top team received two days extra leave with a partner in a hotel at one of our Go destinations. We even put people up in the luxurious Gleneagles Hotel in Scotland (Glynis negotiated a good February rate!). Penalties were huge for not taking the extra time off.

Then we put money into a People Fund that everyone who managed people could use. We wanted the money to be used up each year to buy every single person in Go something special to say thanks. The thank-yous ranged from a team trip to Alton Towers to a bottle of wine. It didn't matter. Even swashbuckling adventurers like to feel appreciated.

I could never put my finger on the atmosphere we created at Go, but it was special. I received an email from Paul Llewellyn-Beard, a Go captain who went on to become our Chief Pilot. He sent a list of Life Philosophies he'd found that he felt

captured many things at Go. One of them was: 'Follow the
three R's – Respect yourself, Respect others, take Responsibility
for your actions.' Another: 'Learn the rules so you know how to
break them properly.' Or: 'When you realise you've made a
mistake, take immediate steps to correct it.' And finally: 'Open
your arms to change, but don't let go of your values.'

These philosophies didn't come from the *Harvard Business
Review*, or even as tips from management consulting gurus
McKinsey. He revealed where they came from when he closed
the note with: 'You weren't into Buddhism in a previous life
were you?!!!'

Chapter Eleven

Picking Routes and Crunching Numbers

Every weekday morning around 5.30 a.m., I heard our fax
machine whirring into action to spit out a copy of Go's daily
report. The night shift of Go Operations sent it across before
heading home to bed. The report had the load factors and
punctuality for every Go flight from the previous day, and I
would eagerly digest the information with a mug of strong
coffee at the kitchen table before heading off to work. At the
weekend, Lauren loved to get in on the analysis, helpfully filling
in the charts with different coloured highlighters. Blue if the
flight was more than 70 per cent full, pink if less than 50 per
cent. There was a lot of pink. Things just weren't working out
the way we had hoped.

This was the difference between plan and reality, fact and fiction. When we crunched the numbers for the Go business plan
we had assumed that our average prices would be 30 per cent
lower than traditional airlines' fares. So, for example, if British
Airways and Alitalia were flying to Italy for £300 return, we
expected to do it for £210. We thought such a big discount
would stimulate an enormous amount of extra travel. In fact,

we spent hours and thousands of pounds with LEK trying to use computer models to predict the increase in demand caused by prices going down. It's at the heart of understanding how to be a discounter.

In the late spring of 1998, we were still wet behind the ears when it came to discounting and new to the realities of start-up business. 'At these low fares,' I said in countless interviews, 'we believe that many new customers will take extra trips.' A sound theory, but the problem was that even though we'd dropped our average prices to more than 50 per cent below the fares of the big guys, planes were still taking off barely half full. As a result, the revenue forecast for the first year's budget was looking ever more rose-tinted by the day. There was a lot of deep breathing as we reviewed our revenue numbers.

'No one ever achieves their business plan,' one colleague said, to reassure himself and me.

'That's true, it's just a rough template,' another would add when faced with our bulging revenue deficit.

The trouble with running a business at start-up is that it's a bit like driving a car blindfolded. You think you're pointed in the right direction, but to begin with you can't really see whether you're on track. You just have to keep going and hope you don't hit a tree before you can see ahead well enough to steer!

The big questions we were asking ourselves were: Will revenues pick up when customers get to know about us? If so, when? Are we charging too much? Or too little? Are we on the right routes?

We had a further disadvantage in that we didn't know exactly when we would get our hands on more planes, because we were taking them only as and when good opportunities came up from the leasing companies. As a consequence, we usually had only six weeks' advance notice to start selling seats on each new route, when ideally we should have started selling at least three months in advance.

The cost side of the picture was also hazy. Again we'd made a host of assumptions about how much everything would cost. As we negotiated all the big contracts – aircraft, engineering, airports, handling – sometimes we did better and sometimes worse than we'd planned. But where did we stand overall? Until we'd systematically worked through the real numbers we couldn't know exactly.

Two members of our top team were vital to navigating our way forward: Lynne Hodgkinson and Steven Horner. Both joined within weeks of each other in March 1998.

Our acting finance director and my fellow creator of the business plan, Simon Harford, returned to British Airways to become Bob Ayling's executive assistant in mid-1998. Although Simon remained a non-executive director on Go's board, Lynne was now in charge of finance. We were lucky to snag such a high-flyer.

A no-nonsense northerner, Lynne trained at Arthur Andersen and came to us via Budapest and Paris. She had spent several years on a string of merger and acquisition assignments in Eastern Europe, where she met Ronald Lauder, the son of perfume icon Estée Lauder. He was successfully dabbling in entrepreneurial ventures in Europe's new economic frontier, and Lynne helped him with acquiring a famous Budapest landmark, the Gundel Restaurant, in Heroes Square. It had been nationalised in 1949 under communist rule and Lauder had spent $25 million returning it to its pre-World War Two splendour. By 1995 it had regained its position as the finest restaurant in Eastern Europe and one of the top ten in the world. Lynne became its finance director, and then worked on the financial planning for a string of initial public offerings for Lauder's media businesses across Europe.

In her early thirties and earning a couple of hundred thousand a year, plus a Louis Vuitton suitcase full of perks, it was tremendous experience, but life was changing for her. She had fallen for an English businessman she met in Berlin and had started looking for jobs to bring her back to the UK.

One morning, sitting in a luxury Paris hotel, she was scanning the *Financial Times* job pages and she saw an advert that said Operation Blue Sky was looking for a finance director. She sent off her application, and in mid-January Simon invited her to meet us in London. In the meantime her Lancashire mum had phoned to tell her the airline's name was now public. 'They're going to call it Go,' she told Lynne. 'That doesn't sound a very good name, does is it, dear?'

Simon interviewed her and was impressed. I then met Lynne at my central London 'office' in HHCL. It was hot and stuffy in the glass-walled room. Apparently I asked a lot of awkward questions about accountancy controls, and she didn't think she had done too well. But she had. She had precisely the skills we needed, and the intellectual depth to help shape our development. She was offered the job and went to meet Derek Stevens, the Chief Financial Officer at British Airways, for final approval.

Arriving at Go was initially a shock to her system. 'I'm a detail person,' she said, 'and I like everything done correctly.' On her first day, Simon plonked a whole pile of spreadsheets, invoices and four one-inch-thick volumes related to our plane leases on her desk. She looked aghast, but rolled her sleeves up and got down to business. She had to sift through all the numbers and countersign all the paperwork to pay the bills. 'There was no accounts department, or credit control or invoicing,' she recalls.

Lynne's hard work, attention to detail and organisational skills were just what we needed to work through the chaos of start-up. She hired an accounts department, set up the systems we needed and was famously tight-fisted in contract negotiations. Lynne also had a big job creating proper budgets that managers could use to run the business from the pre-start-up financial models. Robert Wickham, a borrowed Boston Consulting Group consultant from Trinidad who came via Sydney, spent a number of months with us, developing more detailed financial models from the early work created at LEK. But a model isn't the same as a budget. In this big task, Lynne was perfectly assisted by Monika Rese, who shared Lynne's total commitment to work and had a good knowledge of airlines from her previous experience at Deutsche BA.

Lynne was always well-groomed and wore smart suits in the office. She didn't really feel comfortable with the informality of Go, and among the directors it was she who struggled the most with the ethos of the company. Lynne had taken a sharp pay cut to work with us, because she was keen to become involved with a project where she would have an equity stake. She was well known in the company for driving a decidedly non-low-cost car – a Mercedes SLK 230 sports car. She got a lot of stick for this.

It took months to staff up her finance department and get organised. Lynne's first major task was to reassess our original business plan numbers and completely rework our budget based on what we were now learning about our real revenues and costs. The updated budget said that we were even further from our targets than we thought. Instead of losing £13 million in our first year, we could now expect to lose £20 million.

As reports of our increasing losses filtered back to British Airways, I expected an eruption. Instead they were calmly accepted. I think that British Airways' equanimity had a lot to do with Lynne. She had become acquainted with a variety of British Airways' finance managers, but she was especially appreciative of the Treasury department's assistance in those early days. She also paid calls to British Airways' Head Office to keep them up to date on our performance, and could always explain exactly what was going on. So although the numbers may have been frightening, at least British Airways had confidence that the Go Finance Director had a firm grasp of the facts.

But our performance also depended on where we decided to fly and, increasingly, this became Steven Horner's domain. We had worked hard on initial route choices, looking for destinations that would grow because of our low fares and aiming to avoid direct competition with our established competitors, easyJet and Ryanair. As a latecomer we had the disadvantage that many of the most promising routes had already been grabbed by a low-cost operator. Steven's importance became evident as the routes that Simon and I had chosen for Go at the start turned out to be decidedly hit-or-miss.

It would take him more than a year, but Steven puzzled out the secrets of the low-cost Holy Grail, making routes introduced after 1999 much more consistent winners. Steven was a master of the science of route selection, subjecting each candidate to analyses of market potential, competition and pricing. But it's the less tangible elements that make choosing routes more like an art form than a science. A passionate film buff with a strong artistic streak, he began to work out how to spot the routes with star quality.

Steven was in his early thirties when I received his curriculum vitae and a covering letter in November 1997 from the South of France. He had been immersed in the transformation of Air Littoral, a tiny family-run regional airline based in Montpellier. With Steven's help, the company went into profit after fourteen years of losses.

Steven admits that he was a plane-spotter from his earliest years. Instead of playing baseball like other kids in his San Francisco Bay Area neighbourhood, he would sit at home mapping out imaginary airline routes. He was our kind of oddball: the type of child who would crane his neck skywards and identify the livery of each passing airliner, probably even from his push-chair. While still at school, during his summer holidays he had worked for one of the first US low-cost airlines, the 1980s phenomenon, People Express, and he enjoyed their freewheeling team style.

After completing his degree in aviation management, he joined Piedmont, where he learned first-hand about flight operations. He moved on to an airline consultancy, and then to CanAir in Montreal, preparing ground-breaking market research into the potential demand for regional jets, which carry up to fifty passengers. These aircraft would go on to revolutionise US domestic travel in the 1990s. But when the company was taken over by Bombardier he moved on again to Air Littoral in France.

So, by the time he arrived at Go, Steven was well versed in a wide variety of air travel markets and was eager to have a crack at the European low-cost sector. He inherited our early route choices: Rome, Copenhagen, Milan, Bologna and Lisbon. Then after that the selections were based more on his analysis and judgement.

Steven was stuck with the Milan route. According to our business plan, it was supposed to be our most profitable route. London and Milan were joined at the hip by fashion, football and artistic flair. British Airways and Alitalia were charging outrageous prices on the route, and we presumed we could charge lowish average prices and still be far cheaper. So this was bound to be a knockout route for us, right?

We didn't factor in the dreaded Malpensa effect. The Italian government had built a gleaming new airport about forty-five minutes north of town, and had started forcing all London–Milan air traffic to the new airfield. The other Milanese airport, Linate, is just fifteen minutes from the city and is the place to be. So we discovered that Malpensa was the Milan airport that no one wanted to use. It was awful.

Big and powerful British Airways was protesting against being moved to Malpensa in the European courts, but as a new entrant we had no existing position at Linate to protect. As a new player, we meekly started flying to Malpensa. That made it virtually impossible to attract local Milan passengers. There was no train link at first, and the airport delays made it unbearable. Go lost millions of pounds trying to figure out how to make Milan work. The irony was the route only turned around financially years later when we pushed our way into Linate.

The shock of seeing our most profitable route on paper crumble into sand was huge. But we had to keep pushing hard to grow quickly, and while we were unsure how to pick winners we couldn't afford to be frozen by analysis paralysis. Ed and David said we might just as well have been spinning a huge roulette wheel every time we wanted to choose a route. The next spins of the wheel came up with Bologna, then Lisbon and Edinburgh. Life would have been a lot easier if we had really understood the power of growing markets with dramatically lower prices. But we didn't.

Lisbon – a fantastic city with its vibrant mix of the old imperial culture and a young and progressive people – was also supposed to be a winner. We were eager to start flying to the Portuguese capital that summer because Expo 98 had opened on the same day that Go launched and put the city in the news. Lisbon was expensive to operate because of the high airport landing and handling fees. The Lisbon route would have been successful if customers had been prepared to pay as much as they would to go to Faro, the gateway to the Algarve. But they weren't. To get the travel volume, Lisbon needed very low fares, like Milan or Copenhagen, but it was more expensive to operate. We didn't see all this as clearly at the time. We just kept hoping that we could inch our prices back up as we became more established. Not a clever strategy in a low-cost discounting industry.

By July we started selling seats to Edinburgh. Our three flights a day to the Scottish capital would serve a booming market. Not only was Edinburgh going to be the home of the reinstated

Scottish Parliament, promised by new prime minister Tony Blair and delivered after a referendum, but it was one of the major financial centres in Europe, home to heavyweight UK companies such as mutual insurer Standard Life and the Royal Bank of Scotland, which was about to bid for the National Westminster Bank.

If we could woo business customers on this route then it would be a winner. Establishing a reputation for reliability and punctuality would be the key to success with business people. And there were even thoughts that Edinburgh could become one of our future bases.

Steven recalls: 'The decision to operate a UK route was primarily to diversify our routes. We were flying longer routes and needed some shorter ones to make our aircraft more productive. We were also planning savings in marketing and distribution costs because we were already advertising in UK national newspapers. KLM UK's service to Edinburgh also had gaps in their schedule and a poor reputation for punctuality.'

Outside the company, the barrage of criticism against Go was relentless. Franco Mancassola, the Italian-American who set up his airline Debonair in 1996, a competitor on the Rome and Copenhagen routes flying from Luton, complained about us to the European Commission and was angry when his argument was rejected. Debonair lasted until the end of September 1999, when its cash ran out. He was especially scathing about Go, and later got rather personal about me. He felt strongly, saying that: 'Barbara Cassani didn't create anything. Everything was given to her. She didn't have to risk a dime or scratch her head twice. She created nothing.'

And Richard Branson couldn't resist chipping in, and was reported as saying: 'It was akin to a bleeding competition against a blood bank.'

easyJet pushed on with its law suit in the UK, which was entering a new phase. No longer could we be stopped from flying, but British Airways would be tied up in court for years defending the claims. Stelios also took an easyJet plane to Brussels that summer to complain to the European Commission that Go was pricing unfairly on the new Edinburgh route. We had come on to the route with prices below easyJet's. In due course, the EC action was dropped when easyJet announced that its Luton–Edinburgh flights were, in fact, doing fine and that our entry had not had the dire consequences predicted.

The accusations continued that we were being unfairly subsidised by British Airways and that Go was just a ploy to drive the low-cost competitors out of business. Nothing could have been further from the truth. We were like no other British Airways subsidiary. For instance, we were allowed to disregard the hundreds of pages of British Airways Standing Instructions for subsidiaries. Of course, this didn't stop departments sending us documents for completion to comply with the insatiable appetite of large companies for useless data. We just binned them.

We kept just two important links. Both were sensible and in keeping with our original promise to the British Airways board that we would run Go like a venture capital investment. We stuck to safety and financial reporting. We agreed to be inspected by British Airways' Safety and Security team each year (in addition to standard annual checks by the CAA).

Ed Winter and I took comfort in the thought that we were under close safety scrutiny in those early days. We needed to be safe and professional and used those checks to keep tightening up our new operation.

The financial reporting and control linkages also made good sense. The Go board approved the budget, capital expenditure limits and big items such as aircraft leases. New route launches also came to the Go board for approval. Our board papers were not circulated beyond Chairman Bob Ayling, Simon and

Roger. We never once had a route choice or pricing decision overruled by those British Airways executives. Even if the decision made life difficult back at British Airways, they stuck to their promise. As long as the proposals stacked up and were in line with Go's business plan, they approved our recommendations. I can't remember them turning down any decision we put to the Go board.

By late summer 1998, Ed was on top of operations, David was preparing our first newspaper sales offer, Lynne was rebudgeting and Steven had settled in to take charge of route selection. Three months after our launch, I took a much-needed vacation. We headed off to share a big rented house with our friends Tom and Hilary Stark and their two boys, in Nantucket, an island off Cape Cod in Massachusetts.

The house was near the beach and we mostly wandered around in flip-flops, shorts and bathing suits with the kids. But I wanted to stay in the loop over big decisions that couldn't wait until I returned – like choosing our new routes. By fax and phone, I agonised with Steven and the rest of the senior team over a long list of candidates. We agreed to fly to Munich and Venice, starting in November and December. Work then began immediately on the airport deals that had to be negotiated before announcing the routes for sale. We always tried to keep the airports guessing about whether we would start up a route, so that we could negotiate the best possible deal. But we wanted to announce a new route and start selling seats at least eight weeks before the start of flying. So these routes needed to go on sale in September. Time was getting tight to tie up the airport contracts and organise the marketing activity.

My life had changed for ever since becoming the CEO of an airline start-up. I wore a pager and carried a mobile phone at all times in case of emergency, even on the beach with my kids. Always in the back of your mind there was the possibility that something serious might happen. This was made abundantly

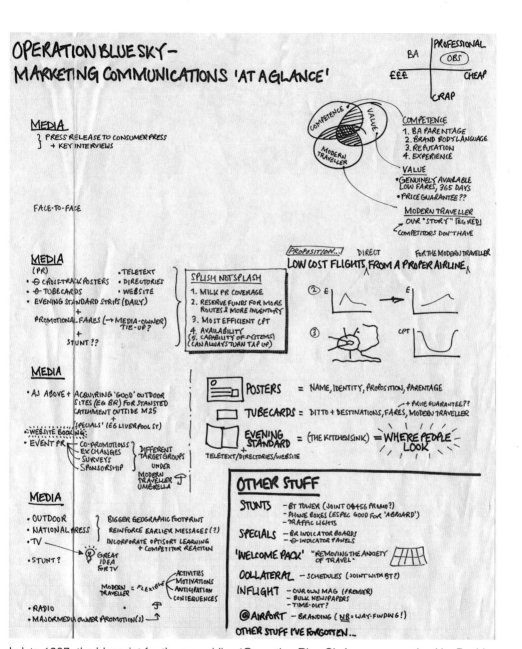

OPERATION BLUE SKY —
MARKETING COMMUNICATIONS 'AT A GLANCE'

BA | PROFESSIONAL
(OBS)
£££ | CHEAP
CRAP

MEDIA
} PRESS RELEASE TO CONSUMER PRESS
} + KEY INTERVIEWS

COMPETENCE / VALUE / MODERN TRAVELLER (venn diagram)

COMPETENCE
1. BA PARENTAGE
2. BRAND BODY LANGUAGE
3. REPUTATION
4. EXPERIENCE

VALUE
• GENUINELY AVAILABLE LOW FARES, 365 DAYS
• PRICE GUARANTEE??

FACE-TO-FACE

MODERN TRAVELLER
OUR "STORY" [EG RED]
COMPETITORS DON'T HAVE

MEDIA (PR)
• ⊖ CROSS-TRACK POSTERS   • TELETEXT
• ⊖ TUBE CARDS   • DIRECTORIES
• EVENING STANDARD STRIPS (DAILY) • WEBSITE
+
PROMOTIONAL FARES (→ MEDIA-OWNER) TIE-UP?
+
STUNT ??

PROPOSITION...| DIRECT   FOR THE MODERN TRAVELLER
LOW COST FLIGHTS FROM A PROPER AIRLINE

SPLISH NOT SPLASH
1. MILK PR COVERAGE
2. RESERVE FUNDS FOR MORE ROUTES & MORE INVENTORY
3. MOST EFFICIENT CPT
4. AVAILABILITY
(5. CAPABILITY OF SYSTEMS)
(CAN ALWAYS TURN TAP UP)

② £ → £
③   CPT

MEDIA
• AS ABOVE + ACQUIRING 'GOOD' OUTDOOR SITES (EG BR) FOR STANSTED CATCHMENT OUTSIDE M25
+
'SPECIALS' (EG LIVERPOOL ST)
• WEBSITE BOOKING
• EVENT PR ┌ CO-PROMOTIONS
           ├ EXCHANGES
           ├ SURVEYS
           └ SPONSORSHIP
DIFFERENT TARGET GROUPS UNDER MODERN TRAVELLER UMBRELLA

POSTERS = NAME, IDENTITY, PROPOSITION, PARENTAGE

TUBE CARDS = DITTO + DESTINATIONS, FARES, MODERN TRAVELLER + PRICE GUARANTEE??

EVENING STANDARD = (THE KITCHEN SINK) = WHERE PEOPLE LOOK
+
TELETEXT/DIRECTORIES/WEBSITE

MEDIA
• OUTDOOR
• NATIONAL PRESS
• TV
• STUNT?
} BIGGER GEOGRAPHIC FOOTPRINT
REINFORCE EARLIER MESSAGES (?)
INCORPORATE OPTISORT LEARNING + COMPETITOR REACTION
💡 GREAT IDEA FOR TV

MODERN TRAVELLER = FLEXIBLE ┌ ACTIVITIES
                            ├ MOTIVATIONS
                            ├ ANTICIPATION
                            └ CONSEQUENCES
• RADIO
• MAJOR MEDIA OWNER PROMOTION(S)

OTHER STUFF
STUNTS — BT TOWER (JOINT 04456 PROMO?)
        — PHONE BOXES (ESPEC GOOD FOR 'ABROAD')
        — TRAFFIC LIGHTS
SPECIALS — BR INDICATOR BOARDS
         — ⊖ INDICATOR PANELS
'WELCOME PACK' "REMOVING THE ANXIETY OF TRAVEL"
COLLATERAL — SCHEDULES (JOINT WITH BT?)
INFLIGHT — OUR OWN MAG (PREMIER)
         — BULK NEWSPAPERS
         — TIME-OUT?
@ AIRPORT — BRANDING (NB = WAY-FINDING!)
OTHER STUFF I'VE FORGOTTEN...

In late 1997, the blueprint for the new airline 'Operation Blue Sky' was summarised by David Magliano's hand-written masterpiece produced for our approval meeting with Bob Ayling. The strapline 'Low Cost Flights From a Proper Airline' started here and evolved to 'The Low Cost Airline From British Airways' which we felt said it all: low prices, good quality *(David Magliano)*

BA CHEAPO

VS

easyJet

Does "the world's favourite airline" really want a low cost carrier?

1. Confused customers wouldn't know what "frills" to expect.

2. Their mainstream business will be hit as customers switch to BA CHEAPO.

3. The unions will hate it.

4. Travel agents may boycott their long haul flights if cut out by BA CHEAPO.

5. They will screw it up and lose a fortune, so making money can't be the objective!

6. The only possible reason for starting BA CHEAPO is to eliminate smaller competitors.

7. And then increase their fares again!

8. This is against the consumers' best interests and illegal.

Fly **easyJet** from London Luton to Amsterdam - Barcelona - Nice - Palma de Mallorca - Aberdeen - Inverness - Edinburgh - Glasgow, also new daily services from Liverpool to Amsterdam - Nice

www.easyjet.com

easyJet used advertising and PR to question BA's motivations for establishing a low-cost airline. This ad plus 'The Beauty and The Beast' were classic examples *(Advertising Archive)*

the **Bus**

148 people who dialled
08456 000 111 paid **£69** and
got on the **Bus** to **Milan**

go direct
fly to Europe for £69

08456 000 111

go direct
London to Rome £69

08456 000 111

Company: **osca**
Destination: **Rome/Milan/Hamburg**
Price: **£69**
Phone: **08456 000 111**
Web: **www.osca.com**
www.bustop.com

The search for a name nearly left us
calling the airline The Bus. Other
options developed by HHCL and Wolf
Olins were Go Direct and Osca. Less
is more in the low-cost airline business,
so we opted for Go *(HHCL)*

We had a bit of fun ourselves by offering a jumbo-sized Go boarding pass to Stelios when he and his colleagues tried to ambush Go's inaugural flight in their orange boiler suits which spelt out GO EASYJET
(David Chancellor)

The distinctive Go branding was used effectively on London double-decker buses to promote our fledgling airline . . .
(David Chancellor)

. . . and London taxis built brand awareness far beyond our meagre fleet in the summer of 1998
(David Chancellor)

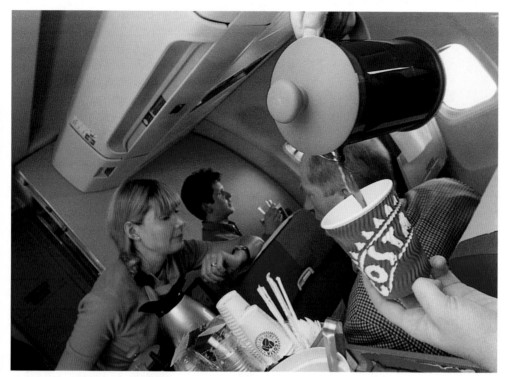

Cafetière coffee was the 'Y' that best captured the spirit of Go. No freebies, but what you bought was good quality *(David Chancellor)*

go discovering

Between Go's colourful, contemporary designs and professional, yet friendly style and people, we won over our customers – who liked us because they could do more of what they wanted to do . . . travel *(David Chancellor)*

Captain John Reed (also known as the cartoonist Figment) designed the birthday card that I personally sent to every employee *(Figment)*

Glo and Phyl (Gloria Wright and Phyl Fay) joined Go colleagues (from left to right) Louise Wheeldon (Cabin Crew), Nathalie Bethall (Marketing), Nicola Biggins (Cabin Crew) and Margaret Oliver (Operations) at the costume party to celebrate Go's first anniversary in May 1999 *(Barbara Cassani)*

Following the crash of a Korean Airlines jumbo jet at Stansted, Go's operations were relocated to the tiny Cambridge Airport owned by the Marshall family. We swamped the airport with our fleet of seven aircraft, but we met our promise of getting customers to their destinations *(Marshall Aerospace)*

Congratulations

This is to certify that

Barbara Cassani

has won a

Go M.A.D
award

This award is a thank you for all your personal efforts and leadership for the last 4 years. It is for the support, respect and achievement that you have inspired in everyone at

go

At the final Go annual party in May 2002, the takeover by easyJet had been announced and my decision to leave the combined airline had been made public. I was presented with my own Go MAD (Make a Difference) award and a gift of an Italian jumping saddle – given to me by the individual donations of everyone at Go *(Barbara Cassani)*

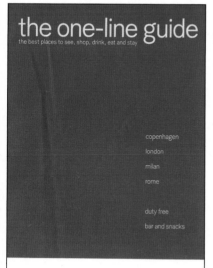

The award-winning *One Line Guide* from its first edition (left) in May 1998 to the last (right) in March 2003. The magazine offered one-liner tips on visiting every Go destination. The magazine celebrated what the airline was about – more travel for more people, at low prices *(Go)*

The astonishing sale of profitable, fast-growing Go by the suits at British Airways is captured in a cartoon in a national newspaper in 2001 (© *Kipper Williams, the Guardian*)

I ♥ **go**.com

Welcome! This site celebrates the airline Go.
I hope that you enjoy it and that it helps to keep the memory alive!

Set up by Scott Fuller (ex-Go cabin crew and airport customer services), a website emerged in August 2003, more than a year after the sale of Go to easyJet. The logo and branding may have gone, but the memory of a great company lived on *(Scott Fuller)* clear in Nantucket that first summer when I got a call from David and Ed.

There was a problem, and at first I thought it must be a practical joke.

'Run that past me again. A Go Captain has been detained in Milan accused of taking an entire aircraft full of passengers hostage?' I queried in my 'I am not amused' voice.

'It's true, Barbara,' said David. 'Bryan Bliss is being held by the authorities.'

Bryan was a very experienced and conscientious pilot who had come to us after a long career at British Airways.

'Well, get on to the PR company and get them to sit on this until it blows over,' I said.

'Hmmm, Barbara. It's too late for that,' said David. 'A TV film crew has just arrived at the office and it's on the front page of tonight's *Evening Standard*.'

'What????' I shouted, in disbelief and frustration.

David later recalled that this was one time when he was glad the Atlantic separated us. Deep in the middle of the media 'silly season', the British press scrabbled around for remotely newsworthy stories and blasted the whole affair over the newspapers and television.

Bryan was unfairly portrayed as a villain. His commitment to on-board safety was so heart-felt that when the cabin crew informed him that an Italian teenager had been smoking in the toilet, he refused to let anyone off the aircraft upon arrival in Milan until the culprit confessed.

There was a little bit of history here too. We had already had trouble with Italian teenagers who were travelling to the UK to attend English language schools. It was a fad at that time among Italian teenagers to wear an airline seat-belt as a trouser belt, and several were stolen on almost every flight – to the tune of £25 each. We also could not allow someone to sit in a seat without a belt, and we ended up losing revenue with empty seats going home. What incensed Bryan about the incident was not only the smoking, but that the culprit covered both smoke detectors in the toilet, making it impossible to detect a fire. So Bryan was expressing the frustration of all of us when he took his tough stance. Clearly he was not taking everyone hostage, but it took some hours to persuade the Italian authorities, and many months for the charges against him to be dismissed.

We weathered the PR storm and Bryan flew the plane back from Milan after he was released. Sadly, going out of town continued to be a hazard. Every time I headed off, something was sure to go wrong.

Back at work, I turned my attention to the nuts and bolts of running the business. We were growing so fast, hiring people, spending millions on goods and services every month. One of my recurring bouts of paranoia returned with a vengeance. I was deeply worried about keeping financial control of this fast-growing beast. Getting the basics right is at the heart of a successful start-up. I was very happy that Lynne had all the instincts to be a tight-fisted bookkeeper, and she set up an efficient and robust process for managing the cash coming into and going out of the company.

We puzzled out how to manage Go through this stage by trial and error, using a lot of simple common sense. But I also listened to my friend Tom Stark, an entrepreneur who offered me plenty of sound advice. Tom had built a sports equipment company in the US from scratch, using his redundancy money from a former employer, eventually selling it for millions.

'Barbara, I think a few basic lessons are important here. Keep control of the company cheque book,' he advised. 'A start-up needs much tighter control of cash than an established big company.'

I signed every cheque over £5000, making sure I recognised every supplier's name. I spot-checked to make sure the prices were in a ballpark I understood (especially important for contracts like airport and handling fees), and I regularly sent back cheques and invoices to the line manager responsible to double-check the numbers before I signed them. Even when our annual expenditure exceeded £200m, signing cheques was a big deal. We upped the value of the cheques I signed to £15,000, still representing a huge number of payments. Once each month I signed aircraft lease payment wire transfers for several hundred thousand dollars per plane. My ritual was to count the number of lease payments every month to make sure it matched the number of planes we had in the air. It was basic, but we needed this to survive. If it mattered to me, the CEO, it would matter to everyone else.

We were also figuring out the reality of what kind of airline we wanted to be. In any airline, shit happens. Rough weather disrupts flights, an aircraft needs a replacement part, a delayed air crew has flown too many hours, there are a myriad things that can go awry, and there is always the chance of something far more serious, so airline operations are regularly thrown into confusion. How you deal with problems characterises your airline, and ultimately what your customers think of you. And we wanted to ensure that we handled issues as best as we possibly could. It wasn't always simple or easy.

If a Go plane went 'tech', it had a knock-on effect, not just disrupting the immediate flight but also causing problems at the airport expecting the aircraft. It was up to the operations team to come up with a solution. For example, they might divert a Rome flight to collect passengers stranded in Milan or vice versa. That way we could still bring everyone home, hopefully minimising the overall inconvenience. Combining flights was possible in those early days because after the initial flurry of bookings most planes were seldom beyond half full. Many customers, and certainly our competitors, assumed that big daddy British Airways would come to the rescue and provide back-up planes. They didn't; that was the deal. We wouldn't have asked. We coped and stuck to the promise that became our mantra: We'll get you where you wanted to go – no matter what. In those early days, we were fortunate that our customers were patient.

It was a difficult juggling act, often a case of choosing which customers to inconvenience the most. On Christmas Eve in 1998, just as I was thinking of heading home for the holiday, Andy Holmes, Go's Head of Operations, popped over to see me from the operations department.

'OK Barbara, you're the CEO earning the big bucks – so what do we do on this one?'

He went on to explain that our last flights of the day from Stansted were ready to leave on schedule, but half our passengers hadn't checked in because they were stuck on badly delayed Stansted Express trains on their way up from Liverpool Street Station. There was a major problem somewhere near Tottenham Hale, and these passengers were anxiously calling us on their mobiles, asking us if we could hold the flights so they could go on their Christmas trips. If they missed their flights, the earliest they could travel with us next would be Boxing Day, because we didn't operate on Christmas Day.

We called the train operator to try to figure out what was going on, and were told that the problem would be fixed soon. We worked out that if the problem was sorted, we could probably get our passengers on board their flights in the next hour and a half, but as a result, most of our flights would be delayed by at least several hours. And if our outgoing flights were delayed, our last return flights would have similar delays. Not exactly what you want for your passengers and crew on Christmas Eve. Andy and I took the decision to wait for the trains, and prayed that the train operator would be true to their word and sort out the problem. We made it by the skin of our teeth.

Needless to say, while we had many thankful letters, we also received some angry messages from passengers who had been on time for their flights, but were delayed because of our decision to wait for the other passengers. When I wrote back I explained that we knew we were going to delay the start of their Christmas celebrations, but we felt that stranding people for Christmas at Stansted was not an option. I'd make the same decision again. I hope those passengers we delayed at least appreciate that it was a difficult choice. Next time they might be one of those stranded on a train.

The feedback from most of our customers was overwhelmingly encouraging. I used to pin their letters and emails up on the notice board, both good and bad, for everyone to read. Monica and Arthur, two customers who lived in East London, extolled the virtues of Go and said that 'Go certainly got our vote as the most friendly airline.' They even wrote a poem about Go for us. Jenny in Wimbledon liked paying less for her ticket and choosing whether or not to buy food. She summarised her views by saying 'Go is brilliant.' We even had a very frequent traveller, Matthew, who had topped the list by flying with us eighty-seven times in our first year. We found him and asked if we could do anything to improve our service, and he said we shouldn't change a thing. In our first six months an astonishing 86 per cent of customers rated us 'good' or 'very good'. Most short-haul airlines (who even bothered to ask) would be thrilled to hit 70 per cent. More than anything else, although our financial results were worrying, we knew we were on the right track where it counted – with customers.

Chapter Twelve

Jack Welch Gives Us a New Lease of Life

We may have been way off the business plan, but at least we had the World Cup in France, Michael Owen and David Beckham, and England's footballing prowess to take our minds off Go's financial position in the summer and autumn of 1998. At best our original plans were only half right. We needed to change things if we were going to make it. And here we got a little help from Jack Welch.

Finding good planes to meet our original plans had been a sticking point. Ed was continually scouring aircraft leasing companies for suitable planes. We had earmarked $235,000 per month in our budget for a five-year-old plane. Then something very interesting happened. Ed identified six brand-new 737 aircraft owned by GECAS which were due to be delivered straight from the Boeing factory in Seattle between November 1998 and November 1999. One problem. Our current fleet of four planes with three more on the way meant that we only needed two more to hit the ceiling of nine planes agreed with the BA board for the second year of operation. This GECAS deal would make us 40 per cent larger than planned at the end of year two.

GE at the time was the world's largest company, and through its finance arm, the largest lessor of commercial aircraft, renowned for its consummate professionalism and the legendary sales skills of its Chief Executive Officer, Jack Welch, then in the final years of his incredible tenure. We also knew of GE's reputation for driving a hard bargain because our first planes were already leased from GE.

Our chairman Bob Ayling knew Jack Welch personally and they got along extremely well. Jack had bought British Airways' large engine overhaul facility for GE at Treforest in south-east Wales in August 1991. Part of the deal was to sell British Airways the new GE-90 engines for its initial fleet of 15 Boeing 777s. Jack says in his own biography: 'It was an unprofitable operation that primarily serviced and overhauled Rolls-Royce engines and British Airways wanted out of it.' The aircraft order was worth a staggering £4.3bn, because it also included a further 24 Boeing 747-400s, powered by Rolls-Royce engines. Rolls-Royce and GE were fierce rivals in the aero engine market.

Bob recalls that from this time they established an excellent relationship. 'Jack's energy and enthusiasm are a tonic. He's been to see me many times on his visits to the UK,' he once told me. So Bob suggested at our April board meeting that I contact Jack. An approach was made through Declan Hartnett, who was the GECAS point person on the Go deal, and I was genuinely surprised by what transpired.

I presumed Jack was tipped off about our interest in the six new aircraft, because an invitation arrived at Enterprise House. Jack Welch wanted me to attend the launch of the CNBC/MSN business news network in June, part of NBC – another GE company. I was impressed that Jack was even interested in our little airline. The flattery began when CNBC's 'Money Honey' Maria Bartiromo interviewed me for CNBC's live TV news programme and I sang the praises of the growing European market for low fares.

Then after the broadcast I had an informal tête-à-tête with Jack. When I spoke to him, it was as if I was the only person in the world. He engagingly discussed setting up a new airline and oozed charm. The evening finished off with dinner at the Grosvenor House Hotel on Park Lane, where I sat next to Robert Wright, the long-serving Chief Executive Officer of NBC and an old pal of Jack's. They even took me home in a GE limo.

When I arrived in the office the next morning a handwritten note from Jack had been faxed from his corporate jet as he flew overnight back to New York. I may have been a doubter about the Moonie-like qualities of the GE culture before my dealings with the company, but it was for real. Besides, Jack's a helluva classy salesman.

Later, in researching this book, Jack was asked about our session. 'I definitely recall the meeting, and having heard about Barbara's new airline, I was delighted to meet her. She was smart, engaging and determined about what she was doing. I considered it part of my job to try and explain GE airline services capabilities to her. It was particularly easy in this case since I was so excited about what she was doing outside the mainstream of British Airways' corporate structure.'

So why was Jack so interested in our low-cost model? 'The Southwest model, or some form of it such as Go's, continues to be the most successful segment of the airline business,' he said. 'The current difficulties with the major airlines may end up with them improving their cost structures going forward, which will come closer to levelling the playing field.'

GE's proposition was clear – they wanted to do a deal with us and would offer a competitive price, but only if we took all six planes off their hands. The prospect of leasing brand-new planes was very enticing. It was hard to find good-quality, reasonably priced used aircraft, and impossible to predict exactly when the older planes would be identified, the lease negotiated and the work done to make them available to fly. A new plane off a production line was more likely to be available on a date agreed months in advance.

Used planes always needed engineering work before going into service, and we knew from bitter experience that additional issues could arise during the maintenance checks. Usually, the leased planes from European or American operators were in better shape and their engineering records were intact. Some of the Asian and South American-operated planes were to be avoided. But this rule wasn't always a helpful guide. Our first two planes were from Philippines Airlines and arrived in good shape. Later we received two planes which had been with Air Liberté in France, and there were so many problems to sort out.

Once we started selling seats, we needed to know an aircraft would be ready to fly. It may sound an obvious point, but it can be devilishly difficult to make happen. Planning growth is easier with brand-new aircraft because the manufacturer's delivery schedule was relatively certain. Late deliveries of used planes were already responsible for part of our current revenue short-fall. In a more mature or higher-cost airline, you would hire short-term expensive airlines to carry your passengers to fill the gaps, but at Go we couldn't afford that luxury.

Growing more quickly was drastic, but we needed to shake things up or we would never get to a break-even point in our third year. At the rate we were going, we'd just keep losing money and an embarrassed British Airways, egged on by a horde of told-you-so directors, would pull the plug on us. Growing faster to spread all those fixed costs over a larger business became our only real chance. And since we were fourth in the UK low-cost market, we thought we'd be beaten to all the interesting new routes from the UK if we grew too slowly. Low prices were here to stay, and we needed to hustle to become one of the lead players in the UK.

That was my speech when I gathered with a dozen of Go's senior management team on Tuesday 11 August 1998 for what I had named our 'Out of the Cornflakes Day'. It was a chance to lift our heads up from the everyday, relentless grind of starting up and running the airline and look at the wider picture. In those early months, it was virtually impossible to carve out thinking time to talk about anything other than the latest delayed aircraft or recruitment crisis.

We borrowed the conference room at our friendly and helpful ad agency HHCL. This was our first management day away from the office in the history of the company. We discussed what we'd done well and some of our early blunders, but after a relentless round of 15-hour days I sensed an air of physical exhaustion permeating the team.

From our early days amid the partitions in the rented conference room of British Airways' pension office in Hounslow, there was a chemistry that bonded everyone together. Back in April 1997 I had written in my notebook that there was a 'need to get high quality people – people who are going to live, breathe and die for the airline'. This meeting was going to be the toughest test so far for Andy Holmes managing Operations, Cath Lynn running Cabin Crew, Dominic Paul in Airports, John Mahon running Flight Crew, Mike Williams heading up Engineering, Steven Horner managing Network and Pricing, and Chris Georgiou running Telephone Sales; plus the directors: Ed, David and Lynne.

Lynne Hodgkinson and I explained the harsh facts of life – that we needed to change our plans already. I never whimsically rocked the boat, but this was not what the team wanted to hear. Ed explained that we had the chance to take the new aircraft, and that while it was fast growth, new aircraft would offer savings in engineering costs, certainty on delivery dates and a chance to boost punctuality and customer satisfaction.

Still, the team was under a lot of pressure and I wasn't sure if they could cope with me upping the pace again. The decision to grow that fast had to have the full support of everyone. As we went around the table, we all shared our thoughts on the pros and cons.

Perhaps the biggest challenge was for our Chief Pilot, John Mahon. When we came to him, we paused. Could he find and train the pilots to fly our new planes? Would he be able to meet both our high standards for pilots and this tight delivery schedule? At that time, pilot recruitment for all airlines in the UK was extremely tight, with growth at traditional airlines, Ryanair and easyJet making it very difficult for us to meet our current more modest plans. John turned slightly pink and took a deep breath.

'Yes, I can do it,' he nodded.

Later he singled out this event as one of the most stressful points in his entire career.

We had the planes and the commitment from the team to grow faster. Now all we needed was the Go board and then British Airways board approval.

With our higher unit costs we could only compete with the bigger boys like Ryanair once we'd built up some muscle. In no-frills airlines, costs don't increase directly in line with revenue. Full or empty, the cost of operating a plane stays about the same. For example, even with just a handful of planes, Go was carrying the costs of the CEO, Chief Operating Officer, Marketing Director and Finance Director. The bigger you grow the easier the cost burden of management salaries and central costs.

The marketing budget was also a big problem. In the first year we spent £12m and took in £31m in sales. We couldn't spend any less, without our advertising getting lost in the noise, but if we kept up that budget we really needed sales of well over £100 million. The media costs for our catchy Go spots were high but raised our profile. Our awareness among travellers in London hit 50 per cent, which was an excellent result for four months of advertising and PR. And the marketing industry liked us too. Go was voted the Most Exciting New Consumer Brand by British Design and Art Direction and David was named Marketer of the Year by the Chartered Institute of Marketing.

Our route decisions were still a headache. With Munich, we chose a route with enormous potential, but we underestimated the competitive response. We took on Lufthansa, the German state carrier, and knew they'd be tough competitors, but their response was brutal. Before we had even opened up our service to Bavaria, they started flying the route, matching our schedule and promotional pricing for all seats. They were impressive and daunting.

We couldn't afford to offer the same low price on every seat for more than a few months, but it was a great way of encouraging customers to try us. We returned to more normal variable pricing, but Lufthansa continued to offer one low price for *every* seat on the plane indefinitely.

I was perplexed.

'Surely they can't do this? Aren't they a dominant carrier with high costs? Don't they even know they're behaving illegally trying to force us off the route?' I asked our lawyers. It's complicated, they said, because of the British Airways' ownership of Go.

Inaction cost Go a pile of money. We lost £2m on the route in the first five months of operation. We kept expecting Lufthansa to behave properly. It seemed incredible to me that they would continue. If we lost that much in five months, I calculated they would be throwing away over £4m given their expensive cost structure.

To make matters worse, we had a disastrous first flight from Munich on an aircraft packed with German journalists. And of course I was on board too. We were in one of the brand-new aircraft and I was sitting near the front giving a series of one-to-one interviews when I was approached by the senior cabin crew member.

'Barbara, the Captain would like to see you.'

I brushed her aside and asked her to tell him that I was busy with our guests, the German journalists.

'Ummm, he'd really like to see you,' was the embarrassed reply after relaying my first response to the Captain.

With a resigned sigh and hope that it was nothing serious, I went to the cockpit and knocked on the door before entering.

'Hi, Bryan, what's up?' I said to Bryan Bliss (of the Milan arrest fame).

'Stansted's fogged in and we're being asked to divert to East Midlands Airport. We can circle above Stansted for a while to see if it lifts, but it doesn't look good.'

'But don't we have Cat. 3 landing capabilities?' I queried, referring to the most modern equipment that enables you to land in all but the thickest fog.

'Unfortunately, we are days away from the CAA-imposed restriction that a new airline must be at least six months old before Cat. 3 can be used.'

I just couldn't believe it. Here I was with a plane full of German journalists, on the first flight from Munich, on a brand-new plane and with our most experienced pilots.

'Let's talk to Andy and Ed to see if they'll ask the CAA for a special dispensation,' was my response.

Andy and Ed were patched into the radio and they explained that they had already called the CAA – the certificate was sitting in a CAA in-tray and no dispensation was available. So we were off to East Midlands Airport.

I wasn't sure how far it was from Stansted. Bryan helpfully pulled out a road map of Britain from his pilot's case and we guessed it would be about a one-and-a-half-hour drive. Wrong. It was two and a half hours. I should know. I did one of the world's longest personal profile interviews with a German national magazine on the coach trip. We were on to my child-hood pets' names by the time we pulled up outside Stansted Airport.

It was not an auspicious start and added to my general anxiety that autumn. And I was concerned about the pattern of sales. When I was in sales at British Airways, business bookings would always increase in September and October as people got back from their summer holidays. This simplistic expectation and the fact that we started up on more business-oriented routes like Edinburgh made me confident that business people would start flying with Go in September. Well they didn't; at least not enough of them.

The forecast profit results for the period July–September were much worse than budget, and forward sales were dismal. Passenger numbers were only 51 per cent of the budget. While Rome was popular, we weren't getting enough interest in Milan and Copenhagen. We had predicted an average price of £76 per passenger in the budget, but we were only getting £58. These results were crushingly disappointing.

Were there any bright spots? Absolutely. On Friday 18 September 1998 we launched our internet booking service. It exceeded our expectations from day one – and the travel industry critics said it was streets ahead of its rivals. It was clean, crisp, quick and perfect for an airline named Go. In Europe, easyJet was the leader in on-line bookings, with us just behind. Interestingly, Southwest Airlines was very slow to pick up the value of on-line booking. It was nice to see we could teach them something! Within two weeks, Go's internet bookings were 5 per cent of our sales and rising. Go built up an email database that became one of our most valuable assets – offering promotions first to this special group of Go customers. Low cost and a direct line to our customers: it was a perfect sales tool for us.

At the September board meeting just before our first flight to Edinburgh, we could see we needed a dramatic change of fortunes. We all gathered around the pushed-together desks that made up the board-table and Bob opened the meeting. He was calm, showing no sense of concern or alarm about our precarious situation. And he asked me to explain the three options we had prepared on Go's future growth strategy.

'This is an important crossroads for us. Firstly, we could stick with our existing plan to operate seven aircraft – that's our existing five plus the ex-Air Liberté plane already on the cards and the one ex-British Midland plane ready to be leased. Or we can pursue the second option which is to grow a bit faster and lease three more planes taking the fleet to ten by 1999, to get slightly more economies of scale.'

Then I paused. 'But, as you know, the third possibility is far more daring. We go ahead with the GECAS deal for the six new planes, giving Go thirteen planes by the end of 1999.'

It was a high-risk strategy and an hour of serious debate followed. But the consensus that emerged was to go for it.

Bob agreed to go for the GECAS deal, provided I could secure a reduction in the monthly lease rate. We were dining with the GECAS team, including the new President, Henry Hubschman, at a dinner originally intended as a celebration at Quaglino's in St James's. We negotiated a further reduction of $7000 per month per aircraft and signed the deal. An expensive dinner for GE, indeed. Including the maintenance savings from running new planes, it was effectively like paying $210,000 a month, a neat $25,000 under budget. It was still a huge commitment to spend over $100 million on the aircraft over the next six years, and it seems more risky in retrospect than it did at the time. But the truth is that if we hadn't gone for the growth, we probably wouldn't have survived.

How Bob Ayling persuaded the British Airways board to approve the doubling of the size of the company while we were forecasting a doubling of our losses I'll never know. It is no wonder some British Airways non-executive directors were expressing fears that Go would become another perpetually loss-making albatross.

The marketplace was also keeping pressure on. We had hoped to overtake Ryanair in capacity at Stansted, but they were powering ahead with new routes and switching to the larger Boeing 737-800 series aircraft, with 189 seats instead of our 148. Larger planes meant lower unit costs, which meant they could keep lowering prices. In the autumn of 1998, Michael O'Leary unveiled his price war strategy to promote all the new seats they were flying out of Stansted. A few weeks earlier British Airways had fired their opening salvo by offering 2 million low-price tickets to eighty worldwide destinations. Ryanair's response was to offer 1 million seats from Britain to European destinations from £16.99.

As he unveiled his promotional banner outside the BA flight shop in Piccadilly, O'Leary was quoted in the media as saying: 'We're doing this deal now to re-emphasise Ryanair's position as Europe's low-fares carrier.'

At Enterprise House, I gathered the team to look at what Ryanair were proposing; £16.99 one-way, not including tax, from London to Prestwick in Scotland; Rimini in Italy, Kristianstad in Sweden, and St Etienne in France. And also £29.99 from Stansted to Pisa, Stockholm and Oslo. I asked Steven Horner to look again at our route costings and see if we could match.

Before we could figure out how to respond to the Ryanair fares, easyJet announced it had teamed up with *The Times* to offer readers cut-price fares. Debonair, increasingly under pressure and running out of cash, also pitched in with 100,000 seats between £39 and £69 return from Luton to Barcelona, Madrid, Munich, Rome and Düsseldorf. Low prices shook people up, made them hop on a plane, and they loved it. In the autumn of 1998, everyone was discovering the joys of a low-cost weekend city break.

The depressing reality for us was that our young company's unit costs were still too high to be able to meaningfully match Ryanair's prices. We had come to the battle late for our share in this increasing cut-throat fight. Why on earth didn't we start Go in 1996? I thought. At least by now we'd be far bigger and have low-enough costs to fight back. It was by now a familiar lament.

But the arrival of the brand-new GECAS planes helped us get closer to a level playing field with easyJet and Ryanair. The phrase that spread around Go as we moved into 1999 was that the company was 'growing like stink'.

I have to confess, I had never heard this expression before, but it neatly summed up our rapid change of pace. And its origins might have something to do with a plane delivered, pristine and shiny, from the Boeing factory in Seattle.

The story is best told by Paul Davies, who was in charge of routine engineering at Go. 'We received reports of a foul smell in the forward cargo hold of G-IGOK – an aircraft that had been in service for some three months.'

Paul had the hold cleaned and disinfected thoroughly three times, and for a short while the problem would abate until the stench returned. It got so bad the baggage crews refused to enter the hold unless action was taken. Even the air crews could smell it during flight.

'I thought the handlers were making a huge meal out of a smell of stale coffee and phoned their duty manager and "politely" requested that he sort out his whinging staff,' said Paul. 'I visited the aircraft accompanied by the cleaning company supervisor to assess the situation. When the plane returned to base, our small entourage waited eagerly in the hot sunshine as the loaders removed the small number of bags.

'Even in the light breeze the smell was noticeable, a mixture of well-worn socks, stale cheese and commercial rubbish bins after a few years' service. The smell was almost overpowering yet the floor and sidewalls appeared clean. I decided the only way to isolate the source was to get into the hold with the cleaning specialist. We climbed into the compartment and closed the hold door to keep the wind out. Inside it was immediately apparent that the door was contaminated,' said Paul.

The door's inside is covered with an insulating thermal blanket that is pop-studded. Paul donned a pair of rubber gloves and reached inside and felt a 'mass' hidden behind the blanket. He eased the object out and asked the cleaner to open the door and pass him a bin bag to dispose of the contents. It became immediately apparent what the stench was: a green fish, seriously decayed, and full of pus and nastiness.

'I would have found it funny had I not been unable to get rid of the smell for the next three days and I was unable to eat my evening meal due to a very poorly stomach,' said Paul.

Speculation abounded as to who put the dead fish in the door. It may have been someone who felt disgruntled in Seattle or Stansted, but I think it was a practical joker who thought we'd find it earlier.

And, for me, that seems the best explanation for how Go came to 'grow like stink'.

Chapter Thirteen

Guess Go's Losses

My first big speech was at the Royal Aeronautical Society's opu-
lent headquarters at Hyde Park Corner on Tuesday 2 March
1999. The evening was sponsored by GE, and this was a public
show of unity to mark Go's lease agreement for six brand-new
Boeing 737s. The whinging by competitors had been incessant
and this was my opportunity to explain to the world the hard-
nosed business approach we were taking to this entirely new
sector. Importantly, I needed to re-emphasise Go's independence from British Airways.

I arrived early and met with Nick Claydon from Brunswick
for a quick debrief on the audience. Then I made my way to
the podium, gathering my thoughts. The speech was based
on my ideas, but had been smartened up by a professional
speech writer. It was critically important that this evening went
well. Many of the Go senior team were there that night: Ed,
David, Lynne, Dominic, Steven, Mike Williams and Andy
Holmes. Even Guy made an effort to break away from his
busy banking schedule to provide moral support. The place
was also teeming with the press. I'd never spoken before to

such a large and illustrious group – hundreds, and all airline experts – and I was feeling my nerves.

As the audience moved to their seats, I stood at the front with the European leadership from GECAS. The place was packed. I spotted all the friendly faces and shuffled my notes in preparation. A hush descended on the room that I interpreted as our cue to begin. Looking up, I saw one last member of the audience making his way to the only place left in the front row. It was the seat directly in front of me. There was an intake of breath as the audience registered who it was, and then all eyes were on me to wait for a reaction. It was Stelios. There he sat within spitting distance. I nodded my greeting to him and launched into my prepared remarks.

I ended with my heart-felt commitment: 'At Go we aim to deliver low prices with great service. We don't accept that low cost means poor service and late flights. We have had a tremendous first nine months and are on track to break even in three years. That was my promise when we launched and I make it to you again tonight.'

And with that, we moved into a question-and-answer session. There was even the requisite question from Stelios about BA's 'cross-subsidisation' of Go. Just what people expected. I batted it back. The evening was a resounding success.

The next morning, Glynis brought a freshly brewed cafetière into my office and placed it on my almost-empty desk. For over a year, we had shared this early morning ritual where one of us would make the coffee and once a week bring in some fresh flowers.

But this morning Glynis, my busy and big-hearted personal assistant, was more subdued as she sensed that my thoughts were elsewhere. It was her turn today. She poured two cups of steaming Costa coffee, added the milk, then pulled up a chair ready to begin our round of executive reports, letters to customers, thank-you notes to colleagues, and birthday cards and baby gifts to be signed and dispatched. She asked about the speech last night and was shocked to hear that Stelios had been in the front row. I laughed and explained that our second public encounter had gone well.

It was five past eight, and there were only a few operations colleagues milling around the open-plan area outside my office. Some would wave a morning greeting. But it was the thin sheaf of confidential papers on Go's financial performance at the side of my desk that was distracting me most. I didn't really take in much of Glynis's cheery chatter, because my mind was engaged by the biggest problem of our existence. The airline was bleeding and on its way to going bust.

I'd wrestled with this precarious reality for weeks. My voice from last night echoed in my ears. 'How on earth are we going to break even in three years? Is there a way we haven't figured out yet?' I murmured to myself.

Then, as I sipped my coffee, Glynis shook me out of my thoughts and I looked up at her.

'You know, Barbara, you should fly our new planes to Alicante.'

Glynis Alghanim told me many times about her holiday home in Mojacar, in sunny Almeria province, a two-hour drive from Alicante. She'd shown me family snaps and then complained bitterly that the UK's package tour operators had it all sewn up and charged a fortune. All those people with their own apartments and villas were getting a raw deal. You had to go for either seven or fourteen days at a time. And the only scheduled service was from Monarch Airlines Crown Service, who could name their price. Effectively, she couldn't go away with her husband and two boys for a long weekend.

'Why do I have to pay £250 per person to fly to Alicante?' she asked me.

And that was it. Hardly a eureka moment, but an idea that made sense. We had been flying to Malaga and Faro a couple of times per week, dipping our toe in the water of the markets. Bookings for July and August on those routes were the only good news in Go's summer schedule.

Steven Horner and his route-planning team had also started to look at further destinations in Spain. We were starting Bilbao at the end of April and Madrid looked good for a July launch. What about Barcelona, Alicante, Seville, Palma and Ibiza? In 1999, more than 120 million people travelled through Spain's airports, and were growing well ahead of the averages around Europe. Aena (Aeropuertos Españoles y Navegación Aerea), which oversees the nation's airports, was investing millions in improving the facilities at Malaga, Alicante and on the Balearic islands. More than 13 million tourists each year were heading out for the Costas, and a huge proportion came from Britain.

There was also the trend of Europe's young clubbers, who were heading for the sun and sin and for all-night sessions in Ibiza to superclubs with names like Hedonism and Manumission. Every time the *Daily Mail* warned about the dangerous amphetamine-filled antics, it seemed to increase the frenzied interest in this Mediterranean island hot spot. My bright executive assistant, Greg Miall, himself in his early twenties, assured me Ibiza was sizzling – and I believed him.

Nevertheless, Go had reached a point of no return. Sure we were flying hundreds of thousands of passengers, but the competition was tightening around our necks and our early routes were not doing well enough. City-breaks to Copenhagen and Milan and business flights to Edinburgh were not growing fast enough to justify new flights that we had put on sale. Even our budding stars like Bologna couldn't take more flights. Alitalia and British Airways had both increased flights to Bologna since Go's arrival, and the market just couldn't absorb that many seats all at once – at any price!

We weren't the only ones expanding. Ryanair launched

Venice just as we did. Then Michael O'Leary announced a 25-aircraft order from Boeing and, like us, they needed new routes to fly. That spring they announced flights to Frankfurt, Genoa, Turin and Ancona in Italy and Biarritz and Dinard in France. easyJet also had a new plane a month arriving from Seattle and added flights to current destinations, making their route network stronger and harder to compete with.

My magpie tendencies of listening and adapting others' ideas were hard at work at this time. Over the past year I had learned that choosing routes was as much art as science, so I now listened more intently to ideas from a variety of sources. And I believed Glynis as she repeated her desire for a low-cost airline to come to Alicante. Then there was Greg about Ibiza and Peter Sissons, the BBC newsreader, telling me about Faro, and Kate Isaacs, who cuts my hair at Michaeljohn, who told me we should fly to Nice and give easyJet a run for their money. They knew where we should fly.

The network team had independently undertaken research, but it was inconclusive. For the routes to work, a lot of people needed to break their habit, fly low-cost then take a lot more trips. But it made sense to me at a gut level. When Guy and I had lived in New York we bought an affordable condominium in Florida. We were able to take two-hour flights that cost on average the equivalent of £125 return. If the prices had been double, we'd have gone half as frequently. I understood how some winter sun on the face is bliss for a jaded city slicker. More and more Britons had enough money to buy a place along the Costa Blanca, Costa del Sol and on the Algarve. Being able to fly down affordably for a long weekend would encourage more to buy places. And then their relations visited too. And their friends – for a free place to stay. There is a multiplier effect that made sense.

As spring ended we projected losses for April, May and June of £6.9 million, which was £5.1 million worse than budget.

That's about as bad as it gets in the start-up world. At this rate, we'd be out of business by sometime in 2000. The future bookings for July and August had picked up, but not enough. We had increased flights to Copenhagen and Milan and there was no way we would fill them up. It was just too much too fast. Our plan had been very sensible. Use the new GE planes to increase flights on the routes we'd launched in the previous year. Great idea, but we were just too far ahead of ourselves.

I felt I should have been nominated for an Academy Award as a leading lady in a short foreign film. In the morning I'd be in board meetings discussing how much longer our cash would last, then after a quick Diet Coke and tuna sandwich at my desk I was doing upbeat press interviews to celebrate our first anniversary. I met the Prime Minister and was fêted as one of the innovative breed of e-business entrepreneurs changing the face of Britain. The constant flipping between roles was taking its toll. In public, I was expected to be the cheer-leader for our wonderful airline, yet privately the revenue figures were unable to match this optimism.

The *Evening Standard* in London loved us, and on Thursday 20 May 1999, on the eve of our first birthday bash, they said: 'If starched uniforms and the smell of school dinners is what you expect from a flight, then Go will not be your thing. The airline is resolutely trendy in a Nineties, Blairite sort of way.'

In the interview it was suggested that I was going to dress up as Olivia Newton-John from *Grease* for the Go birthday party. As it happened I went as Snow White and Ed, Lynne (who struggled with her decidedly unfashionable costume), John Mahon, Mike Williams and a few others were the dwarves. Even better, David Magliano and Dominic Paul were the Jackson Two, resplendent in platform shoes and afros. David tumbled from his high heels and spent the night at a local hospital with a broken ankle.

We thanked customers with a £10 voucher mailed to all the

customers who bought from us in the first year. We needed them all back again in 1999 and I wanted us to be the kind of company that said thank you. And customers loved it. We sent out 250,000 vouchers and close to 20,000 were redeemed. Normally you'd be lucky to get 2000 redeemed.

We then asked ourselves why no low-cost airline had tackled Alicante or Malaga. Since we were always fighting to catch up, did it mean that it just wasn't a great idea? Sure, ground handling charges costs were higher than the UK, but after averaging lower airport costs into the mix, it looked ok. It seems so obvious now that this was a market ripe for picking, but in 1999 it was a risk for Go. If we made a mistake and these routes didn't sell, our company faced ruin.

We took a chance on Alicante, Ibiza and Palma not knowing if any or all would be winners. There would need to be a shift in consumer behaviour – moving away from charters and towards taking more trips.

In May 1999, the senior team sat down together in Enterprise House. The mood had changed. There was an acute air of nervousness, as everyone now understood our future was on the line. But I didn't want there to be any suggestion of panic. We calmly agreed that even though summer was only a few weeks away, we needed to make these dramatic changes to halt the spiralling losses for April and May. No one in Go went unscathed by this radical rewriting of the summer plans. To make matters worse, we also disrupted customers who had already bought seats on the flights we would need to cancel to make way for the new routes. These were precisely the customers we needed onside. The sales and customer support teams had to contact every affected customer about their cancelled flights. Then no matter how hard we tried to contact passengers, some came for flights that had been cancelled. The disruption was a big risk and we needed to make the changes quickly.

Cabin and flight crew had already received their rosters for the summer and their lives were being turned upside down. We had hired these crew promising stable rosters to help with their home lives. For many new employees, this about-face was a worrying sign that the talk and the walk would not match up at Go. There were also whispers around the company that the senior team had made mistakes. Did we know what we were doing?

We couldn't do more about those worries than to explain that we had to do something about aircraft that were less than 50 per cent full. You didn't need an MBA to know that something needed to be done.

There was so much to do to put the plan in place. The airports team had to negotiate new agreements with Spain's Aena and handling agents at an unheard-of speed for brand-new airports Alicante and Ibiza. The marketing team had to make an about-face and switch all the planned marketing activities to launch the new routes. And we needed colleagues from Spain. Just as in Italy, we were flooded with applications for the jobs, and the Spaniards were just as keen and enthusiastic to be working for a new European airline.

Everyone in Go kept this crucial commercial project secret. Internally we called it Operation Summer Sun. It would have been impossible to do in most companies, but at Go, everyone knew we were still fighting for survival. Everyone knew the score and we explained what we were doing and why. And no one leaked our troubles or our solution.

On Monday 7 June 1999, we had our big press launch for Operation Summer Sun. We set up at Liverpool Street Station in London for an early-morning photo-call for the national press. We wanted our event to contrast with commuters streaming out and heading to work, so we hired attractive young male and female students to come along in swimming costumes. I had no intention of emulating Richard Branson's dressing-up stunts and I retained my normal clothes.

Brandon Stockwell, our new public relations adviser from Cohn & Wolfe, who became an integral part of our small marketing team, asked permission from the station owners, Railtrack, to spread sand across the outside concourse, erect a beach backdrop and put up some large umbrellas. But the rain started early that morning and it tipped down. It didn't let up all morning.

I was undeterred, even amused. 'Today, Go announces three new destinations to Spain: Alicante, Palma and Ibiza. Available throughout the summer only, every seat on every flight to these destinations is guaranteed at a fixed low price; Alicante and Palma will be £130 return, Ibiza £120 return,' I told the reporters, as I sat on a sun lounger underneath a huge dripping umbrella.

And I also announced that Go was increasing the number of flights to Malaga, Faro and Bilbao, raising the flights to Malaga from five a week to an amazing three times a day in August.

'Our summer specials let you get away at low prices you can count on, at least £60 to £70 cheaper than anyone else in the market. These fares are guaranteed – so you can take a second holiday,' I said.

And then I pointed up at the dark clouds: 'Hey, and with weather like this, we'll all need a bit of summer sunshine.'

That's what made the papers next day, and the message came across brilliantly. The phones began ringing next morning and the bookings poured through the internet.

The public relations stunt was followed up with television advertising – HHCL's masterpiece of bouncing Go spots developed on an Apple Mac and accompanied by sixties retro music. It was a long way from building film sets and spending a million pounds on ad production. The ads were very effective and helped push our brand awareness in London up another five points to 55 per cent.

We held our breath and watched the bookings pour in. The routes were an instant success with the flying public.

Even a famous entrepreneur of the Ibiza club scene liked our prices. He asked me at a lunch, hosted by the editor of a glossy magazine, if I was a member of the Mile High Club. I feigned a puzzled look for a moment, knowing precisely what he was getting at, but thinking it was all a bit tacky.

'Have you done it at 35,000 feet then, Barbara?' he asked more directly.

'Have you ever been in the loo of a 737? There just isn't enough room,' I replied.

Clearly I wasn't destined to be a frequent flyer to our new destination, Ibiza, but fortunately there were thousands who were.

Operation Summer Sun had pulled us back from the brink of financial disaster. We had found a new market for low-cost travel that hadn't been tapped. It was a heady feeling to finally see the discounting model beginning to work. Lower the prices and they will fly. It worked and we had found the key to a vastly profitable market. We offered low prices relative to the market, but in Go terms the prices were profit-making, especially with full planes. Customers were happy at the good deals and flexible schedules and we were thrilled.

The celebrations over the success of Operation Summer Sun were just winding down when the sobering reality of 'what next?' dawned on us. That's the problem with new businesses. We didn't have a plan for the fast-approaching winter season. One of the challenges at Go was the dramatically different seasonal performance of the routes. The losses anticipated for the winter period were huge, and minimising them was crucial to our survival. And the plans needed firming up in August because in airline terms winter starts at the end of October. Slots need to be requested from airports, crew numbers worked out, and selling under way. We understood the problem but a solution proved elusive. First we needed a plan for the planes that were currently taking sun-seekers to Spain and Portugal. I had personally accepted aircraft number twelve in Seattle, and it had flown back to London to start two months of lucrative summer sun flying. After that period, though, we were unsure where to fly it. Unfortunately, we wouldn't be able to fill three flights a day to Malaga all through the winter in those early days, so we needed plans to redeploy the Malaga plane as well as figure out what to do with plane number thirteen arriving in mid-October, just as the most profitable period finished. That must be why Jack Welch gave us such a good deal from Boeing on those six planes.

We called an emergency meeting of the Go board in late September to discuss the likely financial position through the end of March 2000. For the summer period, it now looked like we would lose £6.7 million compared to what we had budgeted at the start of the year – a small profit. The damage had been done before Operation Summer Sun, which had stemmed the haemorrhage. Unfortunately, we would not be able to claw back those profits in the winter when demand for travel drops, in an airline that had tripled in size in one year.

We were relieved that the summer sun routes had worked, but for the dark months we needed a different plan. We proposed flying the winter corollary of summer sun – winter skiing. We would start flying to Lyons and Zurich in December and take advantage of the short but profitable ski season. easyJet had already started their low-cost assault on flying to the Alpine resorts, using Geneva as its destination. We would follow suit.

Steven Horner had been working all summer to gain permission from the UK and Czech governments to fly between London and Prague. A loophole had been spotted in the UK–Czech bilateral agreement governing air travel between the two countries that would let Go in. Remember, anywhere outside the EU Go had to work through the arcane system of gaining government approval to start flights. The UK government was very pro-free-trade and supported us. Unfortunately, the Czech government had not envisaged low-cost airlines when they'd made the agreement some years earlier. We also had to fight official complaints by British Midland, which claimed we should not be able to fly the route (presumably because they were making very nice profits charging high fares). But we prevailed.

We started flying in the autumn of 1999 and Prague quickly became one of our most profitable routes. It is the perfect low-cost airline destination. Hotels, theatre and beer are all very good value once you get there. The only barrier had been the cost of the flights. So we attracted everyone from opera buffs to stag parties.

The final issue was the thirteenth plane that was arriving in October. At first we thought we'd try to make it someone else's problem and sublet it for the winter. But no one wanted a plane for that period. Then we thought we'd just park it somewhere. But it still costs a fortune in lease payments, insurance and parking charges. The idea that worked came from Ed's team. Why not give up a bit of productivity on the entire fleet to juggle the schedule and get rid of the very expensive overnight stops in cities such as Copenhagen, Munich and Milan? Between hotel costs and inefficient use of the crews, the revenue needed to make these flights break even was just too high. Ed and his team had questioned these night stops early on. Steven and I stuck with them because they were important for attracting business travellers out of the local markets in Europe. But it wasn't happening fast enough to justify the expense. We juggled around the timing of the required annual checks thanks to a bit of flexibility from FLS and changed the schedule to move away from night stops. We had found a more profitable (actually less loss-making!) way of using the thirteenth plane.

Our recommendations to the Go board were the result of real teamwork. Launching Prague and the ski routes combined with eliminating the night stops and juggling the annual checks engineering programme were going to help us limp through the winter. But where did that leave our overall financial position for the year? Even with all these changes, instead of losing £12.5 million we changed our budget for the year ending March 2000 to a pre-tax loss of £21.4 million. I can't even fathom the size of the losses if we had done nothing. But the near doubling of our losses against what we had planned was a blow to our neat progression towards break-even in the third year. We hoped we could improve upon the £21.4 million loss, but it was realistic. The board agreed and we set about implementing this plan of action.

During the autumn and winter of 1999, the challenges of running a much larger company filled our days. We had been busy recruiting cabin crew, especially in Italy and Spain. Some took a little time to warm to our way of working, but I think Donatella Zaniboni, now studying law in Italy and from Castel Maggiore, outside Bologna, summed it up nicely.

'I was a Go cabin crew member from November 1999 until November 2002 . . . and it was fantastic. It wasn't easy to adapt to this kind of life, especially because I didn't have any friends in England when I first moved across. At the beginning, during the training course, I had the impression everyone was trying to brainwash me. I know it's a strong expression but I couldn't understand why the company was spending so much effort talking about our common values. I thought it was an American way and would never do with Europeans. I was wrong. During the years I worked with Go I changed my mind; you simply won me over.'

What Donatella went on to say is something that we set out to achieve from day one. She continued: 'I started to see why you choose to employ a certain type of person . . . it wasn't just a way to make us more productive. Most days going to work was fun, and if a company is a happy place, then people work better together.'

Once or twice the English language went awry with our new

European colleagues, and I was told of one Go flight announcement where the passengers were told: 'Smoking in the toilets could lead to prostitution.' Thoughts of my clubbing lunch companion interested in the Mile High Club flashed before me.

At that same time, the operation was going very smoothly, unbelievably smoothly given how fast we had grown. On 26 November 1999 we registered punctuality of 100 per cent. For an eighteen-month-old airline with thirteen aircraft, this was a special achievement, and the celebrations followed. I wrote to Nick Chapple, Simon Henchie, Jeremy Holder, Kelly Muscutt, Kate Foard and Sarah Owen. They had worked that day and wrestled with the challenges of getting the planes in the right places, crew to the planes, and the vagaries of air traffic control. In fact, some months earlier I'd thanked Kelly, Gordon Poulter and Mark Soanes for the first-ever 100 per cent day with a trip on Concorde (thanks to a little help from Bob Ayling). We were shaping up to have the most punctual low-cost airline. Although another trip on Concorde was not possible, I did thank them for all their hard work and ended with 'We're on a roll!'. Just what we needed to become Europe's best low-cost airline.

When I sent my regular briefing note around the company that autumn, I was up-front about our situation and announced our first year's losses. I reminded the Go team: 'The plan for our first year was simple: get the airline started; become well-known and well thought-of; grow extremely quickly; take an ever-increasing number of bookings; keep the cost low, have happy customers; and be punctual to please customers and prove we can use our planes productively.'

It was an incredible wish list, and we achieved a great deal against these benchmarks. On all fronts, I was staggered by the continuing good will and hard work of the whole team. But our competitors were making fun of our losses, which were £22.4 million before tax. Setting the record straight, I pointed out: 'We have grown faster than any of our competitors did when they started. The faster you grow at the beginning, the greater the initial losses that you make.'

easyJet were even running a competition on their web-site to 'Guess Go's Losses'. It was humiliating, and I was tempted to enter the contest, because we could have used the fifty tickets to take Go colleagues to Nice for a lovely lunch. But it just wasn't our style to enter when we knew the answer.

While our competitors were eager to humiliate us, the true effect was to bond everyone together at Go. We found this out in our first People Survey, which Greg Miall pulled together. We borrowed liberally from the employee survey created by sound system retailers Richer Sounds, created by entrepreneur Julian Richer, and sent them a pile of seats on Go with our thanks. We loved the way Julian Richer had incorporated the employees' views and career development into the structure of the business. And they were delighted to help. I was eager to hear what everyone thought of working at Go. It wasn't enough for me to sit in my goldfish bowl and think what a great company we had.

The results were gratifying. Sarah Spencer, heading up our human resources efforts, proudly told us that we must have had the happiest pilots in the history of commercial aviation. And 90 per cent or more of colleagues were proud to work at Go and enjoyed their jobs.

But there were also worrying trouble spots. Two years without a pay rise was beginning to cause concern. There was not the promise of shares or big bonuses, just the prospect of another year of hard work with no increase in pay. There were also cries for even more communications. My top team and I hit the road to tell everyone more about the company's fortunes.

While running this much larger company, we really wanted to keep the small-company feel. The People Survey hinted at this pride, and our customer satisfaction survey in 1999 told us that customers liked their Go experience a tiny bit less than last year (when every customer got the £100 introductory price). Eighty-three per cent of customers rated us good, very good or excellent. But their rating of Go's people was even higher at 85 per cent. The story that follows says it all.

When one of our flights landed in Italy during a baggage strike by the ground handlers, we were hit hard. Some carriers, such as Lufthansa, returned without unloading bags, and Monarch passengers were left for four hours waiting for their suitcases, bags and rucksacks.

Go's Operations Manager, Nick Chapple, says that in over twenty years working in airlines he had never experienced anything like the Go crews who got on with the job. 'We sent some loaders on the flight to offload baggage, but they were prevented from doing this by the strikers, so it was left to the flight crew of Rob English and Bo Robert to deal with the baggage. Bo pulled a baggage cart across the apron to the arrivals hall and Rob got a police car to tow the other one. Tracey Ellis, who normally worked in Customer Support at Stansted but who came along to help, went to the terminal to give the passengers as much information as possible.'

One of the passengers phoned to heap praise on the crew, saying she had never known anything like it in her life from an airline. The plane was late returning to the UK but everyone got their luggage off. And all those involved received a Go MAD award from their colleagues.

Fortunately, sales began to improve somewhat as the winter wore on. Go's internet bookings continued to increase in importance, with 25 per cent of sales coming on-line. Low fares and the trendy, speedy web-site were pushing sales up and lowering our cost of making every booking.

As we headed into January 2000 we launched a major discounted flights offer with *The Times* and *Sunday Times* to get the year off to a good start. The project was the work of Mireille

Briggs and Dominic Laurie. Mireille was the senior manager responsible for Marketing working for David. She grew up in Biarritz and then moved to Scotland to work for the whisky company United Distillers. She epitomises Go – European, stylish and professional. She's also a very nice person and terrific at marketing. Dominic, in his mid-twenties, came to Go with a degree in Modern Languages from Cambridge University and a classical FMCG (fast-moving consumer goods) pedigree – from United Biscuits. He used his wonderful speaking voice to tape the Go safety procedures to be played on board. It was oddly comforting to have Dominic's voice wafting out on a flight. The two of them had shepherded the deal through News International, which was aiming to sell a lot of newspapers off the back of the offer.

Carol Humphreys, Telephone Sales Operations Manager, confided to Dominic that there was a chance of breaking through the £1 million revenue barrier in one day for the first time since the start of Go. This was special to Carol, because she had been one of the original team who opened the sales centre in April 1998.

'This would be massive for the company,' said Dominic. 'At that time, our big losses were well publicised and we were under pressure both from the media and other low-cost airlines. But hitting the million was going to be touch and go.'

The deal with *The Times* gave Go a stack of exposure, and in return the newspaper's readers got the lowest prices in the market at the time. While the internet was now becoming an essential part of our operation, we were still taking half of all bookings over the phone. There had been teaser television adverts just after Christmas, so that once the phone lines opened there would be an avalanche of calls.

The day started with a bang, the phone lines hummed and the web-site soon jammed. Some callers had to wait half an hour to get through. By lunchtime, the team was rolling along halfway towards the million mark. But bookings slowed after 3 p.m. and so by 8 p.m. the total was £100,000 short.

'I'd been at work since 7 a.m. in time for the first call, but I stuck around wandering from pod to pod to give as much encouragement as I could. I even went on the lines myself, much to the amusement of the agents,' said Dominic. To cope with the extra volume, agents volunteered to work a ten- or twelve-hour shift, but working the phones all day is an exhausting job. Fred Kochak, Go's Head of Pricing, was also working late that night and came to help taking calls.

Fred remembers: 'When the call centre was supposed to close, we were only at £950k! We couldn't settle for that! The problem was that the phone system automatically stopped accepting new calls . . . so one of the team leaders called Carol Humphreys at home to get the password to reactivate the phone. Not only did Carol give the password, but she came into the office herself to help achieve the goal.'

When they overshot the £1 million mark, Dom sent David and I text messages at home and found some champagne hidden away from some marketing agency give-away. Fred remembers that 'amongst the smiles and cheers, we toasted Go's success at hitting another milestone'.

The same enthusiasm for Go was not evident at our owner, British Airways. They had announced their own dramatically worsening financial results in November 1999, and Bob Ayling was under attack for everything from the paint job on the tailfins through to the failed American Airlines joint venture. Our timing at Go couldn't have been worse. This was not a good year to spring Go's larger £21.4 million losses. I was hauled in to speak with a number of the British Airways non-executive directors. A conference call with Captain Colin Barnes and Baroness O'Cathain was followed by a starchy, formal lunch with Lord Renwick at his offices at Robert Fleming. I explained the changes we had made to the business and how the majority of the shortfall had been earlier in the year. I was optimistic and hoped to convince them. They gave nothing away and I left with no better idea of their views.

The heat was on for Bob Ayling in the winter. Even his health was being affected. He was ill for weeks over Christmas and he did not look well when he reappeared in the New Year after the disastrous opening of the Millennium Dome. The press and investment analysts were after him. It didn't bode well.

Chapter Fourteen

Go's Warrior Spirit

My mind was gently shifting into Christmas mode as I slipped on my coat to leave for the evening. Did I have all the Christmas presents I needed? And what about last-minute stocking fillers for Lauren and James? But I was shocked out of my mental list-making by an event that tested us and showed the true spirit of my colleagues at Go.

It was just after 6.30 p.m. on Wednesday 22 December 1999, and before heading to my car I walked over to Operations to say goodnight and check with Marcus Harvey, the Operations Duty Manager who was monitoring flights making sure everything was running to schedule. Most of our fleet was away from Stansted at some Italian or Spanish destination or up in freezing Scotland, so all appeared in order.

Then at 6.38 p.m. Cheryl Casey, one of the airports team, approached me looking grave.

'Something's happened,' she said.

'What is it?' I asked.

Then a pilot reported for duty. He was deathly pale and shaking.

'I think a petrol station at the top of the M11 has just been blown up,' he said.

'Whaaat?' we exclaimed.

In our Enterprise House offices, there were several moments of subdued confusion. Then, piece by piece, the picture began to emerge.

'A plane's gone down,' someone shouted.

As several people rushed to the window to look for some fiery sign in the dark evening sky, our eyes flicked over to the operations room computer screens.

'Where are all our planes?' I asked, seeking reassurance. 'Has anything just taken off?' There was a pause for a few unbearable moments.

'It wasn't one of ours,' said Marcus.

Cheryl dialled the Stansted Airport emergency control room.

'Can you tell us what's going on, please?' she asked.

'There's been an incident and we will give you further information when it is available,' was the officious response.

We blinked again at the airport movements screens, and still everything was normal.

This was puzzling. The screen shows each scheduled aircraft at Stansted, and the Go Operations Team tried to figure out what was happening. There were no scheduled departures or arrivals fitting the time of the crash. It wasn't one of ours, but the plane's identity was baffling. I was concerned that it might be a Ryanair plane full of Christmas travellers, since they had such a big operation at the airport.

As phone calls started buzzing around the airport, it soon became clear it was a cargo plane, and these flights do not appear on our screens.

Tragically, a Korean Air freight plane, UAL 8509, had crashed into a field on the edge of Hatfield Forest, at Great Hallingbury, two minutes after taking off from Stansted. The downing of a Boeing 747, the largest passenger plane in operation today and one of the largest cargo planes, is global news.

Five minutes later, Cheryl took a call from the control room.

'The runway will be closed,' she was told curtly.

Cheryl dashed off to the terminal building to attend the emergency BAA updates, which went on every thirty minutes throughout that night.

Our biggest question was how long would the runway be shut? Originally it was going to be reopened at around midnight, once the inspectors had done a fingertip search of the runway to look for clues to the cause of the disaster and make sure the runway was safe.

The crash and the two ensuing fireballs killed all four Korean crew members and had a devastating effect on the local community because the crash was so close to a village and people's homes. The UK's Air Accident Investigations Branch of the Department of Transport, responsible for investigating all serious accidents, published its findings in July 2003. The report findings concluded that an Altitude Director Indicator in the cockpit was not functioning properly and that the pilot was confused about the take-off direction. The explosion was exacerbated because the plane was carring 2.39kg of military explosives.

The loss of life of the four flight crew was sobering to anyone in the same business, but the next two days proved to be a test that showed Go's true colours. There were only two days left before Christmas and all airports were jam-packed with people eager to travel home to family or head off for a festive break. Thousands of passengers had to be diverted, at Stansted over eighty flights were cancelled – but only ten were Go's. And none of our customers was stranded – we put every one of them on another Go flight. We did our level best to keep flying.

Mike Coltman, Go's General Manager, Operations, had just

arrived home and had switched on BBC News 24 in the background as he settled in for the evening.

'We've just heard that an unidentified aircraft heading for Milan has crashed at Stansted Airport,' the newscaster announced.

An eyewitness, David Murtagh, flashed up on the screen, saying: 'I saw the aircraft, it was on fire. I saw it in flames and it was so close I ducked. I thought: "Oh, My God, it's going to hit me".'

Mike's stomach fluttered with nervousness. He knew Go was the only airline flying from Stansted to Milan, so his logical assumption was that a Go flight had crashed. He grabbed his mobile and dialled Andy Holmes, Go's Head of Operations.

'Mike, it isn't one of our planes, but we're still unsure what has happened,' said Andy.

Rob Platts was driving home from work. He was Go's Financial Planning Manager and was just rounding the curve of the road that runs past the end of Stansted's runway.

'I was driving away from the airport with my wife Rebecca when I saw a huge fireball. At first, I thought it was a crash on the M11, perhaps a fuel tanker or similar, but then paper debris began falling around the car. It was most eerie,' he later recalled. 'I saw the airport fire services mobilising at the south end of the airport and I knew it was serious.'

Oli Wigdahl, Go's Head of Sales, was working at home with the radio on. The sketchy news bulletin reported: 'A plane has come down just before 7 p.m. near to Stansted.' He shivered. His wife, Katy, was due to land at 7.10 p.m. on a Ryanair flight from Dublin. It took nearly two hours before Oli was assured that Katy's plane had been diverted to Luton.

Chris Akinbile was working as a telesales agent. He heard a dull thud outside as he sat in the call centre next to fellow agent Becky Hunter. She had just finished a booking and was removing her headset.

'Did you feel that?' Chris asked Becky.

She looked puzzled: "I'm sorry, what?"

'That thud. Like a plane landing really hard.'

Chris had worked in the cargo section at Gatwick Airport for fifteen months and knew what it felt like when a plane landed heavily. Now he was surprised to feel a familiar vibration when he was much further away from the runway.

Moments later, Anna Marie Burke, the Telephone Sales Duty Manager, rushed into the call centre.

'A Korean cargo plane has crashed just after take-off.'

There was a collective intake of breath.

'Oh, my God,' said one of her telesales colleagues as the hubbub increased.

Anna calmed everyone. 'They're closing the runway, so be prepared for a lot of calls from passengers asking for information.' Then she turned to Chris. 'Here are my car keys. Can you nip down and get my crisis management folder out of my car? It's under the front passenger seat.'

He hurried off to find Anna's car and retrieved the folder. As he returned, he passed Ed Winter, who had been on his way home and was now heading straight back to the office. Back at the call centre, Chris passed on the file and ploughed back into answering the calls that were now bombarding the switchboard.

Ed wasn't the only one returning. Derek Patterson, Go's Financial Controller, who worked alongside Lynne Hodgkinson, and John Mahon, the Chief Pilot, had stopped for a quick drink. Paul Stainsby, our Cargo Manager, was outside Enterprise House when he literally felt the earth move. Tariq Hafiz, a Go First Officer, had just landed at Stansted and the aircraft had turned off the runway to head to its gate. The Korean jet roared by and Tariq watched as it crashed to the ground. They all rushed in to play their part in our longest night at Stansted.

Andrew Morris, Senior Cabin Crew, was at home on a day

off work. He saw the news on television and got up, put his uniform on and came into the office. 'I immediately went to the terminal,' he recalled, 'and began the very long night of putting passengers on coaches, helping people find friends and relatives, and answering all the usual questions.'

Mark Rouessart, a flight operations manager, was also enjoying a day off when a friend, working as a refueller, phoned to tell him the shocking news. He immediately dialled Andy Holmes to offer his services. When he arrived, Andy and Ed were discussing their contingency plans. Marcus Harvey, finishing off a day shift, volunteered to stay on, but it was agreed he should go home. We would need fresh people for the commotion to come.

People from all parts of our small airline came to our assistance – from marketing, finance, telesales, operations, cabin crew and pilots. In the atrium of Enterprise House, the television companies set up a temporary base with reporters and camera teams interviewing officials. The police were on hand for their press conferences and media updates. It was a hive of activity.

There was so much to do but so little information. All we knew in those first few hours was that the runway was closed. Go planes began to approach Stansted to land. Where should they be sent? Equally, passengers were checking in for flights later that evening. Should we cancel the flights for the rest of the evening? How long would the runway be closed? Could we pull out a miracle and keep the airline flying?

The most immediate problem was to figure out where to land those aircraft approaching Stansted and how to get those passengers off the planes and out of the airport. The next issue would be how to get the next flight's passengers to those relatively few planes needed for the final flights of the evening.

A stroke of luck and a dash of extreme good timing helped us greatly. Ed and his team had already prepared a business continuity plan in the event of serious disruptions. With only a single runway at Stansted, Andy Holmes and Go's Security Manager, Peter Griffiths, had started discussions in July 1999 about what to do if the runway was closed. Another runway was planned at Stansted, but that was years away. We needed a more immediate solution.

I had met the charming Michael Marshall years earlier on a flight to America, and we talked about our shared interest in airlines. He had invited me up to look at his family-owned airport at Cambridge, which has excellent facilities and is used by both Boeing and Airbus when bringing new planes into the country for delivery. It was also the home of Suckling Airlines, later ScotAirways. I liked the intimate atmosphere and the can-do attitude at Cambridge.

So, in the autumn of 1999, Andy and Peter visited Cambridge to discuss using the airfield as a back-up should Stansted close. The airport was delighted to help but, being such a small facility, it would not be able to cope with the volume of passengers. Andy and Peter then devised a neat solution for passengers to be checked in at Stansted terminal, cleared through security and then boarded on a coach to Cambridge. Instead of hopping on the plane at Stansted, they would do so at Cambridge.

This was fine in theory, but it needed approval from the relevant authorities. Peter recalls he was just heading off on a short pre-Christmas break when the final word came through that Cambridge had the go-ahead. Peter zapped a note to Andy on 15 December 1999. Not a moment too soon. Within a week the Cambridge plan had become a necessity.

Cath Lynn, at the time still running Cabin Crew, mobilised everyone she could find to run an operation through the Stansted terminal, to the departure gates, on to coaches, out to the motorway and on to Luton on that evening. The next day, the coaches would be heading north to Cambridge Airport, about twenty miles away. She had many volunteers and helpers. And of course the entire Go Airports team was incredible.

Well, that was the plan, but the reality was far more confused, because while *most* of the planes headed to Cambridge, a number were diverted to Luton throughout the next thirty-six hours – which added to the general confusion.

That evening, passengers arrived for their flights at Stansted and were whisked away on a coach to Luton. It was worse for those waiting to collect relations and friends, because we didn't know the precise timings of departures and arrivals. It was a moving target.

Go employees were buzzing around everywhere. Some of our people were also dispatched to Luton Airport. A few Go flights were diverted there in the immediate minutes after the crash, but so were most other services, and Luton simply couldn't cope. We were lucky to have many of our aircraft safely heading into Cambridge ready for the next day's flying.

The Go check-in supervisors at Stansted headed over to Luton with about three planeloads of passengers and baggage. Go's coaches arrived at Luton first, followed by Ryanair's. Soon it was a noisy mêlée. The airport authorities opened up the departure security and made an announcement that all passengers could proceed through the departures area without checking in. The stampede that followed gridlocked the security checkpoint. It was completely chaotic.

At the end of that evening, we had eight aircraft at Cambridge. The airport is so small that the 737s were actually interlocking wing-to-wing. Go Operations had to know who was at the head of the queue or nothing would have moved!

Cheryl recalls: 'I think it was around 11 p.m. that what they thought were aircraft remains were found on the tarmac at Stansted and it was announced that the runway would have to stay closed until morning so that a full inspection could be done in daylight.'

The call centre was swamped by passengers wanting information that was simply not available. The same question was replayed over and over again. 'Do you know if my flight for tomorrow is going to be cancelled? When will the airport reopen?'

That evening, the call centre fielded a record number of calls. There was only a skeleton team, so it was difficult to cope with the onslaught, but they managed. And we told everyone there were delays, but that we were still flying.

In Operations, Gordon Poulter came on as Duty Manager for a night shift that would be busy and eventful. Mark Rouessart had agreed to stay and help for a few hours. He recalled: 'With Go's fleet now heading for Cambridge, we needed someone to build flight plans to figure out how to fly all of the scheduled flights tomorrow. Gordon set to work putting these together from scratch. I then took over the job of swapping aircraft and crews around, trying to prevent further delays. All was going swimmingly well until about 11.15 p.m., when I got a call from one of our crews heading towards Cambridge. He had just been notified by Air Traffic Control that Cambridge was about to close.'

Mark called the Cambridge control tower and spoke to the watch manager. It was true. They had to close, as they had no night shift and the controllers on duty had worked as long as the regulations would allow them.

Now Stansted and Cambridge were both closed and there were still three aircraft expecting to land. 'I rang Servisair at Luton to ask if they could handle our diversions,' Mark recalls. 'They only had minimal night-shift coverage, but said they would do everything they could. During the night they turned round the flights.'

One of the biggest problems continued to be too few people for loading and unloading baggage. It was nearing midnight and the Edinburgh flight at Luton was already delayed by six hours, but a Ryanair flight had to be dispatched first, so some Go people actually dispatched a Ryanair flight for them, including loading some bags and assisting the handling agent. The Irish airline, which appeared to have few people on duty, was experiencing a near revolt from its passengers, and police had to be called in to calm down frayed nerves.

Tiredness was setting in and clipboards were seen flying across the office in frustration. Mark finally got away at 8.30 a.m. having arrived more than twelve hours earlier. Not his most restful day off!

The call centre was also extraordinary. When the clock struck 11 p.m., the usual closing time for calls, no one was asked to stay on, but they all did. Right through until 3 a.m.

Cheryl recalls that the last Go flight to Edinburgh left from Luton about 7 a.m. the next day. 'We all headed back to Stansted and handed over to our colleagues. A nice twenty-two-hour shift to be back at work less than eight hours later! I remember it being my first Christmas Day that I slept in until 10 a.m.!'

As we moved into the next day, 23 December, the airport remained closed, and it was becoming more and more difficult to find crew with enough rest to meet the legal requirements. The delays were so large that crews were literally running out of hours available in which they could legally fly. Meanwhile the terminals were in chaos, and Go Operations were struggling to keep the airline flying.

When the runway at Stansted finally reopened in the early afternoon of 23 December, the chaos continued. With most airlines cancelling flights, the terminal was still overflowing with anxious travellers. It was all hands on deck again if we were to keep the airline moving for the rest of the day.

We tried to address the problem of providing information by asking office people and crew to stand on the platforms at Liverpool Street, Tottenham Hale, Stansted and Cambridge railway stations to help passengers understand the plan. But the Cambridge plan did allow us to take much more control than any other airline. The most critical part was the army of volunteers and our capable operations and ground handling colleagues who had us flying again long before others.

Frank Bishop, one of our senior pilots, was in charge of the coaches going back and forth to Cambridge. He'd make a fine operations director for London Transport! He called coach companies, agreed commercial arrangements, directed coaches to where they needed to be.

While other airlines cancelled flights and left passengers to fend for themselves, we were determined to get every one of our passengers home. This happened not because of orders from me and Ed. Everyone leapt into action because helping out was now second nature.

Catherine Lynn recalls some tough on-the-spot decisions. One of these included whether to leave bags behind. This was pre-Christmas and many travellers were laden with parcels. At Cambridge, the runway is shorter than at other airports and so weight restrictions were placed on flights. Rather than ask a few passengers to leave the plane and remove their luggage, we decided that it was more important for people to get home for Christmas. Perhaps some bags and presents arrived a few days late, but at least our passengers were home for the holidays.

At Cambridge, the correct coachfuls of passengers were delivered to the steps of their aircraft while their baggage was loaded on. As planes arrived at Cambridge, the process was reversed with passengers moving down to Stansted. The trip took about forty-five minutes.

Shifting people by bus to Cambridge was going well, but we had to ensure that everyone got to the right gate and on the right bus. This turned into a Herculean effort. It worsened because Stansted's flight information display system packed in. The digital boards just went blank.

At this point, Derek Patterson and Oli Wigdahl had a brain-wave. They scoured the terminal for a white board so that information could be given to our passengers. 'Frustrations were running high among delayed passengers because they had poor information,' Derek remembers. They sequestered a white board from the BAA, and with a handful of the Go training department's non-permanent marker pens, they were off.

Oli remembers: 'At one point we must have had twenty flights on the board with a status for each and an estimated time of departure based on a call to Go's Operations Team. This went well, and we were praised by passengers for walking around shouting out departing flights that were absent from the screens.'

Andy Knight, who normally worked on developing Go's in-flight sales, was in the terminal. He felt the white boards worked well, 'especially when combined with megaphones to holler at passengers to "follow me for flight 401 to Copenhagen!"'. Passengers were amazingly thankful, and many commented that they would never fly with our Irish counterparts again!'

At check-in, many office people who seldom spoke to customers face-to-face explained the situation. Monika Rese, Jo Parsons, and Rose Giacomo from Go's Finance Department were typical – they handed out Quality Street chocolates with their information.

Rob Platts, Go's Financial Planning Manager, recalls that it might have been every accountant's worst nightmare being asked to go over to a terminal full of delayed people and try to inject some sense of order. But he found it oddly inspiring. He later remembered: 'This summed up the Go spirit. It wasn't something that was written down, a formula to follow. It was basically helping people because you wanted them to go away thinking what a good company Go was. You didn't need formal training to be nice to people. There were one or two situations where people were very angry, but on the whole they just wanted a bit of information.'

Late afternoon on that second day of the Korean crisis. Helen Flack, a Go Captain, said: 'I remember spending a few hours before our flight to Edinburgh in the terminal talking to the hundreds of stranded passengers . . . Ed Winter was there in his yellow Go jacket overseeing everything . . . I think he'd been there all day. When we finally got an aircraft we filled it with passengers. At last, we were all ready to go but for the bags when a voice came on the ground intercom saying that the bags were being put on . . . it was the Chief Pilot John Mahon loading bags in the hold . . .The team spirit demonstrated by everyone at Go was amazing.'

Like many others, Chris Akinbile arrived back at the call centre to start his afternoon shift the day after the plane crashed. He was asked to go over to the terminal and help out with crowd control at the check-in desks. 'My job, along with a few other rather large-looking guys from the call centre, was to create a space where Go passengers could check in. I also had to find out what people were flying with us and advise them of the flight times,' he said.

Chris was amazed. He would ask people if they were flying with Go and the regular response was a genuine: 'No, but I wish I was.'

Some time later, I remember seeing a dishevelled and unshaven Chris at one of our check-in desks.

'Chris, you look shattered,' I said. 'Go and take a break.'

He looked at me and replied: 'I'll take a break when you take a break.'

'OK, Chris, I will be going back to the office in a few minutes.'

Those few minutes turned into another two hours, and that's when the terminal began to clear.

Go had a few expressions that we used to describe how we

worked together, and Warrior Spirit was one of them. It signi-
fied being persistent and tenacious, and most of all, doing the
right thing. Faced with that Stansted emergency, Go's 'Warrior
Spirit' came shining through. We didn't use a crisis as an excuse
to give passengers poor service. On those two days, with a generosity of spirit that I had never before experienced in my
career, Go's people achieved the impossible.

Christmas Day 1999 was a Saturday, and it saved us after the
events of the week. We had made a decision much earlier in the
year not to fly on Christmas Day, which luckily gave us the time
to regroup and get aircraft and crews in the right places. That
day's rest put us back on track as we braced ourselves for the
next week's potential crisis – the Millennium Bug. After the
events of the week before Christmas, we were pleased it was a
peaceful non-event, as Go's systems didn't miss a beat and kept
the airline moving into the next millennium.

Chapter Fifteen

Did British Airways Sell the Right Airline?

After shaking off his persistent cold, Bob Ayling was a picture of health. Lightly tanned and looking rejuvenated after a family holiday in South Africa, he chaired our monthly board meeting on Tuesday 7 March 2000 at Enterprise House. It had gone off without a hitch. Bob steered the meeting with his customary aplomb and we finished right on schedule. A textbook model of how a board meeting should be handled.

Everyone was shuffling from the room, chatting in groups, folders and notes tucked under their arms and heading off to their next assignments, when Bob gently tugged my arm.

'Barbara, can I have a private word?' he said.

'Of course,' I replied with a quizzical look.

Bob stepped back into my goldfish-bowl office and I closed the door.

'I wanted to tell you this before you heard it from anywhere else. I've just been sacked. The British Airways board has asked for my resignation and it will be announced on Friday.'

I was astounded. For once, lost for words. Bob had just ploughed through a two-hour board meeting with all of us. He was warm, witty and attentive; now he was telling me he had been asked to step down from his position as head of one of the UK's biggest and best-known companies? It was a tour de force of character.

He then warned me about what might happen to our low-cost operation. 'It's going to be much more difficult for you and the Go team now, Barbara. The wolves will be circling. I feel uneasy about your future,' he said gloomily.

But he handed me a heartening crumb of comfort. After our months of losses and hard work, he felt after his last meeting as our chairman we were now turning a corner.

At this time, we were still some distance from making a profit, but I was grateful that Bob believed that we were winning the battle. He had been fighting a monthly action to defend Go's performance to the main British Airways board. On a personal level, continual press attention made me uncomfortable. At this time *Management Today*'s survey of Powerful Women placed me at Number 11, behind fellow Americans DeAnne Julius, who was on the Bank of England's Monetary Policy Committee and ranked fourth, and Marjorie Scardino, of Pearson, owners of the *Financial Times* and Penguin Books, at Number 1. I wished I could stay off these sorts of lists until Go became financially sound. The publicity pedestal was pushing me higher and higher, and I was concerned that there was a long way to fall. As Bob was now to discover.

We all knew that the clamour for Bob's head had been increasing in recent weeks – there was even a rumour that executive headhunters had been approached to replace him in his £500,000 a year job – but we didn't believe he'd be forced to leave. Yet he was. I heard that some people inside the airline were cheering. That saddened me but made me realise that his position had become untenable.

I reconvened the Go team later that afternoon and told them the grim news. David and Ed shook their heads in awe at Bob's outstanding professionalism. But we all agreed, the wolves were baying for blood.

After he sped off from Enterprise House, Bob still had more to endure before the announcement would be made public. He was to attend an official opening of his farewell achievement, the landmark British Airways London Eye. That whole week was a nightmare for him, but Thursday was surreal.

As the invited throng filed into the glass capsules of this fantastic 350-ft high landmark which was already captivating London, Bob stood next to Lord Marshall, the British Airways chairman, and Lord King, the airline's president emeritus. To an outsider, it looked like a united front, but the chit-chat was strained. Only a few guests realised their host had just been sacked.

Bob's public execution had been delayed until after the opening. The London Eye had been controversial too. The cost of building such a revolutionary structure had come in at £35 million, massively over budget. But from day one everyone loved it and since then it has become London's most popular paid-for attraction, with more than 4 million visitors a year.

For British Airways' non-executive directors, it must have been the final nail in the coffin. Since May 1997, £4.2 billion has been wiped off British Airways' stock market value as a result of a fall in its shares from a 760p peak to around 299p when Bob left. Yet they seemed to forget that he had also been chief executive in a period of record profits.

By March 2000, British Airways was openly being discussed as a possible takeover target, and the reports in the newspapers had the board's non-executive conspirators telephoning Sir Michael Angus, the deputy chairman and chairman of the nomination committee, to say Bob had to go. Lord Marshall then told Bob after he returned from his South African trip.

With the benefit of hindsight, Bob Ayling had started on a

sensible strategy for Britain's national flag-carrier. A review of future trends in the summer of 1996 had concluded that without radical steps to lower costs and improve shorthaul, British Airways would become heavily loss-making within five years. So under Bob's guidance, a number of cost-cutting measures were put in place. He was hacking costs and staff numbers, reducing the transatlantic fleet and putting the more efficient Boeing 777 on the routes instead of the ageing 747. He was trimming the short-haul routes from Heathrow, using the Airbus A320, and moving towards a more frequent service of capital city to capital city which still had a market for business people and politicians. And he was fully up to speed with the massive low-cost market and realised that Go could be a central player in all that. Hiving off Go might have been one of his future options, but only with Go management support and to raise expansion capital. He could never understand the constant sniping that Go was cannibalising British Airways' routes; his view was that the low-cost revolution was an unstoppable force and British Airways needed to be fighting in that market.

However, Bob's lawyerly style and manner, some said his arrogance, caused resentment and a backlash when he set about implementing these policies. Eventually he took on too many adversaries, including the unions, and he didn't manage to round up enough allies.

As part of the review that had been authorised by the board, in 1996 Bob announced his £1 billion cost-cutting exercise, involving significant job losses. British Airways' pilots threatened to ground the fleet, and an offer of an increase in basic pensionable pay was made in return for more flexible working rules. Only 330 cabin crew went on official strike over the proposals, but around 2000 took time off 'sick'. The disruption was huge and cost British Airways £125m. Bob sent a letter written in his lawyerly manner threatening to either sue or sack those on strike, and it backfired badly.

The strikes were hugely damaging to British Airways, and Bob was held responsible. His friend Lord Marshall was reported to have told a well-known City editor that the disputes were 'avoidable'.

Then Bob's proposals for an alliance with American Airlines fell flat too. Don Carty, American's chairman, hailed the alliance with more flights to more destinations. But when Karel van Miert, the then European competition commissioner, said British Airways would have to relinquish 267 take-off and landing slots at Heathrow, the game was over. Instead, British Airways and American took the leading roles in a watered-down Oneworld grouping that also includes Aer Lingus, Cathay Pacific, Finnair, Iberia and Qantas.

So now, Bob, our airline's chief supporter, was on his way out. He should have been applauded for setting up Go. It was a genuine innovation inside a company that was short on out-of-the-box thinking. A lot later, I smiled when Bob said he wasn't really a chief executive but simply a lawyer. Perhaps he was a better chairman than chief executive. Bob remained a staunch believer in the low-cost airline model and he thought we were a breath of fresh air.

But one outstanding matter required a resolution. It had developed into a running sore throughout the history of Go, and it was of deep personal concern to me and to the founding directors. When Charles Gurassa made the original job offer to write the business plan back in March 1997, I was told that I would have a stake in the value created in the new business. This was the Long Term Incentive Plan, LTIP, designed to give management a cash incentive to build a successful business and to attract someone like me – who was ready to leave – by offering a slice of the action. At the time, thoughts of making millions were too far away to be relevant – it was a matter of a promise and honour.

I had taken a personal risk and a substantial drop in my basic pay to come back from New York. I had been on a cushy expatriate package and made around £175,000 a year, while my pay when I started on Project Hyacinth was £85,000. I would have been nuts to take on the role without a share in the upside.

Simon Harford, who was not a beneficiary of the LTIP scheme, acted as go-between and tried valiantly to agree the criteria and the potential payout sums that summer. Early drafts didn't make sense because the targets were almost impossible, based on hitting a cash flow and a valuation target. The maximum I could have earned was about £1m in three years. The other founders were each to get 50 per cent of whatever I got. I reckoned that the targets were being set to ensure we couldn't get more than half the money.

We continued chatting about it until July 1998, but when we leased the extra six planes from GECAS, I knew the early business projections were now totally incorrect, and I asked for another calculation to reflect the growing size of the airline. That new proposal never came. I verbally asked Bob Ayling about it throughout 1999 and, in frustration, I wrote to him in October 1999 offering my own proposal. Personally, I had always wanted a proper share in the equity, not some calculated bonus, so I suggested that they granted us shadow equity. Guy was instrumental in writing the proposal I sent to British Airways. He literally dictated it to me as I sat at our home computer!

Then a catalogue of fun began. Bob lost the first note I gave him at the October board meeting, then I sent it to him again in November. He agreed after much internal discussion with British Airways' Human Resources Director, Mervyn Walker, in the winter of 2000. I knew something was wrong when Bob called me one Sunday when I was at the cinema with my two children watching *Shrek*. He said he really wanted to push the LTIP proposal along. I was worried because Bob never called me.

So I hired Julian Roskill, a top City employment law solicitor at Mayer, Brown, Row & Mawe, in February, and he began discussions with British Airways' human resources department. But when Bob was fired in early March, I still had nothing in writing except the promise of a stake in my job appointment letter.

The newspapers began their speculation about who would take over, and the *Evening Standard*, among others, even suggested I was a possible contender. Bless them. I was vaguely flattered but not remotely interested. I had an amusing meeting with Lord Marshall in April 2000 when he told me gravely I was not being considered for Bob's job. What a hoot that was. I gravely thanked him for taking the time to let me know.

Then on Tuesday 25 April 2000, British Airways announced the appointment of Rod Eddington as its new chief executive. There was an immediate flurry of interest in such a high-profile position, because he was an Australian airline boss. His formidable intellect was much heralded. He attended the University of Western Australia and was a Rhodes scholar at Oxford University. He had been at Cathay Pacific, the Hong Kong-based global airline, when it won a pile of awards as a long-haul international airline, before joining Ansett in Australia, which went bust the year after he left. He arrived in May, and within days I had received a call inviting me to meet him along with Simon and Roger Maynard, Go's new chairman.

He was very polite, but it was clear from that first meeting that he didn't believe a traditional airline should own a low-cost airline. Simon and I tried to put the case forward fairly forcefully, thinking that perhaps Rod had not heard our side before. But his decision was made.

In the car park after the meeting, Simon and I sat shaking with anger and disbelief that British Airways was willing to sell the only part of the airline going up in value and at the worst possible time in Go's history – just as we announced its second £20m loss. I felt like banging my head on the dashboard. The only positive step was that Rod Eddington agreed he would sort out the LTIP fiasco for me and the founders. Yet there were still months of wrangling, foot-dragging and threats to come.

Back in my office, I took another look at the financial figures sitting in my desk drawer. How come my new boss wasn't interested in hearing about this? We had grown from nothing to 14 aircraft in only 23 months and now had over 600 Go people working as a team. Our turnover was £100 million a year and growing and we were improving the hit rate on the routes we were now choosing. Our planes were 70 per cent full compared with 60 per cent a few months earlier and the Go brand and reputation were very strong. Steven had rewritten the pricing structure to make it easier to get low fares, and it was working. David Magliano had come up trumps again when we chopped the marketing spend per customer by changing our advertising mix and pushing more towards our internet site, which delivered 40 per cent of bookings, and the figures were rising substantially. The economies of scale meant that our costs were coming down, although I could see that Ed and the operations team were working flat out to keep this growth under control. Everyone understood what we were aiming for – break-even by March 2001. I didn't need to exhort people every day to look for lower costs; it was as natural as breathing for us. In fact, it was just the kind of culture that British Airways desperately needed, but they were about to jettison all that. It was Bob and British Airways who had the foresight to stump up the £25 million start-up costs for the hardest part – now as we headed for break-even they were going to lose out on its increasing value.

A few weeks later, the hands-free mobile rang in my Volvo on the way up the M11 and I clicked off the talking book to answer.

'Barbara, it's Simon here. There's an important development you should know. Rod's been talking to Stelios about selling Go!'

It took a second to compute.

'Run that past me again. Rod and Stelios are in talks? You must be joking!'

'It's true, Rod has had a meeting with him and they're in preliminary talks to sell off Go.'

I felt a cold shiver run down my spine.

Rod had made it crystal-clear to me that a low-cost operation was not a fit for him. His argument was that no other global carrier successfully ran a low-cost outfit, so he didn't see how it would work for British Airways. Inside BA, Go's increasing success and profile was becoming a huge cultural distraction, taking on elephantine proportions. It was one thing to want to hive Go off from the British Airways family, but combining Go and easyJet to create a much stronger competitor seemed madness.

Even our new-found success in sweeping into Malaga, Alicante and Ibiza was causing a minor diplomatic incident, as Roger Maynard represented British Airways' minority shareholding on the board of the Spanish national carrier, Iberia, and was being regularly harangued by Xavier de Irala, Iberia's chief executive. We had the audacity to undermine the traditional pricing oligopoly that was fleecing customers all over Europe. Irala couldn't understand why Roger didn't just order Go to back off the Spanish routes. It wasn't too pleasant for Roger, as he had now become Go's chairman.

Yet the revelation was a slap in the face to all of us who had been working so hard to create the new airline. This was one of those startling moments; I had missed a fundamental point. We had all been mistaken in believing that Go was 'our' company. Yes, we had created it, but it was owned by British Airways, and they saw it as an asset to dispose of. We had passion for our business, but not the control.

And so began a game of ownership that lasted two years. It was a game I was forced to play. But one point was very clear to me. We needed to continue to manage the business with the utmost integrity. Doing the right thing for the business was paramount. Throughout the ensuing ownership battles for Go I was clear about my personal position. If I did not retain freedom to run Go the way I wanted, with a significant stake in the business, I would have to leave. No longer was I the good corporate soldier who moved jobs at the bidding of head office.

The press began speculating about Go's future and the questioning hotted up. At a Birmingham business breakfast at the International Conference Centre in July, I was asked if I was considering a management buyout. I remember choosing my words carefully in case they were misinterpreted back at British Airways. I had already been rebuked earlier for suggesting I wanted to go it alone.

'Go has always been structured for a trade sale or a demerger, it was part of our original business plan,' I said in the Midlands.

But in my view, British Airways were not keeping up their side of this bargain. We still hadn't sorted my Long Term Incentive Plan, despite Rod's assurances. Everyone tried to assure me there was no problem, but it was stuck in the sand. Then, for some strange reason, an LTIP proposal was approved by British Airways' Remuneration Committee and then the full board, yet I hadn't seen what they agreed to.

In pure frustration, I went to see British Airways Chairman Colin Marshall. I had always got on well with him, but I didn't hold back in this session when I related the whole long-running saga.

'Please, sort it out for me; otherwise I will be forced to leave Go,' I said to him.

'I don't think you should threaten us, Barbara,' he replied.

'It's not a threat but a promise,' I said bluntly and shook with anger as I left.

It got worse before it got better. When I knew Rod was in talks with Stelios, I fired off a blistering note saying I considered

British Airways to be in breach of contract. Rod replied that there was no contractual problem and he was still working on the LTIP. Then I was asked to meet easyJet's management team as part of the sale process, but I put my foot down and refused until my personal situation was clarified and resolved.

Why was I so bolshy? I was afraid that British Airways would sell the company and we would be left high and dry. I would have taken it to court on principle. And I think they knew that. I don't believe it was maliciousness on the side of British Airways, but there had been too many words of platitude and not enough delivering on promises.

It was difficult being the favoured child of one chief executive and a pariah to the next. Rod wasted three months negotiating to sell Go to easyJet only to have the offer turned down by the British Airways board in August 2000 because it was in untraded shares in easyJet. The British Airways board wanted cash, and until floating on the Stock Exchange easyJet couldn't easily raise the cash. easyJet, frustrated from its quest to grow through acquisition, headed straight into a successful flotation on the London stock market in November 2000 that afterwards valued the airline at £800 million. They raised £220 million of new money to support the growth of their business. The shares that British Airways would have received for selling Go would have been worth around £200 million on paper at the peak of the easyJet share price.

British Airways was also in merger negotiations with the Dutch airline KLM. It had set up Buzz as a low-cost rival to us and we were certainly a bargaining chip to combat possible regulatory issues that might halt the merger of British Airways and KLM.

'You must be nuts. Selling us to easyJet will simply boost the competition. And if you must sell us, you'd make more money if you waited six months for us to break even,' I lectured a senior British Airways director.

The speculation was taking on a life of its own. The *Guardian* reported Rod Eddington as saying 'nothing had been ruled in or out' on our future, but said it all depended on the way the KLM talks continued. The *Sunday Times* business journalist David Parsley, who followed our story closely from day one (since he was married to a sales person at Go!), reported on 20 August that we were attracting potential buyers even before being placed officially on the market. He said Go had been valued at £200 million. And he reported that easyJet had been considering a bid. That, by now, was old news. But he was nearer the mark four weeks later in the same paper on 24 September, when he said Go was to be sold.

'British Airways will soon be instructing Barbara Cassani to consider the airline's future. Cassani has been promoting the demerger of Go since the start of the year and some in British Airways thought she was talking out of turn recommending its independence. She has had offers from venture capitalist firms for stakes in the group.'

Then on Monday 6 November 2000 a public announcement was made at the British Airways' half-yearly results meeting that set off the rush to sell our airline: 'Following the successful establishment of Go as a leading no-frills airline in Europe, British Airways intends to realise the value created and offer the subsidiary for sale.'

Rod had kept his word about sorting out the LTIP, and we finally had a verbal agreement as Go's sale was officially announced. We received final documents in December which said we would be paid cash equivalents of our equity should the company be sold.

Now it was time to make some bigger decisions, as I had been in limbo land for too long. I spoke with Roger Maynard, Go's Chairman and a perennial survivor at the top of British Airways.

'Do you think my management team will be considered as one of the options for the sale?' I asked.

'These things are very delicate. Barbara, you must be very careful of going down this path. You need to remember that your duties are to run the company in the best interests of British Airways and the shareholders. We believe an auction is the best way to get the best price for the company.'

I was being warned off.

But the press speculation had my name in the frame for a management buyout from day one. All of Fleet Street's transport correspondents and business writers, whom I had assiduously cultivated over the previous three years, wanted my comments – and I was allowed to make none. My hands were tied. And I found it hard to keep the rest of our Go people up to speed with events because there was now a well-founded concern about the future.

While still managing the business on a daily level, I was receiving regular phone calls from private equity houses and advisory firms all wanting a piece of the forthcoming action. British Airways didn't want me to meet anyone without their approval and I tried to keep lines open with Roger Maynard. There is a specialised industry supporting mergers and acquisitions, with investors, bankers, lawyers and accountants chasing this lucrative dealmaking. For them, the smell of the chase is everything; they love the high-octane excitement of doing deals. And the smartest and most experienced practitioners know the rules of what is often a game of poker.

The ownership battle for Go was about to begin, and nothing in my previous career would compare. The possibilities were both thrilling and frightening. We had no way of knowing then if we could keep running Go for colleagues and customers; getting it right for them meant the profits for shareholders would follow. But a strong possibility for Go was disappearing into another airline or travel company.

As the sale process kicked off, I realised that the next few months were out of my control. This was not a natural or comfortable state for me. One evening as we sat around our kitchen table, Guy warned me again. 'Remember venture capitalists are better at negotiating than management are for the simple reason they do it all the time. You will only do it once if you do it at all, so you don't want to get screwed over the terms of any deal.' It was typically sage advice from Guy, and instilled in me an increasing sense of paranoia that turned me into a ferocious negotiator.

Chapter Sixteen

The Auction

The sounds of a cello were in the background as waiters attentively served the well-heeled customers tea and cucumber
sandwiches in the grand foyer of Claridge's on Monday 8 January
2001. The Go management team were oblivious to all this splen-
dour. We didn't know whether to laugh or explode over having to
promote the sale of a low-cost airline from the most expensive
hotel in London. The venue had been organised by others.

As the melodious strains wafted into a private – but not
soundproofed – side room behind the afternoon tea sippers, I
stood up to open the first of our many management presentations – this time to a small band from 3i, one of Europe's biggest
venture capital companies, and a bevy of their advisers.

'Good afternoon, I'm Barbara Cassani, CEO of Go. I'd like
to introduce the members of my team who created Go. We will
be talking about our achievements to date, how we manage the
business and Go's plans for the future.'

We were excited to be presenting to 3i. They were the 'civil
servants' of the UK venture capital industry, honourable if a bit
plodding. They originated as a government-funded enterprise

set up to develop businesses. Floated on the stock market in 1994, they were still trying to break away from their old government mentality, and weren't perceived to be bandits in braces. The people we saw didn't match the smart new logo and self-proclaimed status as Europe's largest venture capital group operating in twelve countries. And we knew that for all their marketing bravado, Go would represent their largest deal to date. In our eyes, they had two distinctive advantages: they had made money from airlines before with CityFlyer and British Caledonian; and they had a reputation for being friendly and supportive of management. In other words, they weren't known as 'flip artists', who bought companies and sold them on to a competitor. This was an important consideration given British Airways' discussions with easyJet the previous summer. I had met their lead director on the deal, Tom Sweet-Escott, once before, and Dominic, Andrew and Steven had secretly met with 3i earlier in the autumn when British Airways had refused to give management freedom to look into bidding for the company. They were enthusiastic about 3i and eager to impress. I was neutral at that stage.

There followed a 90-minute whirlwind of why 3i should want to invest in Go. The whole team was psyched up for the performance. David Magliano, Andrew Cowen, Dominic Paul, Steven Horner, Lynne Hodgkinson and Ed Winter knew their stuff and it showed. Steven was now Director of Network Management, Dominic was Director of People and Business Development, and Andrew was being groomed to take over from Lynne when she moved to Shropshire after the sale. He had joined the finance team when Lynne had been on maternity leave and stayed on to pull together the future business plan that would underpin our bid for a management buyout. One after the other they stood up and explained how they fitted into our jigsaw. We were young in spirit, confident and informal, and on top of our game. I was so impressed with each of them.

I was especially proud that we had cracked the mystery of profitably developing our route network. Steven had done some seminal work on choosing routes and new airport bases that would power our growth at even higher profit levels over the next five years.

After British Airways had failed to sell Go to easyJet in the summer of 2000, Rod Eddington had asked us to create a five-year business plan of which Andrew Cowen was the architect. We were feeling very upbeat. The critical summer period had been very profitable and set us up well to make a small profit in our third year. In one of my regular updates to everyone at Go on 15 September 2000, I was uncharacteristically optimistic. Everyone had been working hard throughout the summer; cabin and flight crews had flown a lot of hours; telesales, despite some rumblings, had responded to a tougher sales incentive programme. More routes were launched, new people were arriving, and we were even planning an updated version of our uniform with new shirts for men and skirts for women.

'For once I'm happy with the financial performance of Go. All of you have done a great job making a profit every month for five months (a Go record). You may wonder why I care so much. Our future depends on it,' I said.

And we just kept growing. We had been eager to add to our UK domestic network to balance out the longer sector lengths of the beach routes. The different sector lengths helped balance the operation to make our aircraft and crew more productive and also made us more attractive to business people. We decided to add both Glasgow and Belfast to our Stansted network.

It was helped by some tragic circumstances. A GNER express train travelling from King's Cross to Leeds at 115 mph had crashed at Hatfield on Tuesday 17 October 2000. Four passengers were killed and a broken rail on a bend was found to be the cause. It was more evidence of the decaying railways, neglected by successive governments and starved of investment.

After Hatfield, the rail chaos in the UK went on for many months as almost every piece of railway line in the country was checked and much of it replaced. The West Coast mainline service between Glasgow and London was temporarily suspended and speed restrictions were placed on the busiest railway artery in Europe. Railtrack was in disarray and eventually collapsed into bankruptcy.

But their chaos was a benefit for us at Go. People felt more comfortable going by plane, especially at prices lower than buying an on-the-day rail ticket. And business people, heartily fed up with constant timetable disruption, took to low-cost flying in far greater numbers.

In autumn 2000, I headed north to launch our Stansted-to-Glasgow service, with the Belfast service following a few days later.

'I never take pleasure in others' misfortunes, but the recent problems and delays will encourage many passengers to move on to our new service. We are confident that with fares from £48 return including taxes, we will give the railways a run for their money,' I told reporters at the time.

Then I took a little swipe at Ryanair, saying we were the first low-cost operator flying into Glasgow. 'It's a bit of fun, but Ryanair have been complaining because they say they are flying to Glasgow, but really they are coming into Prestwick.'

The rail disruption and chaos went on for months and months. It helped give Go a real step up with business people in Scotland who loved our punctuality and low-priced flights.

As our financial results improved and our reputation as a quality low-cost airline grew, my colleagues at Go continued to hope British Airways would decide to keep us, but I was trying to nudge their thinking along. We were all proud to be part of British Airways, but if we could get the company on an even keel financially we would be more likely to find a new owner who would support our plans. I felt confident and wanted everyone else to feel that way too. Our ownership was uncertain, but the way we managed the business was crystal-clear.

No matter how much we expected it, the November announcement to auction Go off to anyone with a big enough chequebook had shaken us. We spent the next two months rebuilding our confidence. Damn it, we had built a wonderful company, and whoever bought it would hear our pride and enthusiasm. In my own mind I was clear that if I didn't like the buyer, I wouldn't be part of the deal. Freedom to run the airline safely was critical; I was concerned that venture capitalists might push us too far on costs in the wrong places. Managing colleagues and the customer experience in the Go way was also non-negotiable. In fact, not much about the speed of growth, where we flew, what we flew or how we managed was negotiable in my view. I was ready to walk away if the wrong bidder won Go.

After British Airways' announcement to sell us on 6 November, and well before we met 3i at Claridge's in January, I asked my board for permission to hire financial advisers to investigate a management buyout and solicitors to help Ed and me through the labyrinth of trying to do the 'right' thing while looking at our own bid for the company. Requests to free us to look at an MBO were refused, but British Airways did allow us to hire solicitors to help us understand our fiduciary duties. They must have understood that if a private equity bidder emerged on top, we would be facing an MBO, but *they* wanted to do the choosing, not leave it to us.

So on Thursday 23 November 2000 I went to find the right advisers. As ever, I put my business out to tender, and one of the candidates was Charlie Geffen at the leading London law firm of Ashurst Morris Crisp. He was highly recommended by British Airways' own Legal Director, Steven Walsh, who had earlier worked as a solicitor at Ashurst and had become a non-executive director of Go. Charlie was a genuinely affable guy about the same age as me, and had brought along his fellow partner David Carter.

I grew to trust Charlie and David; they were the perfect foil of velvet and steel, an enormous support in the months to come. Charlie stuck with me like glue throughout the management buyout. Charlie, as head of mergers and acquisitions and private equity, had a gently mocking sense of humour, vital for deflating the stress during tense negotiations, and he liked Americans. David was more serious, but precise and astute, able to recall any one of the dozens of deal issues, and gave great advice.

They thought we would need financial advisers and offered to make introductions, but I politely declined because of the British Airways edict and since I had a world-class adviser at home in Guy. It is not everyone who is married to a mergers and acquisitions expert, and he was my sounding board. While I privately fumed and fretted at home, he was my rock. It didn't make for a quiet home life, but over the kitchen table we would dissect the options and what I should do next. Guy was Go's secret weapon.

At first Charlie didn't understand that I came with a ready-made financial adviser. He recalls me saying: 'Well, my husband knows about acquisitions, I'm going to get him to help me on this one.' He balked, momentarily, thinking: Oooh! Unfortunately I've heard this before and it doesn't usually work. Alarm bells would ring for him if someone said they had a friend or relation who could help in a complex deal.

Guy has always been a clear-headed, methodical person, and he was able to take me through the steps. Gradually, I revealed my developing thoughts to the management team. Ed, David, Steven and Dominic all were vital and agreed to stay on board. Lynne was now expecting a second baby, and we had had several talks about whether Go was right for her going forward. We agreed that she would keep her personal plans quiet and work hard for a good deal. She had a big financial incentive to see it go well – once we had her founder's stake in Go signed up with British Airways in December. Fortunately, Andrew Cowen was blossoming as a new member of Go's senior team.

Go's further fourteen senior managers were proving their ability to run a new airline on a daily basis, but taking on a management buyout was quite a different proposition, so at the end of November I dragged the top twenty senior managers and directors away from the day-to-day for a confidential session in a Go conference room.

Go's senior managers were a diverse group both in experience and personality. Most were in their early thirties, with a few in their twenties, forties and fifties. Together they formed the bedrock of the company. For most, Go was their first adventure outside the safety of a big company. Fred Kochak was in his mid-twenties and ran pricing for us, having joined from American Airlines in Dallas. Andrew Goodrum, heading up cabin crew, and Cath Lynn, running airports, were both from Sainsbury's store management. Mireille Briggs, our European marketing chief, had grown up in classical brand marketing at a large FMCG company. Ralph Anker was heading up route planning and had come essentially from academia. Derek Patterson, our financial controller, had come from traditional roles in Ford. Rob Platts joined us from the oil group Lasmo, to be our financial planner. Sarah Lambie was our in-house solicitor, who had joined us from Wragge & Co. The group was later joined by Blair Stewart, a twenty-something IT whiz who had come from Freedom Air in New Zealand.

Others had been through more change, such as Mike Coltman, Ed's number two in operations, who was an American MBA who left easyJet after several years. Oliver Wigdahl, Go's Head of Sales and internet, had lived through Air Europe's rise and fall at Gatwick and then worked with American Airlines in Europe. Another was Mike Williams, Go's Chief Engineer, who had been disappointed and disillusioned by the decline of British Caledonian and its subsequent acquisition by British Airways. Andy Holmes ran operations and had joined us from several start-ups and easyJet. Paul Llewellyn-Beard had taken over from John Mahon as chief pilot after enduring tough times at Air UK's charter arm.

But none of them had been anywhere near a management buyout. And that put them in good company, since neither had I. We had a lot to learn, and fast.

For several months I had been having one-to-one sessions with David Carter (not to be confused with his namesake at Ashurst), who was a CEO mentor. He was a former high-flying banker who had dabbled in venture capital, started up a leisure business, and floated it on the stock exchange. He was now chairman and founder of Merryck & Co., a unique consultancy of CEO advisers where the emphasis was on improving personal and company performance. He approached me out of the blue and offered to take me on as one of his cases on a pro-bono basis until Go could afford to pay him. That was a style and deal I found hard to resist, and I took advantage of the free help on a pro-bono basis for a year until we could afford to pay. Over two and a half years, we met regularly and talked about my performance and the development of the management team. He helped me raise my game as a CEO. Our sessions every few months became oases of calm reflection amid all the frenzy of running a fast-growing operation. I became clearer about my objectives and the way to manage my top team. When the sale became more of a reality, I realised he had done his own MBO and could offer insights into the psyche of the venture capitalists as well as practical tips on getting the best possible deal for management and employees. Now I asked him and a Merryck colleague to join Charlie, the other David Carter from Ashurst and Go's senior team to explore the ramifications of what we were thinking of undertaking.

This was the pivotal gathering on 30 November because I did not want to be seen as bullying the management into making any commitment they couldn't fully support. We had too much respect for each other and jobs were on the line. An MBO would add financial risks too.

Charlie handed out a helpful booklet called *Management Buyouts from the Management's Perspective* which shed light on what we were about to go through. It explained some of the terms that would soon trip off our tongues such as share capital, vesting, equity splits and ratchets.

Charlie's book stated clearly: 'Generally speaking, equity houses do not like to see management having a completely risk-free opportunity.' And while this didn't mean putting their homes on the line, it required finding out how much each member was willing to risk. David and his Merryck colleague talked to everyone in the team individually and reported the results back to me anonymously. I didn't want to misjudge their appetite for following me over the parapet into battle. This was the acid test for us. If I had approached each individual face-to-face, they would have felt obliged to declare their loyalty. That would have been unfair; this was a decision that transcended allegiance to me. Everyone had to make their own decision, without undue pressure.

Ashurst's David Carter later recalled in a conversation to a reporter: 'Barbara had some financial knowledge and Lynne had worked on IPOs in Europe but the rest of the team had never been involved in something as large as this. But they were a very impressive lot asking tough questions. They were willing to take a risk and learn.'

One uncomfortable consequence was that everyone now understood that as founders Ed, David, Lynne and I would earn money from the sale. It became clear that the founders' stake in the business (the one that was still not agreed and signed with British Airways) would make us rich if Go was sold for a substantial sum. This was upsetting for some. Everyone knew I had a stake, but they were surprised about the others. I had been surprised that one or two of my fellow 'founders' hadn't shared the knowledge of their stakes with their own teams. In the eyes of the other directors and senior managers, this was a fundamental issue about fairness. I had wanted to offer shares more widely, but British Airways was uncomfortable with this approach. I was barely able to extend the share options to Ed, David and Lynne – the only ones who had the promise of equity in their contracts. This was the genesis of a fundamental issue about money and reward that became more important. The unfairness of giving ownership benefits to a few would tear us apart unless we could find a way of sharing the benefits more widely in the post-British Airways era.

By then, I'd developed a firm belief that for a management buyout to work successfully everyone at Go, from the engineering department to the telesales team, through to the Ops department, must be given a stake. They deserved it. Without their concerted commitment, we wouldn't be able to grow as fast as we needed to catch up with our bigger rivals.

Even with the unsettling knowledge that some of us would get rich even before the management buyout, the results of the private interviews were unanimous. Everyone wanted to go for it. The amounts of money they were willing to risk were a huge proportion of their savings. When David Carter of Merryck debriefed me, he was deeply impressed with the intelligence, commitment and bravery of Go's top team. He felt we had a rare thing going. I was stunned and grateful. There would be no need for them to come up with tens of thousands each, but the fact that they would have done it for Go was a tremendous boost to me.

And while their loyalty sustained me, I wasn't sure we would succeed if we jumped up and publicly declared our interest in doing a management buyout of Go. I felt that British Airways might work against us: the negative feelings towards us were that strong. So we played a waiting game, praying that venture capitalists would bid for us – as opposed to another airline. Any venture capital bid, by definition, is an MBO because they virtually always insist on the involvement of the current management.

But in fact, I was still paranoid about my own position and our negotiating strength, and Charlie Geffen gave me pep talks. 'Barbara, don't forget you are in a very strong negotiating position. Remember there are three elements in any deal: power, creativity and persuasion.'

We had power because we had created Go and knew how to run the business. And I was the most critical as founder and CEO. Strict legal duties bound me to act in the best interest of the company and shareholders, thus I was not completely free. Charlie urged me to bite my tongue when I regularly flinched at British Airways' arrogance in taking for granted that the Go management would simply roll over and work for any buyer presented.

Charlie is one of the best negotiators I have ever worked with, and fleshed out the identikit picture of the venture capitalist that David Carter of Merryck had given me. He helped me understand that most venture capitalists are very risk-averse, with an outlook on the world that resembles a caveman using brute-force threats to get his way. Making huge returns on money is their only reason for doing business.

Our greatest strength at this point was that no outside group could run Go if the management group stuck together. It would have been an impossible risk for a new buyer to install new management into a loss-making airline. Like a band of latter-day musketeers, we were 'All for one, and one for all' in agreement to forge ahead.

As pawns in the auction sale process, we were required to meet a whole batch of other possible purchasers. The Sunday papers were full of leaks about potential buyers. I can honestly say that none of our small band spoke to the press, but I can't speak for British Airways, a place known to leak like a sieve. And it was backfiring badly. The speculation about Go's valuation reached a staggering £500 million in the *Sun*. This kind of drip-drip speculative coverage continued until the day we managed to win control of the company. I was astonished that the great Goldman Sachs and savvy British Airways weren't managing the market's expectations better. But I was gagged by them both, having been given strict instructions not to speak to the press about anything but flogging Go seats to the public.

Barring me from taking part in managing the sale of Go increased my own exasperation. There seemed so little proper activity, so I phoned up Goldman Sachs and asked them if they had tried calling jetBlue's investors yet. jetBlue was the latest exciting low-cost start-up in the US, based in New York. Had anyone approached George Soros, the billionaire who ran a private equity arm and was one of Goldman's own clients? For goodness' sake, I said, he and Weston Presidio were backing David Neeleman's jetBlue in the United States; surely his outfit would be interested in us.

Meanwhile, David Neeleman was being fêted in *Business Week* as one of the entrepreneurs of the year for 2000, so well-run, low-cost airlines were obvious sexy.

Have you tried Texas Pacific Group? I asked. They were one of the largest private equity firms in the United States and were involved in the £2.7 billion acquisition of Punch Taverns from Allied Domecq. It was one of the largest leverage buyouts ever seen in Europe. Only problem was that its founder, David Bonderman, who had been on the board of Continental Airlines, was also Ryanair's chairman, and I suspect Michael O'Leary had a few choice words describing us in private.

Although I doubt he could be ruder about us in private than he'd been in publicly describing Go as a dog. I continued to float my helpful suggestions that met with a thud of indifference.

The initial Information Memorandum, inviting bids for the airline and prepared by the bankers, was a shambles. We heard from separate sources that prospective buyers were appalled at how badly it presented Go. It was not at all what we had expected. One potential investor, who knew me well, phoned to tell me later: 'According to the memorandum, the business looked awful, and I would have had no interest in it on that basis.' To be fair, all we had to report were two years of massive losses. It just wasn't the right time to put the business up for sale.

I became a proper pain in the backside. Had anyone called Cinven? Kohlberg Kravis Roberts? Apax Partners? And why were they dragging their feet with other venture capitalists? Of course, most investment outfits didn't like the risky aviation sector. The celebrated value investor Warren Buffett made the now-famous remark that if you totted up all the investment in all airlines since the Wright Brothers started flying in December 1903 you'd find in total they have never made a dime. Candover Partners called me up without going through the bankers, met with us and left enthusiastic. Then their investment committee, adopting Buffett's yardstick, halted the conversations because they just didn't invest in airlines, period.

I met Fred Vinton, of Electra Partners, and a story leaked out to the Reuters news agency on 29 November that I was 'in early talks with private equity firm Electra, about a possible management buy-out'. It made a brief mention on the *Evening Standard*'s City pages, alongside a story about Bookham Technologies, an optical equipment darling that had gone to the stock market in March. Its shares had dived below its offer price. Other technology stocks such as Arm, Baltimore and Logica were all starting to go flat. The Footsie fell 84.9 points to 6,164.9 points with an editorial warning 'brokers fear a full-blown bear market'. These were the ominous signs of a future market melt-down. Not a great time to ask already flighty venture capitalists to stump up over £100m for a loss-making airline.

I also talked with Robert Easton, of US-based venture capital group Carlyle. He is an old friend, an ex-colleague of Guy's, and his wife Elza is my son James's godmother. I called to help Carlyle understand that there was more to Go than was included in that first flimsy sale document. I even eventually spoke with Weston Presidio myself. And then Preussag showed their interest when I received a call from my old boss Charles Gurassa, who had moved on from British Airways. Eventually, we saw some life. Not exactly vigorous life, but enough to think we'd get a few preliminary bids.

The first round of bidders gave such broad ranges that they were virtually meaningless. Because I was kept in the dark by British Airways, at the time I didn't know what anyone had offered. 3i only told me much later that they had indicated a range of £95m–£140m. These bids were the mechanism that British Airways and Goldman were using to decide who could return for the complete dog and pony show from Go management after Christmas. During this time, British Airways also hired Ernst & Young, spending hundreds of thousands of pounds to prepare a financial report on Go to expedite the sale process. 3i promptly rejected the report and then hired PWC to do another analysis costing hundreds of thousands of pounds more. We'd seen enough accountants to exhaust a huge finance department, let alone the tiny band that Lynne, Derek and Rob were leading.

Goldman Sachs continued to offer little hope about the prospects for the sale, citing our lack of maturity, a history of losses and strong competition in the low-cost sector.

I was spitting mad. They could not grasp what we were trying to do in our low-cost model.

Guy, who understood the ins and outs of the investment

banking world, tried to placate me. 'I know it's frustrating, but they are top of the pile among dealmakers and this isn't a big deal for them, Barbara.'

Then one morning I received a phone call from one of their acquisition team requesting a draft of the Go management presentation that would be needed after Christmas for those investors who made it through the first round of bidding. I asked for help, only to be told that most of their clients had strategy departments who could prepare the presentation.

'They just don't get it. We are a start-up, low-cost airline, we don't have a strategy department,' I said to Guy with increasing exasperation after I put the phone down.

But we didn't want to look like a bunch of country hicks. I called up Lynne, Andrew, Ed, Steven, David and Dominic and we invited Peter Smith and Martin Pilkington, our old friends from LEK, to come to our aid. (And British Airways even paid their hefty bill!) In true style, this dynamic duo argued and debated among themselves on how best to describe the company and the business results and came up trumps.

From October 2000, when British Airways decided to sell Go, until January, auctioning Go off to the highest bidder was shrouded in secrecy. I was on the periphery of the deal. It was a confusing time. I had different roles that pulled me in opposing directions. My first responsibility was to the board of Go, that is British Airways – they owned Go and paid my salary. There was also my personal loyalty to British Airways. Then I had special, legally defined duties as a director to do what was in the best interests of shareholders. On the other hand, I was a founder of the business and had a duty to the employees and to our original vision. And finally there was a chance that I might be a buyer of the business. These different roles clashed and made the six months during the sale very stressful.

So at that very first presentation of Go to a potential buyer at

Claridge's in January, I summed up our presentation to 3i after everyone had spoken: '. . . and so my ambition for Go is to use the independence from British Airways to grow, be profitable and create the best low-cost airline in Europe. Then we will head for an initial public offering within three years. I have confidence in this outcome because of the strength of our business and investor interest in the fastest-growing, most profitable sector of the airline industry,' I concluded before sitting down.

When 3i stood up to say a few words, they did not impress, but I didn't care. They didn't need to be orators; we just wanted their money to buy our freedom. We hoped they would bite at the bait offered in our presentation and agree to make a second formal bid in mid-February.

Just a few days later, the team and I were back presenting the Go story, but this time the venue was the Liberal Club on the Thames. Still not quite in line with the contemporary, low-cost Go brand, but at least it wasn't Claridges.

We continued the presentations that week to several venture capital consortia including Electra, West LB and Barclays. They came with overpowering numbers of advisers and we dispatched their questions and issues with ease. They were in sales mode and were obviously trying to gain our trust. The game is simple with the venture capitalists. First cosy up to management, then use the insider knowledge to bid just enough to win the deal, and then once you are in exclusive negotiations you persuade the management to identify all the problems and issues that can be used to negotiate a lower price. They were all pretty transparent in their objectives.

And we were relieved at this early stage in January that the only trade buyer was Preussag. We had been very concerned that easyJet or Ryanair would enter the bidding. Our greatest rival, easyJet, would not be in the race because Stelios and his crew had just completed their stock market flotation and were too busy to make yet another bid for Go. And Ryanair's boss

Michael O'Leary would have been pilloried for even thinking about it, because he had always described Go as a perpetually loss-making no-hoper. Besides, I don't think British Airways were keen to get involved with him after his success in a High Court action against them over Ryanair's rather puerile 'Expensive BA ****ds' advertising campaign. It claimed British Airways was five times more expensive than Ryanair, and Mr Justice Jacob, while describing the behaviour of both sides as 'immature', found in December 2000 that the adverts were not shown to be false. Ouch. So British Airways was not eager for a repeat of a bloody nose from Ryanair. If either our orange friends at easyJet or Ryanair had been involved in the auction of Go, we would have been living our nightmare scenario.

When we presented to the big German travel conglomerate Preussag, though, our hearts sank. It would be just like being part of British Airways, but without the protection of a Bob Ayling keeping the rest of the organisation at bay while we got on with growing and becoming profitable. My old boss, Charles Gurassa, was behind the Preussag interest because he was now their chief of airlines worldwide. Given his extensive experience at Thomson, British Airways and Thomas Cook before that, he knew that the low-cost sector was here to stay in Europe. The vast fleets of charter planes at Preussag were at risk as airlines such as Go grabbed market share to Spain and Portugal. In fact, although Charles lost in his internal battle for Preussag to buy Go, he later launched a lowish-cost airline in Germany to take on Ryanair in Preussag's home market with the catchy name Hapag-Lloyd Express.

Because of my reluctance to believe all the sales hype from the smooth-talking venture capitalists, I had asked for references from companies that 3i and the other venture capital firms had invested in. Each CEO of the 3i invested companies said that 3i were respectful to management and supportive as long as the business was financially on track. Fair enough. On the other hand, I was astounded to take references provided by other venture capital firms where several chief executives told me they'd been personally shafted on the terms of the deal. Can you imagine what their other CEOs would have said? So 3i was lining up as our preferred option.

As it happened, 3i needed a deal like Go. City commentators said that 3i was overcommitted in the precarious technology, media and telecoms sectors and that they should refocus on traditional industries before the dot.com bubble finally popped. As we found out later, they did too little too late to save their shareholders from taking a huge hit. But airlines did fit the bill as a more traditional sector, and were something they knew a bit about. Angela Lane, their resident airline expert, said: 'The low-cost model made me sit up because it was the first plan that I had seen based on creating new market share rather than fighting for existing customers on a route. Low prices meant the traditional airlines – with their hefty costs – could not simply come onto the route and undercut the profits as had happened on traditional airline routes.'

There was a whirlwind of follow-up meetings after the formal management presentations where I had to be well prepared and focused. When I met each of the interested groups I asked them directly how they intended to manage Go and they all agreed the existing team would remain in place and they would support our growth plan. That was a good sign. I was also interested in the amount of equity they were prepared to make available for Go employees and management. And we tackled a thorny concern head-on: how easily could we be separated from British Airways? The answer: 'Without too much hassle and with relief on both sides.'

The joint grouping of venture capitalist Carlyle and KLM with its Buzz subsidiary approached British Airways to enter the auction. At first they tried to interest British Airways in taking a stake in a merged Go/Buzz, but once rebuffed, they worked on a joint bid to buy Go and merge us with Buzz. I was never convinced. Buzz was a commercial mess, Carlyle had a 'tough guy' reputation, and KLM's motives were unclear.

Meanwhile I was darting across to the West Country for secret negotiations for our first base in Bristol, code-named Brazil, while trying to cover our cost position from an unexpected accountancy mishap. We needed to properly implement a new accounting standard on provisions for aircraft maintenance costs and the effect was to dramatically harm our bottom line. And, in the forefront of my mind, we were conducting the first pay negotiations in Go's history, looking at how to reward the hard-working Go people who had gone three years without a pay rise. I was concerned that our captains would be poached by better pay elsewhere. Other airlines were desperate for trained 737 pilots and senior cabin crew, and ours were the best in the business. easyJet pulled a fast one on us and offered a £30,000 bonus to any trained 737 captain who joined easyJet. They must have known that Go was vulnerable during this period when British Airways had signalled a desire to sell us but the future buyer remained unknown. We flapped around and increased Go pilot base pay a small amount, but we should have had more faith in the team. Only one guy left, and he was moving near the easyJet base of Liverpool anyway. Good for him that he got the £30k!

In many respects, Electra was the most credible bidder. They had a long track record and had delivered a number of similar deals. Fred Vinton, an American who now lived in London, and Nigel McConnell, an ex-accountant who had the silky patina of a long-time buyout operator, were both highly experienced. Could I work with them? That was another question.

West LB, fronted by Philip Buscombe, was famous as a debt provider for buyouts but not so well known for taking on the equity side. The glamorous Robin Saunders, whom I met later at a lunch with the business editor of the *Sunday Times*, was their most famous dealmaker. But I couldn't fathom how this could be their kind of territory.

Barclays Private Equity was a smaller outfit, and Simon Henderson was the cheerleader for finding a way for Barclays to participate in one of the bidding groups. They just couldn't commit the capital to do the deal alone or as the lead. They had the most belief in Go because of their involvement in buying Luton Airport, home of easyJet. They originally looked at putting their own deal together, and even approached Bob Ayling to return as chairman. They then teamed up with Electra, but ultimately they left that grouping and joined 3i to become the second-largest Go shareholder, though their stake was controlled by 3i.

It is not clear to me that British Airways ever realised how weak their hand was if the highest bidder came from someone we refused to deal with. We didn't warm to the prospect of dealing with Electra. 'Why don't you think they are the ones for us, then, Barbara?' asked Ed, who was my closest deal confidant, one afternoon as we surveyed the list.

'It seems fairly obvious to me. They don't really see Go as special enough. They haven't properly understood what we are about. I think the most we'll get is 15 per cent of the equity, and they expect it to be distributed among the top management. I wanted a partner who can help us spread the equity to the whole of Go. Besides, they've already indicated they want to make changes in the director team.'

'I agree completely,' he replied.

So what about the Carlyle Group and KLM bid?

I shook my head over the prospects of Go being merged with Buzz.

'I just can't see this being the right move for Go. You know my views on merging airlines. Besides, they have the wrong planes, a fleet of ageing and expensive British Aerospace 146 regional jets, highly paid pilots on KLM traditional contracts, and I have my doubts about KLM,' I said to Ed.

Leo van Wijk, the Chief Executive of KLM, was keen to merge Buzz and Go and he caused me a huge headache with my employees with some ill-judged comments that were reported in the *Financial Times*. I felt that was a taste of things to come.

It was now time for us to play our card. Just before the bids were due I rang 3i on 16 February from Andrew Cowen's junky old commuting car as we headed into Central London to Carlyle for another session to discuss the disastrous combination of Go and Buzz.

'We want you to win the next round and move into exclusive negotiations. I hope you fully understand that we expect to significantly exceed the profit forecasts in the numbers you've seen. Don't lose this bid for the sake of a few million pounds.'

'Thank you, Barbara, we'll do our very best,' Tom Sweet-Escott replied.

We were told that they were the best venture capitalist option for us, and that they would stick by us through the thick and thin of airline life. 3i later said: 'We thought your management team were very impressive. You gelled well as a team and had analysed everything to the nth degree. You had built your business proposition on very sound foundations and that was reassuring for us as investors.'

The deadline for final bids approached, and on 20 February the offers went in to Goldman Sachs and British Airways. We had to wait to receive British Airways' decision on the winner of round two. I later surmised that three bids came in, at £100m from 3i, £90m from Electra and £95m from the Carlyle/KLM investors. I was shocked and dismayed.

'It's been bungled,' I said to Ed, when I heard the top bidder was 3i at £100 million. 'They're all far too low. It's a giveaway at this price.' I was offended because I thought Go was worth £150m. That's what I would have been prepared to pay.

We began to realise that this could play to our advantage.

The bids might undervalue Go, which hurt my ego, but they gave everyone at Go a chance to own a stake in the company at a bargain basement price. And we were relieved to hear that British Airways was prepared to press ahead at this price. We took a ribbing in the press when the price emerged, but I'd rather suffer that embarrassment than miss a bargain.

British Airways granted 3i an exclusive position in March to try to hammer out a deal with management and finish its review of Go's business. 3i was disappointed, once management were free to talk, that we couldn't point to any areas of weakness in Go to drive the price down. Frankly, we were getting a bargain, and as the business performance was good and we were on track for a real profit, I thought British Airways might put the price up, which is what I'd have done in their shoes.

3i also began to relax a bit more as they could see that Go was a fully-functioning company, completely ring-fenced from British Airways. The only tricky issue was the nine aircraft that were leased by Go but with a British Airways financial guarantee. Obviously leasing companies wouldn't voluntarily give up that blue-chip financial backing (and indeed they couldn't because many had securitised the asset on the basis that a world-class company like British Airways stood behind it). My old friends at GECAS agreed to recut the deal without the guarantee, but in exchange for the promise of future business (but only if the terms were competitive), and we agreed to set up financial reserves to protect British Airways from any default by Go under 3i ownership. If it sounded complex, it was. And this was just one of a myriad issues that needed to be sorted through.

3i had a whole host of advisers, including Texan Larry Billett, the former finance director of Pan Am, who was then working with the bank Société Générale, as well as accountants PWC to help review our numbers and Go's financial robustness. Larry came by train to visit us with Angela Lane, who was now assisting with the deal, and advised her in a booming voice: 'Don't go into anything in airlines other than the low-cost sector. If ya wanna invest, this is it.'

And here I should explain why this was quite a different deal from most management buyouts. There are two ways to finance an acquisition: equity and bank debt. Equity is the money you invest yourself, while bank debt is money you borrow to buy the company. The venture capitalists like to have as much bank borrowing as possible, because it increases the return on their own investment. Here's an example: suppose they buy a company for £100 million using £50 million of their own money and £50 million of bank debt. Then if they later sell for £150 million, after paying off the £50 million bank debt, they've made £50 million profit – a 100 per cent return. That's twice what they would have made if they had put in the whole £100 million themselves. But borrowing is risky. You have to make sure that you can pay the interest and not go bankrupt! So in a standard acquisition there is normally a mixture of both equity and bank debt. But the Go deal was abnormal. The money that went into buying our company had to be entirely equity – out of 3i's investment funds. Why?

We simply didn't have the borrowing capacity to go to any banks for loans. We had no tangible assets such as aircraft to provide security for the banks because the planes were all leased and owned by someone else. So when we looked at how much money Go could afford to borrow to help buy the company from British Airways, we agreed that the obligation of all those aircraft leases meant that we effectively already had a huge amount of debt on our balance sheet. Go just did not have any more debt capacity to repay extra loans that would be used to buy the airline. We also were forbidden from taking on too much debt by the CAA, the government body that ensures that UK airlines are run prudently, from an operational/safety standpoint, but also from a financial perspective. In fact as part of the deal, 3i had to put £12.5 million of new capital into Go to bolster our loss-diminished balance sheet to keep the CAA happy. I was relieved to have the regulations of the CAA preventing 3i from engaging in risky financial engineering.

But there were still hurdles to overcome within 3i. The final deal had to go before the 3i Investment Committee, headed by Brian Larcombe, the Chief Executive of 3i. When Tom Sweet-Escott introduced the proposal, Brian put his head in his hands. Brian knew that airlines were a risky business.

'So what's so different about this business plan?' quizzed Brian.

'It's the management team. They are special,' Tom replied. 'They are young and aggressive and they are supremely analytical about what they are doing.'

'Are you sure about this?' said Brian. 'It's a substantial sum.'

Tom's instinct was we were a very hard bunch with a tough commercial culture. And the tougher we were, the more comfort he took. 'If they treated everyone, such as their suppliers and contractors, the way they've dealt with us, then they are doing a great job,' he told the committee.

The 3i deal team had visited us at Stansted and wandered around and saw first-hand how frugal we were. There were no plush offices or thick carpets, we didn't even have a proper canteen – it was a shared area with the company's visitors' reception. We had passed the frugality sniff test.

Once the 3i Investment Committee had given the deal the thumbs-up, it became chaos to get the deal finished. Eating, sleeping, driving, I was consumed by the chase. We had aimed for a 31 March completion date, but it was clear we had months to go. From March through to June we were immersed in the triangular negotiations – 3i with British Airways, management with 3i and British Airways with management. At times I wasn't sure I would ever close the deal with 3i. They tried all the venture capital tricks in the book. The most troubling was when they tried to renegotiate the terms of my own participation. It was standard practice for them but not for me. I balked and would have walked. They backed down. What emerged was a persistent worry that private equity investors enjoyed doing the deal more than the prospects of going to board meetings, working with management and monitoring successful businesses. It is always more interesting for them to either be selling or buying. Ironically, I saw life in precisely the opposite terms.

Chapter Seventeen

Shipshape and Bristol Fashion

While we were nailing down the MBO terms, we had another set of tough negotiations. We were in talks with Bristol Airport about establishing Go's second base. The growth plan and future profits underpinning the MBO required us to add a new base of operation every year. The new airport bases were expected to be more profitable than Stansted. And an attractive low-cost airport deal could turn this airport into a money-spinner for Go. For the airport owners, the expensive redevelopment finished in 2000 would begin to see a payback.

Deciding on Bristol took eight months. It all started with a blanket faxed letter being sent to the Bristol Airport Managing Director, John Parkin, by consultants we used to keep our identity anonymous. We were looking for a new base, and after casting the net widely across Europe, it was down to one of East Midlands, Newcastle, Edinburgh/Glasgow or Bristol. We were indifferent between the various options at this stage, but John was quick off the mark, responding immediately to set up an exploratory meeting.

The negotiations were difficult, because setting up a new

base involves agreeing a lot of complicated issues. We would need engineering support, hangar arrangements for our planes, baggage handling, advertising signage, and we wanted to recruit local people to Go as cabin crew and pilots.

Inside Go a new tier of managers was emerging. Among them was Mike Coltman, who had joined us from easyJet. He had been on our inaugural flight with Stelios as part of the orange boiler-suit gang and was now Ed's number two, a General Manager – Operations. He had in-depth airline experience and was now working closely with Andrew Cowen and Steven Horner, our route director, in the negotiations with Bristol.

It had been going swimmingly in a three-way discussion between us, the airport and Servisair, the ground handling agents. The complex legal arrangements were slowly but surely being resolved, then Bristol threw in a new cost that had been left out of the original proposal. All of a sudden, they wanted to levy a capital charge. The spanking new terminal had been officially opened on Friday 3 March 2000 by the Princess Royal, and the airport's rapid expansion required extra construction work in the ground handling area. The new owners hadn't been kept up to speed with our deal and insisted on the extra charge.

I was livid. They were trying to pull a fast one. The main issue was that it put our costs up; the other issue was that I never want surprises at the eleventh hour. The Go team had been very clear that the first proposal from the airport must be all-inclusive. We didn't want any nasty surprises, thank you. This charge was unacceptable. We didn't accept a renegotiation of our deal with 3i in the MBO and it wasn't acceptable from an airport. In a session with Andrew, Steven, Mike and Ed, I ranted and raved. 'I don't know where all this has come from, but they're trying to put one over on us.'

'I was at the Airport Operators Association's annual dinner at the Hilton Hotel in London as a guest of the Bristol team,' recalls Mike Coltman. 'John Parkin and Mike Luddy, his Marketing Manager, and Andrew Skipp, then the Finance Director, were at the same table and while it was a very civilised affair the new charge came up. I remember pounding the table saying: "We will not pay any more for the services; we need to have an all-inclusive deal so we can work out our budgets." Our position was stated clearly to them.'

Mike, a tall and athletic American, recalls the robust discussion continuing much of the evening. He is hazy about getting home, but it was around 3 a.m. Meanwhile the Bristol party headed home for work next day with precious little sleep.

At 11 a.m. next morning, in my fishbowl office, I held an emergency conference call to break the deadlock.

'Hey, John. How's the head this morning?'

'Probably a lot better than Mike's,' he replied cheerily.

'Well, what can you do to resolve this problem? I'm afraid it's a deal-breaker.'

There was a long pause on John's side, but then he backed down.

Sorting this out was important for both of us. John assured me there had been nothing sinister, only a little problem with his own board. I was clear that the charge needed to disappear and it did.

'The discussions were very honest and Barbara and the others weren't bashful about what they wanted,' John later recalled. 'And the relationship proved to be more successful than either of us imagined at that time.'

While Ryanair had a token presence at Bristol, the West Country was desperate to be plugged into the low-cost craze. The catchment area was along the wealthy and populous Thames valley corridor and the West Country was full of well-off older people with time to spare. It was ripe for our picking but it needed John Parkin's vision. He spoke our language and saw the potential.

John Parkin arrived after the death of local airport legend Les Wilson. Under John's leadership the airport grew from 1.4 million passengers a year to nearly 4 million.

In the close-knit world of venture capital, Tom Sweet-Escott of 3i first met John Parkin when Bristol council put its shareholding up for sale. He backed John in a management buyout but they were outbid by First Group. Tom was impressed that John had still delivered on the plan he presented to 3i for that MBO.

The transport group First Group took a 51 per cent stake, investing £32 million, which helped push the airport up the league table. Then, in January 2001, in the middle of our discussions, the airport was sold to Macquarie and Cintra for £198 million. This had been a potential problem that John and his team smoothed over perfectly. But John Parkin reckoned the Go deal was the most significant of his career. 'You do a lot of deals in business, but this was certainly the most pleasing,' he said later.

With the Bristol deal signed and in the bag in March 2001, we packed a Go aircraft with journalists on a special flight into Bristol and used it to make our announcement of the new base there. It took me by surprise how the local regional daily and evening papers lapped up the news. It was splashed all over the front pages. A front-page picture and lead story in the *Bristol Evening Press* ran with the headline 'Low-cost airline set for £50 Bristol take-off', and underneath was one of our Boeing 737s in Go livery rising into the sky. It was an irresistible taster. We ran a competition with the paper to choose the most popular sunshine destination. It became the buzz of the city, and eventually near the end of March we began selling ten routes including Nice, Alicante, Barcelona, Faro, Malaga and Palma.

We held the official route announcement at the Watershed arts and media complex on Bristol harbour side. It was another bite at the PR cherry for us. We were going to release some helium balloons, but there was an icy drizzle and it became so cold the balloons just didn't want to fly. Our cheery public relations team, led by Brandon Stockwell, was anxious about the rain now tipping down. It was the Liverpool Street Station Operation Sunshine scenario all over again. So with some typical Go ad-libbing we shifted inside for the press snaps. The balloons were set off inside, floating up to the roof of the art centre and revealing our new destinations.

To continue the suspense of rolling out new routes, we went back with models in bowler hats and kilts for a promotion announcing low-cost flights from Bristol to Edinburgh and Glasgow. We had arrived in style and intended to offer the full range of Go destinations as quickly as possible. Prague and Venice followed just a few months later.

The perfectly formed airport was a joy to deal with and deserved its success because John and his management grasped the potential for this prosperous segment of Britain. Their efforts paid off and Go launched a Bristol base on 22 May 2001, on Go's third birthday, with a packed flight to Nice. On the aircraft, customers congratulated me on Go's welcomed arrival into the West Country. Over 750,000 people used the Go services at Bristol in our inaugural year, which was more than the total passengers flown out of Stansted in the airline's first year. Bristol became the fastest-growing airport in the UK.

In among all those press conferences and celebrations in Bristol, the negotiations with 3i's lawyers and investment bank, Société Générale, continued. Discussions revolved around the management and employee equity deal and agreeing how we could work together. Freedom to run the company was non-negotiable and we wanted a big say in the future of Go. I continually tried to negotiate a clause to give management a veto if investors decided to sell. Charlie Geffen worked with me to raise the issue again and again throughout the talks. I managed to get a veto regarding a minority sale to a trade buyer, but given their overwhelming size as the biggest owner, a veto over a total sale was something that 3i, like any other shrewd investor, would not have given away. Besides, we had agreed that floating Go as soon as possible on the stock market was a shared objective.

One big condition emerged that held the key to getting more than the average 10 to 15 per cent of the equity for employees. 3i wanted the founding directors to roll all of their earnings from the British Airways sale into the MBO. We had considered reinvesting a much smaller amount. It was another late session with coffee around the kitchen table with Guy.

'If you can squeeze even more equity out of them, you should roll all the money over. I can't think of anyone I'd rather invest in than you and the Go guys,' he advised.

'And you don't mind? I won't have much cash to show for the first three years. It also means we'll be staying in the UK indefinitely,' I said.

'I think in your heart of hearts you want to keep running Go. You've set it up and it's about to make a profit. You need to see this through,' he said.

I calculated that I would earn just over £2 million from the sale, and even after paying almost half in income tax I'd be able to put in £1 million after tax and still take a chunk to pay off the mortgage.

The big breakthrough came at Merryck's offices in Berkeley Square. I was negotiating with 3i over the phone and had Ed and David beside me. For my £1 million investment, and if my colleagues rolled over half of theirs, we looked close to a deal. In exchange – in a lightning stroke of boldness – David Carter encouraged me to ask for 25 per cent of the equity and I eventually negotiated 22.5 per cent of the company. This was an astonishing proportion. We had secured it with our financial commitment, the only kind of commitment venture capitalists could respect. Frankly, I had never thought we'd get more than 17 or 18 per cent.

So I would put £1.1 million into Go, and David and Ed would each put in hundreds of thousands. And for the other sixteen senior managers, I encouraged them to do what it took to find a couple of thousand pounds to buy their equity. This was going to be the chance of their lives. I never worried for a minute that we would lose any of our money. I was to keep the same 4 per cent stake (which was simply the stake I had under British Airways ownership), while the remaining 18.5 per cent was to be held by current and future employees and management.

Go's employees certainly needed a bigger share of the equity than was imaginable to most private equity firms. The mathematics were simple: we had 750 employees, we were doubling in size over the next three years, and I wanted everyone to be able to at least earn one times their annual salary in shares after three years.

The 3i team had originally assumed that we would distribute stock to pilots and a handful of top people. This was not the Go way. Certainly, I felt the pilots should get a sizeable number of shares, but I wanted every employee to have a stake in what they had created.

Because the directors and I were up to our necks in all the details of the MBO, the senior managers and their teams stepped up and took more and more responsibility for the business. We were all working like crazy, but the airline operations ran fantastically well. I felt justified in fighting so hard for the big pot of equity. It was for the people who would make or break the future for Go.

The three-legged negotiations continued, with Tom and Angela Lane speaking to Roger Maynard and British Airways' dealmaker, Heath Drewett. We were within touching distance of a great result, which was capped off with a final meeting between 3i and Rod Eddington.

3i was now paying less for the airline than they had put in their February bid. It was incredible in a business that had improved its performance during the negotiations and was now profitable. The deal was lowered to £80 million in cash, plus a deferred payment of £20 million to be paid within five years. And a further £10 million if a trade sale or flotation went on within the first few years. There was a 'non-embarrassment' clause that meant 3i would have to pay a big proportion of future sale proceeds to British Airways if 3i sold Go on within a year. Non-embarrassment indeed.

Establishing a new base is an enormous logistical exercise, and the first few months required a huge effort. It took several months to hire and train enough Bristol-based crew, so at first we had to dispatch our Stansted-based pilots and cabin crew by coach around the M25 from Stansted and along the M4 to Bristol. It was a regular two-hour journey, and often longer if you were caught in horrendous rush-hour peaks. There was some understandable whingeing about this. We fielded a lot of complaints. Dominic and Andrew Goodrum became concerned about the extra travelling.

'This is ridiculous having to spend three hours on a bus before we can go to work,' said one exasperated Go colleague after a particularly taxing trip. I was concerned about all the noise and asked Dominic to try and sort the problem until we could hire more people.

Then suddenly, after a few weeks, it all stopped.

'Why has it gone so quiet? What's happened?' I asked one of the cabin crew managers.

'Oh, it's amazing. The crews love going to Bristol, the passengers are just so friendly and appreciate the service. The crews don't seem to mind the commuting so much now.' We need to find more places like Bristol. Andrew and Steven even had a private daydream of making Bristol our main base, moving everyone out of London so we could enjoy a far better quality of life. Hey, not such a bad idea.

The day before we signed the MBO agreement, I took Go's first flight from Bristol to Glasgow with some hunky male models decked out in kilts and bowler hats. I was regaled by customers who were delighted that we were bringing lower prices, now a third of the cost of a British Airways flight. But we were also building a reputation for punctuality and friendliness that made low fares seem too good to be true.

The day after our first flight from Bristol to Glasgow was earmarked as our signing date for the MBO. I had been coy to journalists in Scotland about the timing because of the previous innumerable delays. I rushed back to London after a day of Scottish interviews where I couldn't talk about what was really on everyone's mind. The next morning, I went in early to British Airways' firm of solicitors, Starbuck's coffee in hand, and steeled myself for a day of reading scores of documents and putting my signature on nearly every one. It was a galling reminder of the new world we were entering when the proceedings ground to a halt until the founders and I could prove to 3i that our nearly £2 million contribution to the MBO was indeed invested. Our money went into the deal first.

Poor Ed Winter had flown back from a family holiday in Florida to participate in the signing and money transfers. This was the biggest investment any of us had ever made.

I jumped from the table as soon as the hundreds of documents were signed late in the afternoon, forgoing the champagne on offer. David and I did more than a dozen interviews – I wanted to shout about our independence and brag about how well the business had been doing. The months of agony were over. Go was ours. After that, drained and contented, I headed home to Lauren and James and the entire family played a game of Monopoly.

The press surrounding the MBO had been very positive. After six months of press silence imposed by British Airways, I was telling our story to the *Sunday Times*, *Financial Times* and others in the UK and to all the major papers in Spain, Denmark and Italy – important markets for Go. We decided to prepare for the future and behave more like a public company, issuing monthly traffic growth statistics. These monthly press releases would begin the process of informing potential investors on Go's growth, which would be a major factor behind a successful stock market initial placement offering (IPO).

With the deal out of the way and Bristol successfully launched, I turned my attention to promoting Go in the press free from any constraints and intent upon telling the world about our successes. We were thrilled to announce our first profit. We had said we would break even in three years and we did better than that. We made a profit of £4m, which was better than budget: something many airlines never do, and a huge triumph with the distractions of being up for sale.

All our detractors had said we were just an anti-competitive ploy to kill the low-cost sector. We had a right to hold our heads up high when we announced our first profit. The celebrations went on among everyone at Go. It was the beginning of a new era. We were independent, profitable and adding new bases. There was another reason to be happy. We established a generous profit sharing where 10 per cent of Go's net profits would be distributed equally. In that first year of profits, the longest-serving Go employees each received £1052.

I quickly moved to meet with Jim Parker, a well-known US financial analyst whose reports on low-cost and regional airlines were closely watched by the US investor community – an important target group for Go's IPO. Jim assured me that if we could demonstrate increasing profit margins and scope for growth in the European low-cost sector, we would be in great shape. I felt confident that both were within our grasp. He was eager to have me over to New York to speak at his annual conference in January 2002, and I enthusiastically agreed.

All the internal growth at Go made it even more important to keep running the company well day-to-day. Just a few days after the MBO, I was dining again at Pizza Express in Bishop's Stortford with Go colleagues to explain our plans and listen to what was new. Many sessions led by the director team were spent explaining the share options we gave to every employee. It was complicated because the shares were not yet quoted on the Stock Exchange. Everyone wanted to be able to look up a share price, multiply their shares by that figure and come up with a value. For many this was their first chance to own shares in any company. It took many hours from all of us, but especially Andrew and Dominic, to explain that you couldn't just look up easyJet's price and multiply the number of options to come up with a value. Creative thinking, but it made us pause at the low level of understanding among some of our colleagues. The share options that were issued were for Go's business, we explained. easyJet's share price reflected the value of shares in a completely separate company. While we were both in the same airline sector, you couldn't look at one company's share price and figure out how the other one would do. We explained that an option on a share in Go was a larger proportion of Go than one share in easyJet because we had created fewer shares, and this was important to know when looking in the newspaper at stock prices.

We went on to explain that the shares in Go were valued at just 10p each and that we hoped they would be worth 50 times that or £5 in three years when we went to IPO. It seemed too good to be true. But when we explained our plans of adding at least one new base per year, they could see that those 10p shares would only turn into £5 with an enormous amount of their own hard work.

Many were curious about the distribution of the 22.5 per cent of Go that I negotiated from 3i. Frankly, it was a nightmare. I have always tried hard to be fair to colleagues, but I knew I would make some people happier than others in distributing the shares. My starting point was the nineteen people who had bought their shares – not received options. The founder director and CEO deal was 8 per cent that had been hammered out separately with 3i because we contributed our multimillion-pound investment in the MBO. I then tried to give the other directors the chance to buy shares that might one day be worth a million pounds each, and the other senior managers enough to pay off their mortgages. It was an important moment for me and Guy when we paid off our mortgage. I figured it would be for them too.

Beyond the top team, I had almost 10 per cent more to share with current colleagues and another 3.5 per cent held in reserve for future employees. I didn't want all our new, post-MBO employees to feel like second-class citizens. They would pay more for their shares, but they would have a stake in our future too, since they would be part of building it. With Ed Winter's help and that of a spreadsheet he bashed together one weekend, I divided the shares for the remaining employees roughly in line with salary. Captains and our middle-management team received more than cabin crew and telephone sales people. I had reservations about my own shareholdings versus those of others, but on the whole I was satisfied that we had been fair. One of the early values at Go was to be 'honest and open'. I talked about my salary, bonus, money made on the first deal and all subsequent earnings. Sharing private information as the leader makes you squirm, but it takes away the veil of secrecy and made sure that I was honest about my own package. I was under no illusion that my frank colleagues at Go would have told me if I hadn't earned my keep.

Everyone wanted to understand the implications of the MBO. Ed and I even spent an afternoon with Chris Darke, the General Secretary of BALPA, the union that represents all unionised British pilots. He at first expressed caution on our share option plans, let alone our commitment to share 10 per cent of Go's profits with employees. At the time he shook his head with disbelief, but he came around to our way of working together.

The next step in the plan was to appoint a chairman. 3i and I were to make the appointment in full consultation, so I asked Carol Leonard, the former City journalist and now a leading executive headhunter and managing director of Leonard Hull, to seek references from a short list of possible candidates. On the list was a professional chairman called Keith Hamill, who had a strong finance background as Finance Director of Forte, the hotel group, and WH Smith, the high street retailers, and as chairman had guided a number of companies through stock market flotations. He had been an accountant and corporate businessman at a senior level for nearly twenty-five years, yet he was only touching fifty. Cigar-puffing Keith was driven up to Stansted from Chislehurst in his chauffeur-driven BMW to meet me on 2 July.

Keith was grounded in the traditional business world and was not yet experienced in the discounting model. He had come from the hotel and retail world where increasing prices was a virtue and costs were to be contained. It was a case of the New World discounter meeting the Old World value-added profit-taker.

'The investors know how tough you can be,' he said bluntly. 'So they don't want a shrinking violet as the chairman, do they? The Go chairman mustn't be a doormat and the investors need to have confidence about that.'

And I was equally clear that while I agreed that his job was to fire me if I didn't produce results, I wouldn't brook any interference in the running of the company. I needed help in preparing the company for flotation and grooming Andrew Cowen to become a public company finance director. I had worked well with my previous hands-off chairmen, Bob Ayling and Roger Maynard, and I didn't want any big changes. We got on just fine. We agreed on the way to run board meetings, and Keith's military control of the agenda was impressive. My next task was to find two more non-executive directors who could complete the board to enhance the prospects for a successful stock market flotation.

In those summer months after we completed the MBO, 3i were the model of restrained venture capital owners. They would dutifully turn up at board meetings with good questions. They remained 'observers', since 3i at the highest level were concerned about having 3i on the board of an airline. Presumably they felt this would somehow shield them from criticism should Go have a crash. Who knows, but they stuck to their curious observer status until the end. Barclays were more straightforward, and appointed Anton Wellenreiter as the board representative for their £20 million contribution to the MBO. They even approved with ease our decision to start World War Three by opening up flights between Dublin and Edinburgh and Glasgow Prestwick in Scotland – another strand of our strategy to make Scotland a secondary hub for Go.

Of course, we didn't realise that Michael O'Leary would take the move as a personal affront. We had insider reports of him screaming and swearing a blue streak when he heard the news. Go was becoming a threat to Ryanair, and they wasted millions of pounds of profit starting up on the Edinburgh route and dropping prices to £10 one-way on Glasgow too. You know you have a competitor's attention when they break a promise at the heart of their business model just to get you. It was general knowledge that they had promised no new routes from Dublin until their new airport deal was agreed with the Irish government, and to avoid flying to BAA's Edinburgh Airport until they lowered their charges. We were more of a threat to Michael O'Leary than high costs. Now this was a new tune. We didn't know whether to cheer or cry.

The Go board also agreed with the huge opportunity we

identified to move the more than 2 million ferry travellers between Northern Ireland and Scotland from sea to air. We ran ads encouraging people to avoid seasickness and sold seats at £25 each way. Unfortunately, easyJet either had the same idea or heard about our plans (probably from loose-lipped airport operators). They announced plans to start in summer 2001, whereas we were planning to begin in September. We leapt to the challenge, leased planes that allowed us to start up early, and beat our orange nemesis by starting up in early summer. Fares were ridiculously low, but the air market grew dramatically between Scotland and Belfast. We were determined not to be thwarted in our plans to grow Scotland into an important base for Go on our way to becoming Europe's best low-cost airline.

In those early months at Bristol we learned about the different customers in the West Country. In general we received rave reviews, but then we suffered a setback that was shown on local television. Some passengers were paying as much in excess baggage for their golf clubs to escape to the Algarve or Spain as they had for their seat. We shrugged and said 'tough' in the first instance, but the shouting grew louder. The success or failure of Go in Bristol would rest on these sorts of discretionary trips. After much analysis and deep intakes of breath, we did the right thing. We allowed customers to take a bag of clubs (or skis for that matter) with them as part of their luggage allowance, bending the rules on the precise weight. It felt dishonest to con people on board with very low fares then charge them a small fortune to bring the luggage that was the reason for the trip in the first place. The small loss of excess baggage revenue was more than offset by the loyalty of customers.

Making this kind of commonsense compromise with customers made excellent business sense too, since we were making millions in profits from these beach, golf and ski routes. Alicante, Faro and Malaga were stars out of Stansted and were sure to be in Bristol. We liked our golfers and wanted them to know it.

As a result of all the time I had spent with lawyers, investors, bankers and accountants doing the MBO, I felt a bit disconnected from the airline and day-to-day issues. Andrew Goodrum, Go's Head of Cabin Services, had himself trained to be a working member of crew. He regularly updated me on the issues facing cabin crew. At this time, they were finding the long flights and demanding customers to Faro and Malaga hard work. One of them retorted to Andrew that he and I should work with a crew one day to see how hard it was. So we did. It was the day from hell, but I wouldn't have missed it for the world.

On 10 July we started first thing out at the gate, tidying the aircraft for departure. A glitch was reported by the flight crew and engineers, but, no problem, we were lucky to have a spare plane nearby that we could steal to keep ourselves from being more than an hour late. Upon arriving at plane #2 another technical hitch developed and we were forced to wait several hours for the problems on plane #1 to be fixed.

So we decamped to the terminal to chat to the delayed passengers about this indeterminate, rolling delay that ended up at three hours. The crew were mortified to have me and Andrew Goodrum along, but they were brilliant.

Finally, everyone was boarded, we took off and I began my duties as the 'galley slave' (all I was good for, since I was not a qualified crew member and I was never a great waitress) making pots of cafetière coffee, tea and hot chocolate, while delivering supplies to colleagues serving these demanding customers. They may have been demanding, but they bought a lot of food, which was profitable for Go and earned the crew a tidy commission.

So far so good, until the captain was instructed by Go Operations at Stansted to divert our Faro-bound plane to Malaga to provide one of our extra crew members. Andrew

Goodrum was the fourth member, only three were legally required on our flight, and he would be rescuing a stranded Malaga–Bristol flight where a Go crew colleague had fallen seriously ill.

After much negotiation with Go Operations (and some unnecessary input from me), we did it all – saved the stranded Malaga flight (leaving Andrew Goodrum in Bristol and his car at Stansted!), delivered the London-to-Faro customers, and collected the Faro-to-London customers who were now four hours delayed. I spoke with customers and took flak from one who would probably miss a Madonna concert in London. I assured him that rock divas were usually late and hoped that Madge would deliver for me. On his way off the flight, another man thanked me for sticking my head above the parapet and said it was the only reason he would consider using us again.

My colleagues, Steve Traveller, Sylvia Goodchild and Natalie Holmes, were terrific, and I now graphically understood that delays were a huge burden to crews' lives as well as to customers. We were all shattered.

Notwithstanding my eventful day in the business, that summer of 2001 has to be seen as Go's golden age. In July and August alone we made over £10 million in profit. The Stansted operation was humming and the Bristol first summer surpassed our expectations. The 6 September board meeting was about growth and impressive profits. We thought the next six months would be busy with new base selections, choosing between Airbus and Boeing for new planes and preparing for an early IPO in late '02 or early '03. But there was a big dark cloud with Ryanair written on it.

'We misjudged it and we got a bloody nose on the Dublin route,' Keith Hamill, our chairman, later recalled. In July we announced that from September we would be taking on both Ryanair and Aer Lingus, with return flights from £50 to Edinburgh and £45 to Glasgow, including taxes. The management team had been unanimous about this decision – except for Andrew Cowen. He had urged caution and wondered if we knew what we were getting ourselves into. Wise man. Call it an adrenalin burst from the success of the MBO, but the rest of us (me included) thought we could pull it off.

Gung-ho Michael O'Leary must have been pumped up for this fight. 'This is going to be a disaster for Go,' he told the *Irish Times*, 'because the best they can manage is £45 as against our £29. Nobody will be flying with them except for the passengers they take off Aer Lingus.'

Then he snorted that we didn't even qualify as a low-cost airline! 'Their fares are 60 per cent higher than Ryanair's and they have a crap schedule. Their first flight out is at 10 a.m. We will be out and back at that stage. Goodbye Go,' he taunted. We got a thrashing on the route as Ryanair slashed prices even further. Going head-to-head cost us millions and we withdrew wounded.

We learned another crucial lesson about discounting. You can't take on someone with lower costs because they dig deeper than you to lower their prices and still make money while you're bleeding. There was no partial membership in the discounting game. We knew Ryanair's costs were much lower but easyJet's weren't. Andrew and Rob Platts did a special analysis comparing the three of us and explained how we could inch our costs down. Their conclusion? That we could lower our costs below easyJet's within months if we restructured our schedule to use crew more productively, reduced selling costs using the internet, and took advantage of falling aircraft lease costs.

Keith Hamill admitted that he initially did not buy into Go's discounting strategy. The received wisdom in the UK's retail industry over the years had been that you battled to get a dominant market position – then you bumped up the prices. He had done just that in the whisky industry fifteen years earlier. It was an accepted way to do business. In retrospect, he acknowledged, it was a lazy and destructive way to deal with customers and made your business vulnerable to nimble innovators. By the late 1990s, in many areas of the UK, deregulation and global competition was forcing change. Increases in technology were helping cut costs and the customers were now more demanding.

'The customer is becoming much more aware that they are being gouged,' he said. 'Which is why discounting is here to stay.' Keith was well on his way to becoming a discount disciple too.

Chapter Eighteen

September 11 and the True Discounters

My parents' generation used to say they knew exactly where they were when they heard of the assassination of John F. Kennedy in 1963. But I was too young to remember. I was only three and the death of the US president in Dallas on 22 November went right over my youthful head.

September 11 2001 was another such day. It was unimaginable that hijackers could fly two jets into the World Trade Center, killing close to three thousand people and causing the tallest buildings in New York to collapse. It was even more horrific because we watched it happen.

The day for me had started up like many Tuesdays. I was up at 5.30 a.m. to head up to Bedfordshire to ride Peter (a retired advanced eventing horse known competitively as Huntwyck). He and my coach, Nick Turner, had kept me sane over the previous two years of Go craziness. An hour's ride before work put a spring in my step, readying me for the day. I needed it this day.

I first heard the sketchy news during a lunchtime meeting in my goldfish bowl at Enterprise House. The first reports suggested that some joker in a light aircraft had flown too close to

the Twin Towers. Then one of the guys in the office logged on
to the internet and the full horror began to emerge. At 8.46
a.m., New York time, just before 2 p.m. in London, an
American Airlines Boeing 767, Flight 11 from Boston, with
nearly 10,000 gallons of fuel on board, hit the north face of the
North Tower of the World Trade Center. From that moment
the world changed for ever. We did not have a television in the
office at this stage but we followed the day on various web-sites
with increasing alarm. About fifteen minutes after the first
crash, a second airliner, United Flight 175 from Boston, hit the
South Tower of the World Trade Center. All flights across
America were grounded and every airline in the world went
into a major security alert. We then heard that another plane,
American Flight 77, hit the Pentagon. Just after 10 a.m. in New
York the South Tower collapsed, followed under an hour later
by the North Tower. It was chilling to think that this atrocity
could happen in the city where I use to live and work and have
many friends.

Then the fourth plane, where the passengers are believed to
have overcome the hijackers, crashed in Somerset County,
Pennsylvania. What these people went through in their last
moments of life on what was meant to be a routine internal
flight across America is still too shocking for me to dwell upon.

The sense of danger and foreboding was even more real for
all of us at Go because we were running an airline. For the next
few hours after the two Boeing passenger jets were flown into
the World Trade Center, we were concerned that a plane could
be heading for the tall buildings at Canary Wharf in East
London. What was more troubling – it could be one of our
planes.

The confusion of that day would stay with us all. As an airline
chief executive on the day of the disaster my overriding priority was to ensure my planes were safe and all our passengers and
crew accounted for. The struggle afterwards was to keep the

airline running in light of the new security measures and to do all I could to restore faith in air travel.

But we had to be professional and decisive to deal with our own problems. Stansted Airport is one of the most secure in the UK, but a feeling of confusion nevertheless began to set in. Faxes came sputtering out of our machines from the UK government and their significance had to be interpreted by our head of security, Peter Griffiths. But we were left scratching our heads on some of the directives. Peter, Ed and I tried to understand what we needed to do.

That afternoon Keith Hamill, our chairman, was heading to the United States on business. He later recalled: 'I was on a flight ready for take-off at Heathrow and we were stuck at the edge of the runway. As the delay went on we were allowed to switch our mobiles back on and Barbara rang me.' I'd phoned him to keep him in the loop. It would have been a gaffe if a reporter had phoned him first and he hadn't been up to speed.

Keith said he was impressed with our initial responses. 'I thought they did a terrific job under the circumstances. Barbara and her team put in place their emergency contingency plans very quickly.'

Go's passengers were subdued and crews mechanically completed the day's flights. Passengers viewed each other suspiciously and kept a close eye on the cockpit door – a practice that has stayed with many. The thought of what all those crew and passengers went through in America just a few hours earlier cast a pall over the operation. Flying would never be quite the same again.

Security was the most immediate issue. In the late afternoon of the 11th, Peter Griffiths, Go's head of security and a Go pilot, received a fax from the British government with a series of changes to security procedures for UK airlines and airports.

We spent a long night's vigil at Stansted trying to understand what the UK government wanted us to do given the higher risk we all now faced. Late that night, I even spoke to Mike Hodgkinson, then the Chief Executive of the BAA, who was liaising with the Department of Transport. I was very concerned that the procedures for searching planes and passengers weren't fully thought through. They appeared as across-the-board instructions for all airports and seemed illogical.

Separating arriving and departing international passengers is a major part of good security. Unlike Gatwick and Heathrow, Stansted was already one of the 'cleanest' airports in the UK, with a very high degree of separation.

'We really need some guidance from you here. How long are you going to shut this airport? Are you satisfied that we are complying with the government's new security procedures? When are our passengers going to be able to fly and what do we do next?' I blasted down the phone late into the night of the 11th.

'The picture is still very hazy, Barbara, and we are trying to find out what the government is expecting of us,' Mike replied.

In my increasingly heated conversation with him, I said that if the UK government didn't want us to fly, then we would have to shut the airline operation down until the level of threat was better understood and the security procedures agreed with airlines.

While I was fighting with the top security brass, my colleagues at Go responded with speed and good humour, once again demonstrating our finest characteristic, Warrior Spirit. We also stuck to the mantra we often repeated to ourselves when we were tackling the crisis of the moment: 'We'll get passengers to where they paid to go – no matter what.'

The UK government ruled that all bags must be X-rayed and random searches conducted at the normal security access point, but then searched once more just before boarding. The difficulty was that we were given the instructions by the government just a few hours before we needed to start checking customers in on 12 September. We worked with the airport to establish additional checkpoints to hand-search all carry-on bags and passengers again before they boarded the plane. There was no possible way that the airport could hire all the additional security people required, so the Go employees volunteered their time to stand beside trained security people to conduct the searches that did not require special training.

By now, the airport was in a real mess, but we were the only airline with finance people, telesales agents, marketing, pilots, cabin crew, management and others talking to customers to explain the new security procedures. We had quite a job persuading passengers that nail scissors needed to be confiscated but ballpoint pens were acceptable on board. People came in on their days off to help, and some joined the security team.

The Go team were brilliant. There were more than a hundred volunteers. To speed up these secondary searches, we asked customers to take an absolute minimum on board as hand baggage. Go colleagues handed out WH Smith carrier bags for passengers to transfer a few necessities from their hand baggage that now needed to go in the hold. Karna Gupta, Adrian Cairns, Tom Edwards and Pak Chen Ho from Revenue Management were particularly adept at sweet-talking the critical carrier bags from the WH Smith sales people. According to their boss, Fred Kochak, they even did their best to answer unanswerable queries about delayed flights, flights not appearing on the airport monitors and cancelled flights. (Once or twice, they even had to do a bit of foreign language translation! Adrian speaks French, Karna speaks Spanish, Chen speaks Cantonese and Tom speaks German!)

The first few days were chaotic, but quick thinking and offering passengers as much information as possible kept Go's operation running much more smoothly than any other airline at Stansted. We were also asked to step up security around the aircraft themselves. Challenging people without a valid, visible

ID was part of the new vigilance. We alerted our cabin crew and flight crew and assigned additional duties to enhance our own security.

The mood was very serious, as we all were concerned about additional terrorist attacks. But there were lighter moments too. Rob Platts, Go's Financial Planning Manager, agreed to take on some plane-guarding duties until the crews could be properly briefed.

'Armed with my calculator and ruler, I headed out to keep an eye on the aircraft in those first few hours after September 11. I was then redeployed to take nail scissors off little old ladies as they boarded the plane. Being a finance professional at Go certainly widened my horizons!' Before joining Go, Rob had been a financial analyst for oil exploration and production company Lasmo. Talking to airline passengers was a long way from spreadsheets and analysis of oilfields.

Changes in Europe's airline industry started with full deregulation in 1997 and had allowed the low-cost airlines to gain a foothold. Now the pace of change would increase dramatically because of the September 11 attacks. What otherwise would have taken years occurred in months. And Go was well positioned to survive and prosper. Within days, the catalogue of airline casualties grew longer. Already suffering from the weakening US economy, many traditional airlines in the US and Europe faced a mortal blow from the loss of revenue from a halt in US domestic and transatlantic traffic. This loss of revenue was particularly devastating because many of them were already in poor financial shape, with bloated costs and inefficient operations.

After the Gulf War in 1991, seven US carriers were forced to file for bankruptcy, with three – Eastern, Pan Am and Midway – consigned to history. After the Twin Towers attacks, most of the major American airlines faced ruin. United Airlines chopped 20,000 jobs, as did American Airlines, while Northwest cut 10,000 jobs. Boeing, faced with a collapse in orders, laid off 30,000 workers, and even Southwest deferred delivery of their new Boeing 737-700s. In late 2001, President George W. Bush, who couldn't be seen to allow terrorism to succeed, signed a $15 billion aid package for the airline industry to ease the financial crisis, which the US Congress approved.

But financial difficulties were not restricted to the US. Virgin Atlantic moved quickly and shed 1,200 jobs, while British Airways was forced to lay off hundreds of pilots. The Belgian flag-carrier Sabena said it would not last beyond the year end, and didn't. Swissair ceased operations and Lufthansa, Air France and KLM all felt the heat. The mayhem was then compounded by the ensuing Afghanistan conflict and threats of war in Iraq. Even Australia's second biggest airline, Ansett, Rod Eddington's old company, which was teetering on the brink of bankruptcy, folded on 12 September, pushed over the edge by the acts of violence in the US.

And while these airlines turned inwards to try to survive, Go was recruiting pilots from all the troubled airlines. We found ourselves with excellent candidates from the UK and the Continent who had almost instantly lost their jobs. Go was one of the very few airlines in Europe continuing to grow.

Go was also one of the first airlines back in the newspapers advertising low fares on Monday 17 March. We knew customers would need more incentive to fly than usual and we gave it to them. The strong summer profits of 2001 had been fabulous for Go, and we were on track to hit our planned £10.8 million profit. But by mid-September bookings had collapsed. We were looking at empty planes from October onwards. Travellers were cautious, and fewer people took a holiday during the normal school half-term break. A financial plan to lower costs was quickly put together by Derek Patterson, and we followed its progress as if it were a military campaign.

At one of our emergency team meetings we made a vow –

that no one at Go should lose their job. It was Dominic, our Director of People, who put it most eloquently: 'We've asked everybody to believe in what we are doing here at Go. We asked them to work with us without a pay rise for three years. We said that everyone would share in our success after the MBO. We just cannot make anyone redundant, it would be wrong.'

Dominic was spot-on. I think our new investors and directors, Tom, Angela and Keith, were shocked; they had never seen a business that acted like this. But they could see by the look in our eyes that we meant it, and we got results. So they humoured us. Paul Sterbenz was 100 per cent on our side as he attended one of his very first board meetings.

Everywhere I went, Go colleagues would ask for my thoughts and opinion. I wanted to be as optimistic as I could be. Constant communication was the only way: through regular emails, memos and group meetings. People appreciated my weekly message, recorded from my mobile phone late on Fridays or in my study at home on a Saturday morning after I'd been out for my early morning canter. They were chatty and informal. I wanted everyone to feel that they were sitting right there with me.

'We will explore every alternative idea rather than chopping jobs,' I said. This was my first hint that the upcoming round of pay discussions was not going to yield a rise. We were all lucky to have our jobs.

We were extremely lean, but there was always one more squeeze to be made. I wrote a begging letter to all of our suppliers asking them to help us. I explained the dire situation. I even phoned some of our bigger partners: 'I'm sorry, I really don't like doing this, but I am asking that you review your costs with a view to taking a 10 per cent reduction.'

You could sense the silent gulps on the end of the line.

'I'm doing this right across the board,' I would then assure them. 'If we can lower our costs now, we will be one of the winners next year who will be growing and developing. That will be good for your business too. How many airline customers do you have who are planning for 40 per cent growth next year?'

Under normal circumstances, most would have told us to go and take a hike. Perhaps rightly so. But one by one we received their backing, as it meant keeping hold of our business. Even with reduced margins they would benefit from our healthy growth in the future. But some projects had to be shelved, like our plan to spend £1 million on a parallel web-site, which was postponed indefinitely. It would have been nice to have a back-up system, but we were fighting to secure a future for the airline.

A bright spot was the plummeting cost of leasing a 737-300 aircraft. Prices dropped below $150k per month, making our original leases at $235k seem very high. Growing when you could source high-quality planes at historically low prices was a huge competitive advantage.

Our credibility with Go colleagues and suppliers was helped by our bold decision to start up on Newcastle–Stansted. Derek Wright, a First Officer with Go, came from Newcastle and had been sending me emails for some time extolling the virtues of flights between Stansted and Newcastle. He regularly popped in to see me and Steven Horner to make sure we hadn't forgotten about Newcastle. The route had been on Steven's radar, and he heard that a few days after September 11 Gill Airways, based in Newcastle, was shutting down for ever and the route was going to be wide open. Steven, his team and colleagues around the airline did the swiftest-ever airport negotiations and route analysis. We brought the recommendation to the Go board at the end of September and were flying by the first of November. Steven's decision was brave, swift and correct. We made money from the start. The growth impressed our suppliers that we were here to stay. It also helped everyone at Go feel more secure to see the company growing when the rest of the airline world was falling apart.

Amid the security repercussions, another brewing nightmare was the rising cost of insurance. There was even fear that insurance would be permanently withdrawn for airlines. High levels of cover are required as part of the leases we hold on the aircraft. No insurance, no planes. This was getting serious. The UK government stepped in temporarily as the insurer of last resort and kept UK airlines flying. But as the private insurers began to regroup and reassess risk, we saw our annual insurance costs skyrocket overnight from £1 million to £6 million.

In late September, Stelios, Ray Webster (easyJet's Chief Executive), Ed Winter and I met with the UK government to plead our case for the government to intervene and control insurance costs. We all agreed that subsidies should not be offered to airlines, because the traditional airlines would use them to subsidise routes they had no business flying. We didn't make much progress on the insurance costs, but the subsidies to British Airways, bmi and Virgin didn't happen. It was one of those rare moments when we were on the same side of an issue as easyJet.

We felt we had no choice but to apply an insurance surcharge on every seat sold. We couldn't recoup the higher costs from passengers who had already bought a seat, but we were able to cover the costs of future travellers. It always feels like a failure to a discounter to increase prices, but we ring-fenced this one to make sure we could reduce it if insurance costs came down again.

There was a lot of speculation in the newspapers that the heightened security would destroy the low-cost sector. Some of our competitors complained that punctuality was never going to recover. Of course, in the early days we did incur extra delays, but soon we had integrated the changes into our ways of working. We weren't going to use the changes since September 11 as an excuse for being late. We just had to dig deep, find other areas to compensate and use that Go Warrior Spirit. It worked: in November, Go's domestic flights had an amazing punctuality record of 89 per cent of flights leaving within fifteen minutes of schedule.

We felt we were really beginning both to crack the new security regime and to manage our operation well as we headed into November. So you'll understand why I exploded when I received a phone call from David Magliano telling me that the *Daily Mirror* newspaper was about to run an exposé on how a reporter managed to stroll on to a Go plane in the engineering company FLS's facility unchallenged by any of the engineers or security people.

David and Brandon Stockwell at our PR firm, Cohn and Wolfe, tried to contain the story, but at 3.00 a.m. David woke me with the bad news.

'It's worse than we expected, Barbara. We need to be ready for all the news services to pick this up.'

I had consulted Ed Winter and Mike Williams to understand the security breach.

'How could FLS have let this happen?' I wanted to know.

'It was not supposed to happen. I knew that FLS's secondary hangar facility was less secure and told them not to use it for our planes,' explained a frustrated Mike.

'I want to speak to the CEO of FLS, now,' was my response.

And I had a few choice words for him and left him in no uncertain position that our business was at risk with them. As I calmed down, I also began to listen to Mike and his team. The security breach was important, but that aircraft would never have been brought back into service without a thorough search. None of Go's passengers or employees had been at real risk, but it was an embarrassment we just didn't need.

So we were ready when the early BBC's morning newspaper review mentioned the *Mirror*'s front-page splash. And it really looked as bad as it sounded. The tabloid reporter and a photographer walked unchallenged into an airport servicing area and then climbed on board one of our Boeing 737s, which was being worked on by FLS, the Danish conglomerate who did all our engineering.

The *Mirror* reporter was pictured at the flight controls on the front page and the paper devoted pages 1, 2, 3 and 4 to saying that 'an astonishing security lapse at one of Britain's busiest airport is exposed today'. There was even an editorial from Chris Yates, an aviation security expert, who said 'the appalling complacency must end'.

The two journalists spent an hour inside the engineering area.

'We've really been caught out on this one,' I moaned.

We took advice from a number of sources. The advice was pretty clear: 'The only way to deal with this is to acknowledge the lapse and say what we're doing to fix it.' So we did just that. No interviews, just a written statement and soft discussions behind the scenes by David Magliano. In a statement I told the paper that we'd been equally shocked, outlined our discussions to tighten things up with FLS and Stansted Airport, and I thanked them for their sense of public duty. Another calm moment in the life of an airline CEO.

All the low-cost players were now back in the market, discounting and trying to get the travelling public back on their planes. Ryanair began an aggressive ad campaign challenging people to stand up, be counted and show those terrorists by taking a flight, using General Kitchener in their ads. Their prices were unbelievable, so were ours.

At a board meeting in mid-November, Steven Horner, David Magliano and I all spoke like born-again evangelists about the merits of discounting. It was the moment of truth for our venture capital backers and our traditional 'push the price up' chairman. Sam Walton, the Wal-Mart creator, was right all along. You had to believe that continually lowering prices – in our case to fill up the planes – was the best way to run the business. It was counter-intuitive for those who had worked for traditional businesses, but it was time to become full members of the discounting club

'There is a conflict between pricing and profitability,' explained Steven Horner. 'We have been trying to maximise profitability. At first we thought that making our lowest prices hard to find would help push our average prices up. Instead it means you fly around with half-filled planes and develop a reputation for being only lowish-priced. But if we keep our costs low and fill our seats, then revenues and profits will follow. It is an act of faith. Customers need to know we're always low-priced. We have to behave more like Asda and Wetherspoons if we are to win our share.'

In November our load factor was 83 per cent which compared to 77 per cent the year before. More and more seats were being sold at the lowest price – now at 60 per cent of seats.

Steven was right. Keith Hamill admitted later: 'I was moved by the persuasiveness of all of this, and so was Tom. Barbara and the team were telling us to drive up volume and the profit will look after itself. It was a brave thing to do.'

Hallelujah, here were two more hardened old-school business types embracing the gospel of the discount disciples. It must have been a permanent conversion, because Keith subsequently went on to become chairman of a no-frills hotel group.

Even though the profit picture was still uncertain, we took the decision to set up our third base in the East Midlands, which was announced on 13 December 2001. We were working hard to keep the company in the news as a low-priced aggressive competitor who was going to emerge a winner from the mêlée of post-September 11. In September, October and November, I kept Go in the public eye, speaking to several thousand people in speeches in London, Norwich and Glasgow. The company may have been sent reeling from the temporary impact of September 11, but we were beginning to see how we might emerge stronger.

I also began to take a more aggressive stance on the need for airports to get their costs down if their catchment areas wanted the benefits of low-priced air travel. At a business breakfast in Glasgow I announced that we would be opening a new international base. Much applause! But there was only one hitch: it wasn't going to be in Scotland. Between sips of coffee and nibbles on breakfast, I discussed the benefits of East Midlands as our next new base, with flights to Alicante, Malaga, Faro and Prague at £59 return – and Glasgow and Edinburgh from a startling £25 return. The Scots were stunned and felt snubbed. The reasons for choosing East Midlands over Scotland were simple: lower airport costs and more people. Go would not be opening a base in Scotland until the airport costs came down. It made me check my croissant for arsenic, but the message had to be clear. I blamed the airport operator, BAA Scotland. Their intransigence had also kept us out of Gatwick. I completely disagreed with easyJet's decision to fly from Gatwick paying the undiscounted airport charge, because I thought it would destroy their cost structure. I was disappointed to walk away from Gatwick and Scotland, but keeping our costs low had to be a mantra. Once they escape from your grasp, there's no getting them back. A lesson easyJet would no doubt learn.

Our decision to use East Midlands as a base gave complacent British Midland an electric shock, and they woke up with the announcement of bmibaby, their improbably named low-cost operation. We had a good laugh at the name but took them seriously. British Midland had an established position in the area. We knew we were in for a fight, but we were ready. Go was much tougher and more aggressive now, and we started flying from East Midlands on 14 March with 56 flights a week, giving away over 10,000 free seats for starters. bmibaby was too little, too late, and Go captured the imaginations of the people in the area.

And as we headed into Christmas 2001, we eagerly awaited

the all-important New Year's booking surge. We felt we were on track. Costs were lower, we'd returned to our normal high punctuality, our colleagues had come through by supporting our request for no pay rise, Bristol was a shining example of what a low-cost airline can do for a community, the new Newcastle route was an early success, and East Midlands had the hallmarks of a winner.

But until we saw the post-Christmas sales, we wouldn't know whether we'd turned the corner financially. I hoped and felt that it could be the turning point. That would be something. Even after September 11 dried up travel and insurance costs skyrocketed we were clawing our way back. When I make a financial commitment I like to keep it.

Back in the office after Christmas, Dominic Laurie and the marketing team were making final preparations for the advertising and selling blitz. Prices were lower, ads were more aggressive, and our first indication that we were on to a winner was when we released the summer schedule to our favoured email database customers and they bought up seats to the Med in droves. Life was returning to normality; people were planning trips for the summer.

September 11 and the events of the next few months were testing, but we emerged stronger. We were now real discounters, proud of it and with full planes to prove it. That autumn also saw us winning some prestigious travel awards. We were voted the best low-cost airline in Britain by the readers of the *Telegraph* (ousting easyJet from its top position over the two previous years). We also won the top low-cost award from *Business Traveller* magazine. I collected the prize from the Princess Royal with Nicola Judge and Sheila Mahon, the top Go MAD award winners.

The award that meant the most to me was winning a write-in election vote against Stelios from readers in the *Telegraph* for the honour of Entrepreneur of the Year. The award was special for several reasons: it was for men *and* women, it was a vote among regular readers (with my in-laws, Shirley and Terence Davis, and their friends responsible for many of the votes!), and it was from those same readers who had also voted Go their favourite airline. The award sits proudly in my living room today.

With survival assured, business picking up, a dramatic 40 per cent growth planned for 2002, and accolades rolling in, we felt poised to make huge strides towards our goal of floating the company and becoming Europe's best low-cost airline.

Chapter Nineteen

Going Easy

As Christmas 2001 approached we were steaming ahead with our plans for flotation. We had agreed with 3i that taking the company to the stock market in three years would be ideal. They wanted a return on their investment and I wanted control of the company more widely dispersed. We had also begun work on the biggest and most audacious decision we had ever contemplated – a $2 billion aircraft order that would propel our growth for years to come. The flotation was an integral part of our plans, because the new capital we would raise from the stock market would allow us to finance the purchase of these planes at the lowest possible cost.

With a view to our future public company status, our board was now first class. Keith Hamill was fulfilling his role as chairman preparing us for flotation. We looked to Wal-Mart and Southwest Airlines, both global leaders in discounting, for our other board members. I asked our old friend Paul Sterbenz to join the board for his management wisdom and superb low-cost airline credentials to chair the board safety committee. Richard Baker, then a senior director at Asda (owned by Wal-Mart) and now Chief Executive of Boots, was introduced to me by 3i and we hit it off immediately. He is a retailer who believes in low costs and low prices, and he shared our views on customers and employees. I knew he would help us fulfil our discounting ambitions while challenging the team constructively. This was a board that would help build the business and would look great in an IPO prospectus.

Most important, we had overcome the September 11 crisis. When we'd sat down in October to assess our financial position we thought we'd be lucky to make £3 million profit for the year because forward bookings had slowed down so much. But all of the work to increase revenue through higher loads and lower prices was working. And our cost-cutting results were better than hoped for. The whole of the low-cost sector was benefiting from the turmoil of the traditional airlines. We finally saw Lufthansa withdraw from Munich–Stansted and SAS withdraw from Copenhagen–Stansted. They could never make money competing against us and were unable to afford their spoiling tactics any longer. Our base at Bristol had been profitable from day one and continued to perform well. Bookings for the winter season were well up on the previous year and early bookings for the summer season were promising.

In early December, as I was on my way to Blackfriars Tube station, Keith phoned with a bolt from the blue. He told me that both easyJet and Ryanair had approached 3i and were interested in buying Go. My initial reaction combined shock – we'd only just done the MBO for God's sake! – and annoyance that 3i hadn't called me directly themselves. But as I thought more, I quickly concluded that these approaches were going to be just an annoying distraction, not a real concern. After all, hadn't 3i built their reputation through patiently backing management – not by flipping their companies to shark-like competitors for a quick buck? Besides, 3i had committed to work with us towards a flotation within three years and we were on track to get there.

3i said that easyJet's interest was probably just a ploy to get a look at our books. Keith had also been pretty robust when he got a call from Amir Eilon, a Stelios sidekick who had been an investment banker and was now the dealmaker on easyJet's board. 'Now look, we're not interested in selling Go unless you offer us a crazy price. Goodbye,' he said, and put the phone down.

Nevertheless, 3i wanted to pursue discussions, and as the majority shareholder they had that right. But I was irritated that they were prepared to even consider selling out, and wasting our time along the way. When I pushed for a reason their response was a non-committal insistence that all enquiries of interest in their investments must be investigated. I suppose the DNA of any venture capitalist is programmed never to close a door on a potential deal. And so, against my wishes, discussions began.

I resolved to quietly endure the distraction. I briefed the directors, as well as Andrew Cowen's deputy, Derek Patterson, and Ed Winter's deputy, Mike Coltman, on the approaches and asked them to provide 3i with the analysis and information they wanted for their discussions. I brought my indispensable assistant, Julie Naulls, into the loop too. She had been a huge help during the MBO and I always confided in her. She would have to keep the project secret and support me keeping the office running smoothly – even remembering birthdays and Go weddings. But I was determined that everyone else would stay focused on running our business, preparing for 40 per cent growth in 2002, and making progress on our massive $2 billion aircraft purchase decision.

The Ryanair enquiry quickly proved to be a red herring. Their investment bankers, Morgan Stanley, appear to have been just fishing around for possible deals to occupy their M&A team in the post-internet boom deal drought. In any case, why would Michael O'Leary want to buy us now, having turned down a much less expensive opportunity to buy us just six months before and after endlessly bad-mouthing us in the press? But easyJet was more persistent.

Andrew and Derek spent some time putting financial information together for 3i for their discussions with easyJet, but our real focus was on buying planes. Which aircraft type should we buy? Would it be Airbus or Boeing? How many should we order and how would we pay for them? These were the fundamental choices taxing our combined brains. Our $2 billion aircraft decision would have repercussions for the next twenty years.

The conditions were perfect for making such a bold move. After September 11, the bottom had fallen out of the aircraft market. Orders from the traditional airline customers had dried up and the low-cost airlines were the only game in town. So the aircraft manufacturers were offering fabulous deals to get business from the low-cost carriers. Boeing had just secured a big order from Ryanair, and we were aware that easyJet was also in the market for new planes. We were worried that the best deals would disappear if both Ryanair and easyJet had placed their orders and so we were in a race against easyJet.

We were initially tempted to hire external consultants, but decided to rely on our own analysis. I preferred to build up our in-house understanding rather than use assistance from outsiders whose motivations could be suspect. Call me cynical. Ed and Andrew led the work, with help from Steven Horner, who had acquired so much knowledge from his time working at the regional aircraft manufacturer Bombardier, some years earlier. Rob Platts built the financial models, learning and improving them as we went along. Andrew was understandably very careful with the analysis, because we had never bought planes before. But we hadn't started up an airline before tackling Go.

Ed and Andrew met regularly with Boeing and Airbus to

negotiate the lowest prices and best terms. We had three options: we could switch the entire fleet to Airbus; we could continue to fly Boeing but buy their new generation 737-700s or larger 737-800s; or we could take advantage of the bargain-basement price for young but used 737-300s – our current plane in the used aircraft market.

Our best option was to go for all new Airbus planes. The ideal fleet would comprise A320s as the workhorse, together with a few larger A321s for use on high-volume routes to Alicante and Malaga. This mix of planes would give very low unit costs, because both had more seats per plane than our Boeing 737s and we could still use flight and cabin crew interchangeably between the aircraft. If planes were not completely interchangeable the risks increased of having stranded customers when a technical problem occurred. By buying new, we would also have low maintenance costs for the first five years. The main drawback was that we would have to go through the arduous process of changing over from our existing all-Boeing fleet, because we could not afford the added complexity and considerably higher engineering costs of operating with planes from two manufacturers. So an important part of the analysis was arranging the transition to reach an all-Airbus fleet in a minimum of time.

Planning the financing of the planes was complicated. We wanted to take advantage of the generous financing that Airbus was offering, but this depended on whether we would have sufficient capital to make the down payments to buy the planes ourselves, or would have to lease from one of the aircraft-leasing companies. Up to that point all of our planes had been leased, because our limited capital had been used to finance start-up costs. We preferred to buy if we could because the overall cost would be lower.

We were beginning to make good profits, but they were needed to build up some financial reserves to keep the CAA happy. A flotation would give us the opportunity to raise the capital needed to buy the planes. As we met with the leading executives at both aircraft manufacturers in late December to increase the pressure to get the best deal, the thought of selling out to easyJet could not have been further from our minds.

But easyJet's interest continued, and just after Christmas Amir Eilon called Tom Sweet-Escott of 3i again with the terms of an offer: 'We've been to see our bankers to get their support to make an offer for your business. We'll give you £390 million, some in cash and the rest in easyJet shares. And that's a firm commitment. But we are only talking if you don't involve anyone else,' he added.

Tom was obviously intrigued. Keith and Tom reached me on a conference call: 'Barbara, at this price level and seriousness we have no choice but to let them go ahead with due diligence.' That's the process which allows them to look very closely at our business and financial accounts.

'I still think they are trying it on, Keith. And I don't see the point of going further if Go could be worth three times as much in less than three years. The only cash deal you should be willing to look at is a minimum of £500 million.' I was still highly suspicious.

3i still wanted to pursue it, and hired investment bankers Greenhill, an M&A boutique not unlike the one Guy had worked at for a decade, to help with negotiations. I wanted Charlie Geffen at Ashursts on the legal side, and 3i acceded. None of the Go team attended any of the discussions.

My main concern at that stage was to limit the amount of sensitive commercial information we handed over to easyJet and their advisers. Access to route-by-route profit information was non-negotiable. They would have to own us to see the secret to our success – the Summer Sun routes. I was unimpressed with the offer, and I had been through enough inconclusive deal negotiations to know that discussions could be called off at any time. But for the first time I was worried. Would 3i really want to sell out so quickly? From their point of view, £390 million looked one hell of a good deal compared with the total investment of £137 million just six months before.

But we had bigger ambitions. Our business was going so well. When I walked through our offices, or visited the check-in area, or went to our new base in Bristol, I was energised by the positive Go culture that we had created. I could feel the Warrior Spirit that had seen us through our period of punishing start-up losses and kept us strong through the September 11 crisis. When I went down to deliver some decent coffee and donuts to the early morning flight crews I could see they were tickled to see me there at 6 a.m. There was a powerful connection that spread around Go like a happy virus, a mood of real optimism in the air.

I could see that 3i found easyJet's offer attractive, but I felt that it was a steal compared to what Go would be worth in a flotation. So, at my insistence, throughout the winter we held a series of meetings to discuss the attractiveness of an early stock market flotation versus a sale to easyJet. We looked at the stock market valuations of easyJet, Ryanair and other similar US airlines. Basically, for a back-of-an envelope estimate you take profits before depreciation, financing and leasing costs and multiply it by a magic number. This estimates the value of the company before deducting your debt and the capital value of your leases. The magic number multiplier for low-cost airlines was significantly higher than that for traditional carriers. The multiplier relates to how profitable the company is and whether the growth prospects look good. For airlines like British Airways it was around 7 or 8 times. For Ryanair it was over 20 times. We settled for a conservative multiplier of around 12 times – much less than easyJet or Ryanair – and came up with a valuation of close to £1 billion in less than three years.

None of this was really news to 3i, because it squared with our joint analysis when we came together to buy Go from British Airways just six months earlier. Our spring and summer season revenues had taken off in January, and I now began to think that we might even exceed our £10 million profit target. And if we could do this well in the year of September 11, imagine how well we could do without a crisis! We were doing our bit by creating the profits and the stock markets were doing their bit by giving low-cost airlines good valuations. So, to my mind, why would you take easyJet's £390 million if you could have £1 billion? All we needed was a little patience from 3i.

For six months, Andrew and I had been planning a trip to New York in late January to present Go's plans and results to Jim Parker's important low-cost airline investor conference, which would be attended by several hundred investors who already understood the sector. I hoped this trip would help convince 3i to bide their time and wait for the big payout.

The presentation in New York couldn't have gone better. Andrew and I had an early spot on the agenda and we told the Go story with gusto. But we were reminded again of easyJet's unwelcome interest by Stelios's slightly eerie presence at the back of the enormous hall taking notes on our slides before he talked about easyJet's successful first year as a public company later that day.

We then met with individual investors. Some were so eager to invest in Go that they proposed investing before we floated on the stock market. I thought that this might be a good option if 3i were so eager to get some of their money out. On the way to JFK to fly home, I shared a taxi with an investor from Los Angeles who told me that there weren't many opportunities to invest in low-cost airlines. She had just been forced to sell some of her valuable position in Ryanair because the company had grown so big and was eager to invest in other publicly traded shares in fast-growing low cost airlines. So with a skip in my step, I headed back to London confident that we would all wake up soon from the bad dream of easyJet's bid.

But one aspect of the trip to New York nagged at me. The US investors assumed that the money raised from selling Go shares on the stock market would be used to fund growth – i.e. new aircraft purchases and setting up new bases throughout Europe. This would make it difficult for 3i to take their money out of Go. Andrew and I mentioned 3i's interest in getting their money out and the New York investor looked quizzically at us and asked why would they want to? To his way of thinking, 3i should want to stay in to get an even greater return. It sounded sensible to us, but 3i weren't on the same page.

The debate with 3i and Greenhill about the stock market value of Go and their negotiations with easyJet continued through the winter. As our financial performance and position continued to strengthen, I became more and more convinced of the folly of pursuing the easyJet offer.

The talks picked up pace throughout a bleak and chilly February. My drive to work in the darkness was punctuated with snatched mobile calls and with listening to Ayn Rand's *Atlas Shrugged*, a book about how the 'system' crushed one woman's efforts to keep a transcontinental railway alive. Once a week, I would treat myself to a ride to Stansted with Stephen Phillips, who ran his own chauffeur-driven Mercedes people carrier. I paid with my own money and made sure people knew. There would be no CEO Jags at Go. This was my time to catch up with all the documents and analysis being generated for the negotiations. I used to lay them all out on the other empty seats in Stephen's people carrier.

In February, Guy and I took the children to Gleneagles Hotel in Scotland with Denise Pritchard. We stayed for a few days and rode horses, swam and explored the lovely wintry Perthshire countryside. Between activities, I disappeared into our magnif- icent suite with its view of the foothills of the Highlands (upgraded courtesy of the management with my thanks!). I sat for hours of conference calls with Greenhill, 3i and Ashursts debating tactics. It was all very hush-hush and I had to collect secret deal faxes personally, much to the surprise of the helpful team at Gleneagles who would have been happy to hand-deliver them to me. As I sat on the phone I struggled to contain my impatience and continually tried to steer the conversation back to the potential stock market value of Go.

At a critical meeting at 3i's offices at Waterloo in March, Ed, Andrew, Steven, David, Dominic and I were outnumbered by investment bankers and 3i. Once again we argued that Go's performance was excellent. Profits were now above budget, the new Bristol base was humming, and our unit cost reductions were pulling us ahead of easyJet. Damn it, we were on a roll. The prospects for a successful stock market flotation were excellent, weren't they? Andrew chimed in that the new New York-based low-cost airline jetBlue's upcoming spring flotation in the US was looking very good. The brokers were expecting it to be heavily oversubscribed, even with the nervy post-9/11 stock markets.

Then there was a silence. easyJet had by now improved their offer and were offering £325 million in cash and £75 million in easyJet shares. Tom spoke slowly.

'By my calculations, even if Go successfully floats in late 2002, 3i would not be able to cash in its investment in Go until 2004,' he told us.

Our arguments hadn't worked. 3i had already made up its mind. They couldn't resist the prospect of cashing in on easyJet's offer. The debate on the public flotation was over.

Inside the Waterloo headquarters of 3i the pressure had been mounting for several months. Their performance had been woeful. In October they had announced a drop of £1.1 billion in investment value for the previous half-year, including over £700m losses on investments in the technology sector. Their share price was taking a hammering. By March it was down below £8.00 having peaked at nearly £18.00 in late 2000. 3i needed to recover these losses from somewhere. There was a desperate desire for a serious piece of investment success. Go was now 3i's biggest investment, and taking Stelios's deal meant a massive 280 per cent return on the investment in less than a year.

I suppose I should have realised that 3i was nervous about its investment in Go from the moment they decided not to take up their board seats. They had also been eager to further syndicate their holdings in Go, and I assisted where I could, speaking to institutional investors and even a non-airline trade investor. But putting a value on Go shares was difficult from the moment of the MBO because the company was doing so well financially. Investors still had aversions to airlines, and others found a sizeable increase in the share price in just months unacceptable on principle. 3i procrastinated, which may have added to the sense of nervousness.

In fact, there had been a connection even before 3i handed British Airways the cheque to buy Go. It emerged that 3i's CEO, Brian Larcombe, had gone to Harvard Business School executive training with Stelios some years before. They had stayed in touch and the initial approach had come from Stelios to Brian. Tom told me that Stelios had rung Brian late in November 2001 with the idea.

Looking back comparisons between Brian Larcombe and Rod Eddington are irresistible. In their time as owners of Go, neither visited the company nor experienced the business as a customer. They both sold the business long before it had fulfilled its promise. Both decided to sell because of corporate pressure and expedience – not robust commercial analysis. Each made a good return as a shareholder but missed out on the much bigger payoff that was on the cards. It felt as though both spent more time discussing Go with Stelios than with the Go management.

From that moment on, I prayed that easyJet would blow it. And it was not beyond the realm of possibility. They didn't have the cash to do the deal and were relying on issuing more shares to existing shareholders. Their shares had recovered strongly after falling to 250p when the September 11 crisis hit, but the stock market was jumpy about economic uncertainties ahead, and a big complication for the markets was Stelios's desire to sell some of his shareholding. I also soon after found out that not everyone at easyJet was keen on the deal.

When 3i agreed to exclusive takeover talks with easyJet in early March, I was asked to dinner with Stelios and Ray Webster, easyJet's Chief Executive, in a private room at Mark's Club in Mayfair. We were going to talk about the future.

From the start, I could tell who was the real enthusiast for this deal. Ray clearly had major reservations about buying Go. I felt buoyed that there was disagreement at the top. Surely that might mean the deal would fall apart?

Nevertheless, Stelios launched a charm offensive. My only reason for going to the dinner was to find out what they had in mind for Go's people. I wanted to know what to say to the management team and the troops. They reassured me that they wanted to take the best from both companies and that everyone would have jobs.

They asked about the likely reaction to the takeover and were shocked when I told them that the people at Go might not be thrilled to become part of easyJet. I gently pointed out that they had been trying to destroy and humiliate us in the newspapers and law courts since the day we were conceived, but they brushed this aside, saying that it had all been aimed at British Airways. It had felt pretty personal at Go.

They even vaguely suggested that I would have 'a senior commercial role' and that one day Ray might retire. Stelios later recalled my private response in the *Financial Times* as 'Give me a call when Ray retires.' I didn't want anything to do with this deal.

My failure to play ball must have intensely annoyed them, because they made a great deal of my opposition to the acquisition when the news later broke and the press offensive ensued. Then Stelios said in an interview with BBC's *Business Today* programme that I had allowed 'emotions and ego to cloud my judgement'. The subtext was that I was just an emotional female.

I'm not against capitalism. I just believe you get better results for customers, colleagues and investors if you worry about the people first. Business models don't make profits, people do. Passion, honesty and emotional commitment to people and the business produces excellence; mediocrity is the result without them. And it was a privilege to work with some of the best people I've ever met. They were worth fighting for.

And my disagreement with the deal was more than an emotional reaction to 'my baby' being painted orange. I was a seasoned airline executive who had learned the hard way that airline mergers don't work. More than a decade earlier, I had been a senior member of the management team merging Dan-Air into British Airways. That didn't work. It didn't achieve its objective of transforming British Airways' business and the two cultures didn't meld. My US experience was even more convincing. US Airways was a financially weak hotchpotch of route networks and bloated cost structures without a culture of its own as a result of merging all those regional airlines.

I believe that low-cost airlines are at even greater risk in trying to make a merger work. They need an enormous amount of flexibility and good will from employees to work through the inevitable operational glitches. Some of that flexibility comes from the way you write job descriptions, but most of it comes just from employees feeling they want to help out. You can't get rid of the glitches, so your operation and customer satisfaction simply falls apart unless people lend a hand to help out or come to work even with a headache when you need them. You cannot mandate the kind of good will we saw at Go during the Korean crash crisis at Stansted. You can't buy or sell that good will, and it's near impossible to keep it in a merger.

Even the great Southwest has done only one acquisition in its thirty-year history. Paul Sterbenz, when he was Vice President of Flight Operations, was responsible for merging the flight crew of acquired Morris Air into Southwest. Paul told me that Morris was only 10 per cent of the size of Southwest, but he believed it almost tore Southwest apart. Even for the very talented managers at Southwest, it ripped at the relationship with existing employees and it took a long time to build up trust from people acquired as part of a deal.

And that was why I didn't like KLM and Carlyle's idea of merging Go and Buzz back when British Airways was selling Go. I'm not Superwoman, and even though I had the best team of managers working with me, I don't think we could have made it work. So that's why I thought Go's takeover by easyJet would become a nightmare.

Growth through internal expansion is a much better route. Yes, it may mean that you can't put as many of your flags on the map as quickly, but it is a truer, more consistent kind of growth. An airline built to last needs to grow from within. I learned that from looking at Southwest Airlines and from my own, painful, experience. And that's what we were trying to build at Go.

In a surreal twist of fate, just as I was facing up to the premature end of our extraordinary adventure at Go, I found myself in mid-April on the short list of finalists for Veuve Clicquot's Businesswoman of the Year award. Months before, David Magliano and the PR team at Bell Pottinger had decided to nominate me for the award; they'd been supported with independent nominations from Marjorie Scardino and Lady Young. I was vaguely aware of it, but I was pretty preoccupied!

At the photo call with the other very accomplished women nominees I secretly wished that one of them would win. I remember commenting in one of the press interviews that I hoped a British finalist would win. But given the perversity of life at that moment, I had a funny feeling it would be me.

The award is a huge honour, but I really couldn't face all the added public attention just as I was fighting, and losing, the biggest battle of my career to date. The ominous caption underneath the photo printed in the *Financial Times* the next day said that the award had come to be known as a kiss of death to the careers of the winners, and they wondered if this year's winner would suffer a similar fate. Indeed.

By the end of April it was official. I had won the award. In another irony of the moment, at the Claridge's award ceremony, I was presented with the requisite bottle of champagne by Sue MacGregor, who, ironically, had a few years back warned me about being overexposed in the press with an air of disapproval. But the people at Veuve Clicquot were warm and eager to welcome me into their family. I particularly enjoyed my stimulating chats with their CEO, Cécile Bonnefond, a savvy Frenchwoman who had spent time in the consumer goods world of Kellogg's before heading into the luxury world of Bernard Arnault.

I have never been comfortable with the 'woman in business' thing. It makes us sound a bit like zoo animals to be admired for overcoming our natural instincts. I honestly don't think that I've ever been given or been barred from a role because of my gender. I've always tried to use my strengths and overcome my weaknesses in wanting to do well and accomplish things. Being a woman is one of many characteristics that makes me me. I am mildly annoyed by the attention, but David Magliano and I were both aware that my gender gave Go more free press coverage. So I decided to put up with the 'mother of two starts airline' quips in order to get better coverage on Go's announcement of profits, new routes or anything else we were trying to push. That's life and you have to go with it.

May was the worst month, because the battle was all but over but I now had to ready everyone at Go for the new 'orange' world and face my own fate. On 1 May I held the most difficult meeting in my life. I gathered together my senior colleagues who had helped create Go and had used their savings to help buy the airline from British Airways.

The five directors and Mike and Derek had known about the deal since January, so they were prepared. But for the senior managers this was entirely unexpected. They had noticed the flurry of meetings and stress, but they were hoping it had to do with the new aircraft order we'd been working on, or even an early flotation of the company.

I didn't do well. I broke down at work for the first time in my career and turned to Ed to explain our situation. I recovered enough to explain the efforts I'd made to persuade 3i to stick with Go.

In the middle of the shocked silence, Julie came in with a note. It was Brian Larcombe on the phone, wanting me to come out of my meeting to speak to him. That did it. I obviously refused, finished the sombre meeting and returned to my office. When I returned the call, I listened silently as Brian made some small talk until I brusquely asked why he had called. He had never called me before, and we had not met except at one social dinner seven months earlier.

I guessed that he might be calling to say: 'Gee Barbara, I'm sorry we're selling your company, but times are tough at 3i.' I would have respected a call like that. But instead he chastised me for moving slowly to provide certain information required to make the deal happen. I was stunned. He had the nerve to chivvy me along. The group of people I had just dropped a bombshell on flashed before my eyes. I honestly can't remember the precise words I used, but I clearly indicated that I did not appreciate the call. Folklore at 3i claims I used much more colourful language.

I didn't expect the leak to the newspapers on 3 May, two days later. I still don't know where it came from. We hadn't made our normal careful preparations for communicating news inside Go. We had to wing it. I stood on a table in telesales and told everyone in the company straight up what was going on. I also explained that the deal wasn't done until the fat lady sang, but that she was warming up her voice. There were tears, shock and disbelief.

The attention from the press reached crazy proportions. Just after the easyJet news was leaked, a pleasant but persistent photographer from a major London Sunday paper camped out at my front door at home in London to get a picture of me (presumably hoping for red eyes from crying!). My long-suffering husband went to the front door in his old red towelling robe and patiently explained that I didn't want to be photographed. The guy was fortunately not from the paparazzi, and the two of them chatted about his previous assignments as a conflict photographer. War zones to West London? I wonder who he had offended at the newspaper.

At this point our extraordinary team at Go began to move in different directions. We had been so strong and powerful together, but our assessment of the situation and motivations began to diverge. I explained my rationale for leaving to the group that had done the MBO together. Andrew Cowen, Steven Horner, Mike Coltman and Mireille Briggs felt the same way as me. Ed and David's motivations were difficult to fathom. David felt he positively wanted to join easyJet and was eerily calm about the Go brand disappearing. Ed was very quiet, then took a logical approach: 'Really, Barbara, as much as I understand what you are saying, I don't think there is any choice now. Let's be pragmatic about this, you can't blame 3i for wanting such a huge return on their investment, and if it's going to happen, I want to be there to influence easyJet.' Dominic reluctantly said he would agree to join easyJet after the sale because he felt it was inevitable and he wanted to make sure Go's people were taken care of.

The other senior managers were, frankly, too shocked or uncertain to understand the implications. They had not had months to get used to the idea. Even with a tidy payoff in the hundreds of thousands of pounds, most needed a job.

Much as I wanted united opposition to the deal among my colleagues, I encouraged each of them to make their own decisions, for themselves and their families, just as we had done before embarking on the MBO. In my heart, I have to say that it was a huge disappointment to me, but everyone had to make their own mind up about how they saw the situation. For me, I just could not bring myself to work with easyJet. There was too much history, and in my view they did not share the same principles of running a business or a low-cost airline.

And relations with 3i remained frosty. At a long negotiating session at Ashursts, it became clear that 3i were going to accept another price cut from easyJet. My job was to steel 3i's resolve not to give one inch on the price or terms. My fear now was that they would allow the price to drop well below the £400 million mark. I reminded them that Go's profits were strong and now above budget. easyJet had based their first offer of £390 million a few months back on a rough estimate of a profit target of £8 million. But the revenue picture had improved so much that we would in fact report a profit of £12.5 million. If anything, the price easyJet should pay for Go should be going up, not down. But I now knew how eager 3i was to get the deal done. I stonewalled any further cooperation until the deal for employees was protected. We then proceeded to negotiate a better price for Go employee shareholders at £384 million. This meant that 3i and their partners received a price of less than £370 million. I just couldn't stomach a lower price on a business where we were ahead of the planned profits that underpinned the original offer price. It was infuriating.

Back at Go, with the reality of the deal bearing down on us, all work had stopped on aircraft purchases and the future of Go. Instead, Andrew and Derek were working like dogs to understand the financial effect of the deal on every single employee. The idea of employee ownership is great, but it means a huge amount of admin. I received a somewhat embarrassed call from Derek asking me what I wanted to do with the extra 2 per cent. What 2 per cent? I asked. You know, the shares being held back for the new employees. He explained that some of the pot had been used up for new employees, but that there was more than 2 per cent left. I thought the fairest solution would be to distribute it in proportion to everyone's share holding. The only problem with this solution was that I was the biggest winner. It bothered me. I was already going to earn a fortune from the sale. So I suggested to all the senior team that we should forgo our share of the extra 2 per cent and distribute it to everyone else in the company. Just two colleagues on the senior team supported my proposal. Sadly, money does change people. Given the vast fortune of £10 million I was to receive, I decided to share my extra bit (worth around £1 million) with everyone except the top managers. But I forced the two generous colleagues to keep their extra share. So the price per share for everyone except the top team was enhanced by £1 and each share that cost 10p was going to be worth around £14.15. An incredible rate of return that none of us will ever see again. I learned a lot about money and human nature that day.

I suppose that was it. I eventually conceded defeat in late May. In the end the sale of Go was forced upon me. The final price was £374 million, with Go employees enjoying a price of £384 million. It meant we had increased the value of Go by around £22 million a month since our management buyout. This was a phenomenal success in anyone's books.

Yet, in my view, it was not the best option. I still marvel at 3i's decision. They were shrewd investors, with the good sense to buy Go when many others didn't see the opportunity. They were good owners who let us get on with developing a winning business. But they sold us out for a quick profit, and in my view let £600 million of potential return go begging – mainly because they needed a quick victory to offset their failures elsewhere.

Brian Larcombe was quoted as saying: 'We are delighted to announce this deal which would deliver an exceptional return for investors. Our job is to deliver above-average returns for our shareholders by backing dynamic entrepreneurs in growth sectors to build valuable businesses. There could be no clearer example of this than Go.' I'm a hero to the venture capital world. Go's sale was the *European Venture Capital Journal*'s deal of the month – and certainly 3i's deal of the year. I can just about see the funny side of that now. Just about.

The City analysts didn't miss the significance of 3i's treatment of Go. One said it was ironic that 3i, long nursing a reputation for being a 'patient' investor, was now in danger of being seen as 'a quick-flip merchant' as a result of efforts to make decent returns after its technology stocks tanked.

In my own statement to the press, who had been clamouring for my attention for days, I tried not to lose sight of the positives, because everyone at Go needed to begin the transition to 'orange' as positively as possible. 'easyJet's acquisition is a tremendous compliment to all of us at Go on our achievements since starting up four years ago. I'm particularly pleased that everyone at Go will share in the rewards from our success.'

Stelios had won. I announced I was quitting. The takeover allowed easyJet to leapfrog Ryanair to become the biggest no-frills airline in Europe, with more than 2,800 people and 63 planes.

The deal was finally agreed and announced on 16 May, but would still take months to be finalised. Feeling as though my world had caved in, I turned to my friend and CEO coach, David Carter, for advice. All through the ups and downs of Go he had been full of wisdom and encouragement, and this time he didn't fail me either. He counselled me to run Go until the day I left in the way I would want to be remembered. And that's what I did. I kept a close eye on the financial results, watched punctuality like a hawk, and still talked to customers on the planes.

In the next day's *Independent* Ray Webster paid me a compliment I appreciated. 'I respect Barbara's views and I think she has done a fantastic job in taking a fledgling company to where it is now. Naturally, she is disappointed she can't see the company she's brought on through to a flotation.'

The messages from customers simply bowled me over. I received hundreds of emails from all around Europe. Customers didn't want easyJet. They liked Go. Since they currently had a choice, they exercised it. Soon they would have no choice. A few made me smile. One lovely gentleman wanted to do a whip-round of Go customers and to drop the buckets of change and notes on 3i's doorstep to try to get them to stop the sale. But the overriding sentiment was one of the pity of it all. It was such a shame to lose a company whose prices and service they liked very much. I was also encouraged to start up another airline. A sweet but perhaps impractical suggestion.

The Go annual birthday party on 23 May took on an entirely new significance when the sale of Go was announced. The modest venue for three hundred was replaced with the impressive Chilford Hall, with a capacity of more than a thousand.

I was determined to have a great time and give my personal best wishes to as many people as possible. The party was extraordinary, with six bars and party rooms, live bands and DJs. I even had a respectable go on the bucking bronco, proving my riding skills to the doubters in the crowd. Everyone was invited – even former Go colleagues.

The real hero of the night was Peter Lashmar, who was responsible for communications (and parties) at Go. He was the glue holding the place together. Lively, outrageous and lots of fun, that's Pete. He had a surprise in store for me. Afterwards, he got in touch to remember that I tried to step off the stage after I spoke for a couple of minutes thanking everyone. 'But people wanted more, and so having asked everyone if they thought that was enough, you returned onto the stage accompanied by the clapping, cheering and shouting of everyone. It was at this point that I asked everyone "Who has won a Go MAD award?" Lots of shouting followed. Nicola Judge and Sheila Mahon – the two annual Go MAD winners – then came onto the stage and presented you with your Go MAD certificate and pin. Then it was present-opening time, and as you opened the box I remember you saying "I know what this is, how did you get hold of it?"'

Everyone in Go had contributed to buying me a beautiful Italian jumping saddle. Those thousand people joined together and bought me the saddle. The next day, I took Peter (the horse!) for a spin in it and emailed the digital photo to everyone at Go.

My final act as Chief Executive Officer was to set up sessions with every department in the company, and I did a road show. Here's what I said:

> Things happen in life that are not what we planned. It's how we deal with them that counts. I did not choose for this to happen, but it has. Each of you needs to keep an open mind and give easyJet a chance. At some point in the future, you need to stop, look at yourself in the mirror and ask yourself if you're just going through the motions or whether you are really committed to this

new company. If you're not committed you owe it to yourself, to me and to everyone who is committed to easyJet to go do something else. Life is too short. Be happy and productive.

I hope you've learned a lot about how important you are by working at Go. If you don't like the way things are being done in your department, speak up. If you think there are better ways of serving customers, speak up. And if you think there are injustices in the workplace, speak up. They can buy our company, but they can't buy your soul.

Finally, I am very pleased that you are all fellow share-holders in Go and that you will receive a nice big fat cheque when this is all over. I know some of you will be using the money to do very responsible things like pay down debts or help out a relation. Can I ask you to please do something for yourself? And then remember Go with my thanks. Take care of yourselves.

I did that speech countless times – in Scotland, in the East Midlands, in Bristol and especially at Stansted. I met with small groups from all departments – engineers, telesales agents, the marketing team, cabin crew team managers, our customer sup-port team, the airports team, finance colleagues and everyone else who worked in the office. Pilots and cabin crew walked in and out of my office all day with their good wishes. It was exhausting but it felt right. On my last day, I just packed up, drove down to London and went to lunch. We had taken over a small restaurant in Hammersmith called the Odd Spot, owned by John Steans and Harvey Simpson. The group I'd done the MBO with were there, plus John and the assistants: Julie, Mo, Claire, Fiona and Karen. We had a lovely meal, a bit of wine and I said a few words of goodbye and thanks, finishing with: 'Best of luck, and let me know if any of you decide to start up your own businesses. I'd love to be an investor. I can't think of anyone else I'd like to back more.' And with that, Steven Horner presented me with my very own cappuccino machine and I headed home.

Index

Index